THE
FOOTBALL
HALL
OF
FAME

▶▶▶▶▶▶▶▶▶▶▶▶▶▶▶▶▶▶▶▶▶▶▶▶

ROBERT GALVIN
FOREWORD BY SIR BOBBY CHARLTON

PORTICO

This edition published in the United Kingdom in 2011 by

Portico Books
10 Southcombe Street
London
W14 0RA

An imprint of Anova Books Company Ltd

Artefact images © National Football museum

Player photography courtesy of Mirrorpix and Getty Images

Designed by Blokgraphic

ISBN 978-1-906032-46-3

A CIP catalogue record for this book is available from the British Library.

10 9 8 7 6 5 4 3 2 1

Printed and bound by Toppan Leefung, China

This book can be ordered direct from the publisher. Contact the marketing department, but try your bookshop first.

www.anovabooks.com

CONTENTS

▶▶▶▶▶▶▶▶▶▶▶▶

INTRODUCTION

▶▶▶▶▶▶▶▶▶▶▶▶▶▶▶▶▶▶▶▶▶▶▶▶▶▶▶▶▶▶▶▶

The National Football Museum launched its Hall of Fame in 2002, to celebrate the all-time greatest players and managers in English Football. The Museum recognised that an English football hall of fame had been long overdue. The achievements of many stars of the game had not been recognised as fully as they could have been during their lifetimes. While the displays of the Museum, which opened in 2001, feature the greatest names in English football history, it was recognised that enrolment in a hall of fame was the best way to honour the all-time greats.

To select those 'legends' from over a century of football history to be inducted into the National Football Museum Hall of Fame, the Museum established a selection panel of some of the greatest names in the game, including President of the Museum, Sir Bobby Charlton, and the Museum's Vice Presidents, Sir Alex Ferguson, Sir Tom Finney and Sir Trevor Brooking.

The Hall of Fame was the brainchild of the then Museum Chair of Trustees, Brian Booth, who took over from the Founding Chair, Bryan Gray, in 2002. Brian died in 2004 and is greatly missed. Under the

↗
England manager Fabio Capello celebrates the induction of the England 1966 side into the Football Hall of Fame with members of the team, in 2010. Left to right: George Cohen, Gerry Byrne, Gordon Banks, Geoff Hurst, Nobby Stiles, Martin Peters, Paul Dermody (chairman of trustees of the National Football Museum), Jack Charlton, Fabio Capello, and Ian Callaghan.

current Chair of the Museum, Paul Dermody, the Hall of Fame has continued to grow in stature. The National Football Museum Hall of Fame annual award ceremonies are attended by a glittering array of star guests and attract substantial media coverage, making them one of the outstanding events in the English football calendar.

The selection criteria for inclusion in the National Football Museum Hall of Fame are as follows: a manager or player must have managed or played in England for at least five seasons. Players must have either retired from playing, or be over the age of 30. Inductees are then selected from a list of eligible nominees from votes of the selectional panel made via secret ballot.

This edition of the book has chapters on all the inductees selected between 2002 and 2010, comprising 81 male players, 10 female players and 22 managers. In addition, there have been a small number of inductees in special categories. In 2004 Joseph S. Blatter, President of FIFA, was inducted in an Ambassador of Football category, during FIFA's centenary year. In 2008 Michel Platini was presented with a special European Player award.

Reaction to the National Football Museum Hall of Fame by the greatest names in football has been extremely positive, as the following quotes demonstrate:

'I'm really proud to be included in the National Football Museum's Hall of Fame. It's a great honour. If you look at the names included I have to say I couldn't argue with them. They are all great players and people I would love to have played with. And I think it's great that the Museum has secured the Hall of Fame for the benefit of future generations of both footballers and supporters.'
Sir Bobby Charlton, President of the National Football Museum

'The reason I love the Hall of Fame so much and the Museum itself, is because it gives people the chance to reflect on the history of football.'
Sir Alex Ferguson, Vice President of the National Football Museum

And from one of the greats of the game who is sadly no longer with us:

'It is one of the proudest moments in your life when someone calls to say you are in the Hall of Fame. Words cannot describe it. The museum is a

fantastic place to go and should be congratulated for the Hall of Fame. It is a marvellous thing. Let's keep it going.'
Alan Ball

The Museum is grateful for the support it has received from the Professional Footballers' Association, the Northwest Regional Development Agency, Kitbag and Sportech, without which the development of the National Football Museum Hall of Fame would not have been possible.

The exciting new National Football Museum is opening in Manchester in 2011, with a dedicated Hall of Fame gallery. This will be a fitting tribute to these legends of our national game.

Kevin Moore – Director
National Football Museum
www.nationalfootballmuseum.com

Former Arsenal players honour Thierry Henry following his induction into the Football Hall of Fame in 2011. Left to right: Nigel Winterburn, Freddie Ljungberg, Thierry Henry, Robert Pires, Martin Keown, Ray Parlour and Lee Dixon.

FOREWORD BY
SIR BOBBY CHARLTON

Many great footballers and managers have never been afforded the recognition that they deserve in the game. So I was delighted when I learned, in 2002, that the National Football Museum was to create a Hall of Fame to honour those individuals who have made a lasting and outstanding contribution to English football.

Although the Museum's exhibitions tell the detailed story of the game, I believe that the Hall of Fame and its annual Gala Celebration Awards dinner are vital in highlighting the careers of some of the game's greatest names. Sadly, some of these individuals appear to have been forgotten, firmly justifying the role of the National Football Museum and its Hall of Fame.

Rewards are few and far between in football, so to be inducted into the Hall of Fame is hugely satisfying. The huge salaries on offer to today's top players may compensate for the lack of silverware but many of the Hall of Fame inductees were not fortunate enough to have financial security by the time their careers came to a close. To be recognised by their peers in the Hall of Fame is some compensation, I'm sure, as it ensures that their legacy is never forgotten.

Keane, Finney, Banks, Best and Bergkamp are all names that trip off the tongue, but what about the less familiar names of Doherty, Wharton, Chapman and James? All well respected during their careers but less well known today. We must never forget these players and managers and how they have helped to shape the game that we know and love.

On a personal note, it gave me pleasure to be on hand when Nobby Stiles was inducted into the Hall of Fame in 2007. Bearing in mind our long association as players at both club and international level, it was wonderful to see Nobby receive such an important honour. Sometimes, the scale and importance of the contribution made by a player is only fully appreciated with the passing of time. That has proved to be the case with Nobby, who did not receive all the credit he deserved during his playing days.

In 2007, the National Football Museum introduced a new category for the Football Hall of Fame – the great teams of the past, as selected by a panel of eminent historians, including the author. In doing this, the Museum is celebrating collective, as well as individual, excellence.

It has been my great privilege to be a member of three of the teams to be inducted – England (1966), Manchester United (1956–58) and Manchester United (1966–68). In addition, I had the good fortune as a player to pit my wits against the might of two other outstanding sides that are now such deserving members of the Football Hall of Fame – the Spurs double-winning team of 1961 and the Manchester City side of the late 1960s.

Beautifully illustrated and painstakingly researched, the information and detail in this publication will evoke some wonderful memories and explain why the Hall of Fame inductees mean so much to so many.

I am delighted to write this foreword in support of the Hall of Fame book. Robert Galvin deserves every credit for his diligence and knowledge. All the inductees deserve to be remembered and this publication is a fitting tribute to their efforts on the pitch or in the dugout.

Sir Bobby Charlton
President of the National Football Museum

Bobby Charlton leads out the
Manchester United team at Old Trafford.

FOREWORD BY
GORDON TAYLOR OBE

I am delighted to welcome readers to this latest edition of the National Football Museum's Hall of Fame book highlighting many individuals who have enriched the historical tapestry of football since the establishment of the Football Association in 1863, followed by the formation of the Football League in 1888.

The Professional Footballers' Association have been willing sponsors of the Hall of Fame since its inauguration in 2002 and, as the oldest professional sporting union in the world, enjoyed our centenary year in 2007. We are very aware of the great debt we owe to football icons of the past, and the world they helped create for our present heroes.

The very first time I was fortunate enough to see a football museum was in 1988 when I travelled with England for a European Nations qualifying game taking place in Yugoslavia, as it was then, playing at the Red Star Stadium in Belgrade. The Yugoslavians were excellent hosts but in particular I was most impressed – having been born in Ashton-under-Lyne, Greater Manchester and being brought up with the delights of Bert Trautmann at Manchester City and Matt Busby's 'Busby Babes' – to find that inside the bowels of the stadium was a tremendous football museum; its very centrepiece was a tribute to the Busby Babes who played their last match there before the tragic flight from Munich in February 1958. Such a tribute made me realise the importance of acknowledging the history of our game and its heroes throughout the world.

Long may the National Football Museum continue to flourish and long may the Hall of Fame pay tribute to the game's heroes.

Gordon Taylor OBE
Chief Executive
The Professional Footballers' Association

↗
Gordon Taylor at the National Football Museum with the Premier League trophy.

↖
Gordon Taylor during his playing days.

FOREWORD BY
HOWARD WILKINSON

I can trace the beginning of my love affair with football to two special days. One was 2 May 1953, the day of the 'Matthews Cup Final'; the other was 11 March 1950, a sunny but violently windy day so typical of early Spring. Sheffield Wednesday were at home to Preston North End, watched by 49,222 people, nearly all of whom, it seemed, sported a flat cap. I got in free. Though seven years old at the time, my dad said that I was five! Once inside, I was passed down the Spion Kop, overhead, and by hand, to the front, where children enjoyed the safest spot and best view.

Howard Wilkinson.

Preston won 1–0, with an early headed goal from Tom Finney. Later in the match he fractured a cheek bone in a clash of heads. After a spell of treatment Tom played on, as heroes do. Derek Dooley made his debut for Wednesday that day. Two years later Dooley broke his leg, ironically, against Preston – an injury that ended his career as complications and the onset of gangrene meant his leg was amputated below the knee. His record for Wednesday was an amazing 62 goals in 61 appearances.

Tom Finney was already a hero and a legend. Derek was a hero, later to become a legend in the eyes of the people of South Yorkshire, as his contribution to both Sheffield Wednesday, Sheffield United, and all sections of the game widened, demonstrating that football legends need not have worked at the very highest level.

From the opening pages, outlining the career of Arthur Wharton, the first black professional in the 1880s, to Dario Gradi's remarkable 28 years' service to Crewe Alexandra, and Joan Whalley, the best female player for two decades and, as we learn, a classmate of Tom Finney, the portrayals in *The Football Hall of Fame* are painstaking in their detail and generous in their admiration and praise. These three, and many more, are afforded their rightful place alongside the likes of Bobby Charlton and Bobby Robson.

Sixty years on, my memories of that day in 1950 remain vivid. Heroes have that effect on people. Heroes are admired and respected, sometimes worshipped. In return, they entertain, enthuse, excite and inspire all races, creeds and genders to come together and participate in some way in what is the most played, most popular, most supported and most watched game in the world.

The Football Hall of Fame takes the reader on a wonderful journey, paying tribute to those included, and revealing a fascinating insight into the fabric and social history of our game. The National Football Museum should take much credit for the great contribution it makes to the heritage and wellbeing of football.

Howard Wilkinson
Chairman, League Managers Association

THE FOOTBALL HALL OF FAME

FOUNDING MEMBER

PREVIOUS MEMBER

NEW INDUCTEE

TEAM INDUCTEE
SHEFFIELD FC
▶▶▶▶▶▶▶▶▶▶ 1855–1866

May 1855

Cricket is an established sport in Sheffield, and two of its finest practitioners in the area, Nathaniel Creswick and William Prest, a first-class player with Yorkshire, are pondering ways by which to keep fit during the winter months. The two friends come up with the idea of forming a football club. The game, though popular locally for many years, has been played informally, without a codified structure. This is all about to change.

24 October 1857

A group of football enthusiasts meet to discuss their participation in the game. Although there are conflicting theories as to the date of formation, the first recorded minutes in existence carry this date, according to Brendan Murphy, the author of *From Sheffield With Love*, an account of the early history of the game in the city. Sheffield FC, the oldest football club in the world, as officially confirmed by FIFA, is up and running.

October 1858

The formation of the Football Association in London is still five years in the future. Several different codes are being played at various public schools, in the absence of a universally recognised set of rules. So,

members of the Sheffield club formalise and then circulate their own. The game they envisage is still some way from the game we know today. For instance, one of the initial 11 rules allows for the ball to be caught by players, in specific circumstances. Sheffield Rules, a specific form of football, comes into existence.

December 1858

After an exhaustive search the Sheffield club finally find another set of players who are prepared to play a fixture under Sheffield Rules. The opposition is made up of soldiers from a local regiment. For the first time, a competitive game is played by a football club. The violent nature of the encounter is confirmed when two soldiers sustain fractured ribs.

26 December 1860

A rival club soon emerges, and on Boxing Day Hallam FC host Sheffield FC at their Sandygate Road ground – the oldest football ground in the world. Sheffield prevail 2–0 in a 16-a-side game that attracts the attention of the *Sheffield Daily Telegraph*. According to

Brendan Murphy, this is the first example of football journalism: 'No serious accidents occurred – the game was conducted with good temper and in a friendly spirit.'

May 1863

There has been surge in enthusiasm for football in the city, and more than a dozen amateur clubs are

↗
Charles Alcock, a leading figure at the FA and a friend of Sheffield FC, 1872.

organising fixtures against each other, all played under Sheffield Rules.

26 October 1863

The representatives of a dozen clubs meet in London 'for the purpose of forming an association with the object of establishing a definitive code of rules for the regulation of the game'. Thus, with the birth of the Football Association, a rival powerbase exists in the game. Although Sheffield FC retains – for now – its own rulebook, the club makes the highly significant decision to become a member of the new organisation. For two years they will remain the FA's only presence in the provinces. Although isolated geographically, their influence on the development of the game will be profound and far-reaching.

8 December 1863

From the earliest days of the fledgling Association, Sheffield FC have contributed a vital northern perspective on matters of policy. In a letter to the FA, Sheffield club secretary William Chesterman encourages the introduction of a crossbar, then argues against clauses dealing with running with the ball, charging, holding, tripping, hacking and wrestling the ball from an opponent's grip. Sheffield helps win the day. The dissenters break away to establish a rival code – the Rugby Football Union, in 1871. The FA Laws, as subsequently published, include many Sheffield ideas.

February 1866

At the latest meeting of the FA, the ruling body accepts Sheffield's use of a fixed crossbar, and move closer in line with the Sheffield view on offside. In the future, a player is offside unless three opponents stand between him and the goal when a forward pass is made.

Over the years, other innovations from Sheffield will include the introduction of referees, corner kicks, heading, penalty kicks, indirect free-kicks and free-kicks for handball, as detailed by Brendan Murphy.

31 March 1866

Having suggested a fixture between the clubs of the two cities, Sheffield FC organise a side to take on London in a challenge match in Battersea Park. It is the first representative match to be played by the Football Association, according to the ruling body's official history. As such, it can be seen as the forerunner of all representative and, in a sense, even inter-

↖
The Sheffield FC team in 1857.

national football. London win the game comfortably.

As loyal and vocal advocates of amateurism, Sheffield FC soon fell away as an on-field force, to be eclipsed by professional clubs, most notably Sheffield Wednesday and Sheffield United. Their contribution to the national game, however, cannot be judged in terms of trophies and honours. Rather, it is the collective vision and insight that merits our gratitude. Put simply, they did so much to shape the way football is played. Indeed, so much of the spectacle and excitement detailed in the pages that follow is down to the players and administrators of Sheffield FC – the oldest football club in the world.

ARTHUR WHARTON

▶▶▶▶▶▶▶▶▶▶▶▶▶▶▶▶▶

1865–1930

Arthur Wharton, the first black professional in English football, and once the fastest sprinter in the world, played in goal for the best team in the country in the 1880s.

An outstanding all-round sportsman who also played professional cricket, Wharton reached the pinnacle of his footballing career in 1886–87 when as an amateur he represented Preston North End – a team soon to be known as 'The Invincibles'.

His agile, athletic performances during the late 1880s prompted calls from the influential *Northern Echo* newspaper, based in Darlington, for his inclusion in the England team for the annual fixture against Scotland, describing him as 'one of the most capable goal-custodians in the country ... deserving of a place in any international team'.

↖
Arthur Wharton, circa 1895.

PLAYER • INDUCTED 2003

'The general cry of "Good old Wharton" came from the crowd behind the goal who have the best view of his work.' – Stockport newspaper report

The Football Association, however, overlooked him. Though perhaps sympathetic to the discriminatory racial beliefs then prevalent in Victorian society, the selectors may also have harboured concerns about Wharton's occasionally eccentric antics between the posts.

The *Football News and Athletic Journal* once described him as a 'skylark', referring to his

A drawing depicting football in 1887.

favourite tricks, which included grabbing the tape then utilised as a crossbar and pulling it towards him so that shots missed the target, catching the ball between his legs, and dumping onrushing forwards into the net. Across the country crowds loved him for his antics. Moreover, Wharton was courageous and skilful. He was also very quick, as he proved in setting a world record time of 10 seconds flat for the 100-yard dash at the national athletics championships in 1886.

In 1886–87, Wharton played in all six of Preston North End's ties in the FA Cup, helping the club reach the semi-finals. On the way the team conceded only four goals, three of which came in the defeat to West Bromwich Albion.

As the *Athletic News* newspaper stated after one of those Cup games: 'Wharton is, indeed, a born goalkeeper; he never loses his head, and his hands are always in readiness. His was one of the best exhibitions of goalkeeping I have seen for a long time.'

Born in Ghana, Wharton was sent to England in his teens to train as a Methodist minister. Once here, he was undoubtedly treated differently because of the colour of his skin. Newspapers, for instance, routinely referred to him as a 'darkie' and occasionally questioned his intelligence, implying it was a matter of race.

Whatever disadvantages he experienced, Wharton countered prejudice with a personal magnetism and appeal as a footballer that

won over many reporters and the majority of supporters at several of his clubs.

Later in his career, in 1896, while playing for Stalybridge Rovers in the Lancashire League, one newspaper reported that he was 'lionised' by the majority of supporters for his antics. The team even became known as 'Wharton's Brigade'.

At Stockport County, then playing in the Second Division of the Football League, 'the general cry of "Good Old Wharton" came from the crowd behind the goal,' another newspaper reported. Wharton played for County in 1901–02, his last season before retirement. His other clubs included Sheffield United, for whom he made his only appearance in the fledgling Football League, and Ashton North End.

TEAM INDUCTEE
PRESTON NORTH END
▶▶▶▶▶▶▶▶▶▶▶▶▶▶▶▶▶▶▶▶▶▶ 1886–1889

September 1886

A preview of the forthcoming football season in the *Birmingham Daily Post* analyses the methods of Preston North End in these terms: 'They play with a machine-like accuracy and rigid unselfishness. They have brought the "short-passing" game to the highest point of perfection ever seen.' When the action begins, Preston go on to win 42 matches in succession.

▶▶▶▶▶▶▶▶▶▶▶▶▶▶▶▶▶▶▶

5 March 1887

After defeating The Wednesday 3–1 in the sixth round and Crewe 4–0 in the semi-final, Preston are strong favourites for the FA Cup final at Kenington Oval. On the morning of the game, the Preston players watch the Boat Race. Then, before kick-off, several Albion players shy away from the offer of a wager on the result, even though the odds favour them. It turns out to be a shock: Preston 1 West Bromwich 2. Afterwards, John Goodall, the celebrated Preston centre-forward, stands alone in the centre-circle, unable to comprehend the outcome. 'We got starved to death on the Thames bank and could not warm up again before the match,' full-back Bob Holmes later explains. 'We were daft.'

▶▶▶▶▶▶▶▶▶▶▶▶▶▶▶▶▶▶

8 March 1887

Major William Sudell, the Preston manager, is phleg-

↗
Preston North End 'Invincibles', 1889.

matic about the shock setback for his side. 'A man who cannot lose is not fit to win and though it would be useless to say I am not disappointed, I shall have another try, and if I am knocked down next year I will try again and again. It will be our turn to win it some day.'

▶▶▶▶▶▶▶▶▶▶▶▶▶▶▶▶▶▶▶

17 April 1888

The Football League is inaugurated during a meeting in Manchester. Preston North End are one of 12 founder members.

▶▶▶▶▶▶▶▶▶▶▶▶▶▶▶▶▶▶▶

30 July 1888

Supporters are shocked when Nick Ross, 'a demon back', according to *Athletic News*, formally informs Everton that he is ready to sign for them following a dispute with Sudell over wages. Can North End overcome the loss of such a talismanic figure?

▶▶▶▶▶▶▶▶▶▶▶▶▶▶▶▶▶▶▶

8 September 1888

This new football landscape offers promise for the future, according to *The Times*. Looking ahead to the new season, the newspaper notes an improvement in standards: 'The perfection to which Association football is fast being brought about is very noticeable.' On the opening day, Preston are too good for Burnley, winning 5–2 at home.

20 October 1888

Accrington are the first team to gain a point against Preston, having held the League leaders to a goal-less draw.

10 November 1888

At the halfway stage of the season, Aston Villa earn a point at Deepdale. Such are the high standards set by Preston, one local newspaper describes the result as 'a disgrace'.

5 January 1889

Preston are champions, with four games still to play, following a 4–1 defeat of Notts County. Key to the success has been the brilliance of John Goodall at centre-forward, the prolific goalscoring of inside-forward Jimmy Ross, the consistency of Scottish half-backs Sandy Robertson, David Russell, and John Graham, and the courage of Jimmy Trainer, the 'Prince of Goal-keepers'.

2 February 1889

With the League programme completed, Preston now turn their attention to the FA Cup. 'Each year seems to invest the competitions for the National Cup with fresh interest,' *The Times* reports. As a result of a surge in the number of entrants, the Football Association hand byes to the leading clubs, including Preston, until the competition is down to the last 32. In their opening tie, Preston are too strong for Bootle, winning 3–0 away.

16 March 1889

A goal by Russell gives Preston victory over West Bromwich Albion in the FA Cup semi-final at Bramall Lane.

30 March 1889

As play begins in the final, a nervous Major Sudell walks the touchline at Kennington Oval. Playing in their customary white shirts, Preston are harried in possession by the heavier, more robust Wolverhampton

↖

James Ross, the Preston North End forward, circa 1896.

↗

Drawings depicting the 1889 FA Cup final.

Wanderers players. When captain Fred Dewhurst opens the scoring, however, Preston assume control. In his address to the crowd following the 3–0 victory, Dewhurst describes Sudell as the 'father' to the team, adding: 'If it had not been for his exertions I don't suppose that we would have been able to win the Cup.'

3 April 1889

'Last evening supporters accorded the team a welcome quite as brilliant and unique in its way as the magnificent manner in which the North End won the Cup,' the *Lancashire Evening Post* reports. 'Since the victory was accomplished the enthusiasm of Prestonians has been almost unbounded.'

Looking back over the season, *The Times* notes a tactical development in the game. 'Each forward now has a distinct position, allotted to him, and the ball is transformed from one to the other in a most systematic manner.' Preston are changing the way football is played.

THROUGH THE AGES
VICTORIAN FOOTBALL

▶▶▶▶▶▶▶▶▶▶▶▶▶▶▶▶▶▶▶▶▶▶▶▶▶▶▶▶▶▶▶▶▶▶▶▶▶

THIS PAGE: **Above** Players await the presentation of the FA Cup, 1899. **Right** William 'Fatty' Foulke, circa 1896.

OPPOSITE: **Above left** Bob Crompton of Blackburn Rovers.
Below left England team, 1891. **Above right** Billy Meredith.
Below right Drawing of the FA Cup final at Kennington Oval, 1883.

TEAM INDUCTEE
ASTON VILLA
▶▶▶▶▶▶▶▶▶ 1894–1897

25 April 1894

At the end of the season, Aston Villa sit on top of the table, six points clear of runners-up, Sunderland, with a total of 44 points from 30 games. 'The plaudits this season are directed toward Birmingham,' *The Times* reports, listing Villa, Everton and Sunderland as the most powerful sides in the country.

▶▶▶▶▶▶▶▶▶▶▶▶▶▶▶▶▶▶▶

20 April 1895

In the first FA Cup final to be played at Crystal Palace, Aston Villa take on West Bromwich Albion. The final is decided by a goal in the opening minute from Villa's talismanic forward, John Devey. A local lad and first-class batsman for Warwickshire, Devey is injured in a clash of heads with Albion centre-half, Tom Higgins, but both players return to the fray.

▶▶▶▶▶▶▶▶▶▶▶▶▶▶▶▶▶▶▶

22 April 1895

In its match report, *The Times* pays tribute to Aston Villa's 'splendid lot of forwards, who dribbled and passed in a way that often promised a heavy score, and their halves were also very skilful, especially Reynolds, who has reduced his play to quite a fine art. It was the Villa's forwards who made them so much the better side, and an easy precision marked their play'.

14 October 1895

In the space of six days, Villa earn more than £900 from a couple of home fixtures – and the additional income covers the signing of Jimmy Crabtree, the international back from Burnley, for a fee of £250.

▶▶▶▶▶▶▶▶▶▶▶▶▶▶▶▶▶▶▶▶▶

April 1896

Aston Villa regain the championship, finishing four points clear of Derby County. The Villa players are popular figures. There is James Cowan, a 'granite-faced and sternly muscled' Scotsman, according to one newspaper; Howard Spencer, the England right-back and 'Prince of full-backs' who is renowned for his sportsmanship; captain Devey; and the celebrated winger Charlie Athersmith. Throughout this period Villa is managed by club secretary George Ramsey.

▶▶▶▶▶▶▶▶▶▶▶▶▶▶▶▶▶▶▶▶

November 1896

'Football among the great professional teams has become as uncertain in its nature as cricket, and little reliance can be placed on form,' reports *The Times*. Villa lie one point behind Bolton Wanderers, although they have a game in hand. The game's

John Devey, 1894.

growing popularity prompts daily newspapers to devote more space to 'football intelligence' – news about the leading clubs and players.

16 December 1896

Aston Villa are described in *The Times* as the most popular club in the country, ahead of Everton and Derby County. 'Their fine football is an example to all,' the newspaper states.

12 February 1897

On the eve of the FA Cup tie against Notts County, John Devey writes: 'I don't see why we should not bring off the double event in winning the League trophy and the English Cup. It has been done before and it will be done again – and we were very near it in 1893–94. I should think 42 points will win us the League championship.'

9 April 1897

Aston Villa are champions, with a total of 47 points, five more than Devey predicted. The captain now turns his attention to the FA Cup final at Crystal Palace, where Everton await. In a preview of the game, *The Times* refers to 'two great provincial centres of the game'. A sign of the growing professionalism within the game, the newspaper reports that 'both sides have been carefully trained' for the final.

10 April 1897

Following Villa's thrilling 3–2 victory over Everton, the final is described as one of the most entertaining games in the history of the competition. 'Aston Villa's

Aston Villa, 1897.

work was of the most brilliant description, and only slightly inferior was the exhibition of the beaten side,' one newspaper reports. Villa have secured the League and Cup double, and their achievements gain them great popularity in the capital.

17 April 1897

As holders of the double, Villa play their first fixture at their new ground – against Blackburn Rovers. They have been playing at Villa Park ever since.

Epilogue

In a book published in 1906, William McGregor, the founder of the Football League and a great servant of Aston Villa, writes: 'If there is a club in the country which deserves to be dubbed the greatest, few will deny the right of Aston Villa to share the highest niche of fame.

'Never since that day in 1897 has there been a club eleven so crowded with celebrities as the Villa team. Whitehouse in goal; Spencer and Evans at back; Reynolds, Cowan and Crabtree at half; Athersmith, Devey, John Campbell, Wheldon and Steve Smith, the forwards. It was a side the equal of which we have not seen since. If there was one man, however, who made the Villa side more than another, that man was John Campbell. He was the one man in the football world who was suited to Villa's methods.'

BILLY MEREDITH

▶▶▶▶▶▶▶▶▶▶▶▶▶▶▶▶

1874–1958

A hero in the eyes of the Edwardian working class, Billy Meredith was the most famous footballer of his era and a pivotal figure in the emergence of Manchester as a stronghold of English football.

During a career noted for its remarkable longevity, at the outset of the 20th century the moustachioed, bandy-legged winger – a trademark toothpick in his mouth – helped, in turn, both City and United claim their first major honour.

Here was football's first 'star' player, a man hailed by the *Daily Express* in 1907 as 'the greatest outside-right playing football'.

Tactically, wing-play was regarded as a vital aspect of attacking play, particularly when it came to circumventing the more restrictive offside law then in place. 'In the ability to dribble past the half-back and full-back none can compare with Meredith, the Welsh Wizard,' *Football Field* stated.

Billy Meredith practises ball skills, 1915.

PLAYER • INDUCTED 2007 • 48 CAPS • 2 DIVISION ONE CHAMPIONSHIPS • 2 FA CUPS

'His method is to be as near offside as possible. Therefore, he uses his speed to make sudden breaks and cause confusion.' – *Football Field*

Celebrated and often caricatured in cartoons, Meredith gained a popularity akin to that enjoyed by music-hall stars of his day. 'Those 90 minutes of consummate ball control and trickery every Saturday, to the roars of an adoring multitude, were Meredith's one means of communion with his fellow men,' the *Manchester Guardian* reported.

↖
Billy Meredith passes the ball, 1924.

Not even scandal could seriously diminish his popular appeal. Implicated in a match-fixing conspiracy, Meredith was cheered to the rafters on his return from suspension. To his dying day, he strenuously denied any wrongdoing.

At the age of 49 Meredith played in a Cup semi-final – a longevity at the top bettered only by Stanley Matthews in modern times. In the 1930s the two men met, as Matthews recalled in 1948: 'I've never forgotten the advice the great Billy Meredith gave me when I was a kid of 16. He told me to aim crosses to the far post, and that's what I try to do.'

Off the field, Meredith fought against what he regarded as 'the tyranny' of the maximum wage and the transfer system. A lifelong union man, Meredith chaired the first meeting of the players' union, in December 1907.

A native of Chirk, a mining village in North Wales, Meredith signed amateur forms with Ardwick in 1894. Five years later, following a change of name to Manchester City, the club won promotion to Division One for the first time.

In 1904, when City players paraded through the streets with the FA Cup, huge crowds cheered them on. Manchester had never witnessed anything like it before.

Then came the bombshell. City were ordered to sell many of their players, including Meredith, as a punishment for their part in the match-fixing and subsequent illegal bonuses scandal. Local rivals United took full advantage.

The return of Meredith from suspension in January 1907 generated enormous public

interest. 'It was a scene of wonderful enthusiasm,' the *Manchester Guardian* reported, 'an amazing tumult of waving arms and handkerchiefs.' The debut of Meredith proved to be a vital turning point in United's history.

The following year United won the championship for the first time, and followed that success by lifting the FA Cup in 1909. High attendances generated enough money to fund their move to Old Trafford in 1910. The following season, a second title was won.

In 1934, David Jack, the former England forward, wrote: 'There is not a William Meredith in present-day football. His crossing of the ball was *par excellence*, true in delivery and directed towards his colleagues in the goalmouth with almost uncanny accuracy and strength.'

STEVE BLOOMER

▶▶▶▶▶▶▶▶▶▶▶▶▶▶▶▶

1874–1938

More than a century after his first appearance at the Baseball Ground, Derby County fans still sing the praises of Steve Bloomer, the great England inside-forward.

There is more to this lingering admiration than a remarkable capacity for scoring goals, though Bloomer's total of 352 goals in League football for Derby and Middlesbrough has only been bettered at the highest level by two men in history – William 'Dixie' Dean and Jimmy Greaves.

For Rams supporters, Bloomer was one of them – a local lad who proudly and loyally served the club either side of World War One in a succession of roles – player (twice), coach, scout, and 'general assistant' on the ground staff.

For 14 years in succession, Bloomer was Derby's leading goalscorer; on five occasions – between 1896 and 1904 – he topped the division chart. Asked to explain his secret, Bloomer replied: 'I try to get there first'.

Steve Bloomer travels by boat to Canada, 1922.

PLAYER • INDUCTED 2008 • 23 CAPS

'I never faced a more twisting tormentor or wonderful shot than Bloomer.' – Ernest 'Nudger' Needham, Sheffield United and England left-half

His fame spread when he broke both the England appearance and goalscoring records during the same calendar year – 1905. In tribute, and reward, the Football Association commissioned his portrait and established a national testimonial fund – the first time such a gesture to a player had been sanctioned.

Those achievements only added to the sense of shock and consternation the following year when Derby sold the terrace hero to Middlesbrough for the then hefty fee of £750.

Bloomer spent four successful years at the newly-built Ayresome Park, during which time he averaged a goal every other game and made the last of his 23 England appearances. A century later, his tally of 28 goals still earned him a top-10 place on the all-time scoring list. 'I never faced a more twisting tormentor or wonderful shot than Bloomer,' Ernest 'Nudger' Needham, the Sheffield United and England left-half, once said.

Speed of execution was also vital, according to Ivan Sharpe, a one-time team-mate and amateur England international. 'Bloomer's shot came from nearer the toe than the instep, which enabled him to make the effort a moment quicker than other men who took a bigger backlift.' A 'sudden shot', as Sharpe described it.

↗
Steve Bloomer wearing his England shirt, 1895.

During his first stint in Derby, his goals helped establish the Rams as one of the leading English sides. And one of the unluckiest. Three times – in 1898, 1899 and 1903 – they reached the FA Cup final, and three times they lost.

Worse times soon followed in the League, however; and many Derby fans were con-

▶**talking point**

Football crowds appreciated Steve Bloomer for his commitment and enthusiasm.

In his early days as a professional, Bloomer often celebrated a goal by doing a cartwheel, at a time when such flamboyance was almost unknown. At other times, instead of walking back to the centre circle or modestly shaking the hand of his team-mates, as was the norm, the more animated Bloomer would, in his own words, 'take a great jump in the air and whoop aloud'.

'As I grew older, though, I took my successes and failures more philosophically,' he explained.

Age may have mellowed him in many ways, but he would remain an unforgiving critic of team-mates who failed to reach the standard he expected.

vinced that Bloomer's shock departure in 1906 was the reason behind the club's relegation the following season.

Throughout his time away newspapers in Derby reported his progress with Middlesbrough. On his return to the Baseball Ground in 1910, he received a rapturous welcome, and the transfer fee of £100 was quickly recouped at the turnstiles. His popularity soared again in 1911–12 when he led Derby to promotion as champions.

In 1913, the year before he hung up his boots, the *Football Players' Magazine* stated: 'He is the greatest inside-forward who has ever played for England and his name has for years been a household word wherever football is played.'

TEAM INDUCTEE
SUNDERLAND
▶▶▶▶▶▶▶▶▶▶ 1912–1913

31 August 1912

Although Aston Villa, Newcastle United and Everton are rated the most likely champions, *The Times* acknowledges the 'clever array of men' on Sunderland's books. 'Sunderland have proved disappointing for several years,' the newspaper notes. 'This year may pay for all. On names alone, they are capable of the highest honours, and, given a good start, there are more unlikely things than that Sunderland will be champions at the end of the season.'

▶▶▶▶▶▶▶▶▶▶▶▶▶▶▶▶▶▶

10 September 1912

A crushing 4–0 defeat at Blackburn Rovers, the champions, prompts one national newspaper to describe Sunderland's performance as 'disappointing in every respect'. Only the outstanding work of goalkeeper Scott keeps the score down.

▶▶▶▶▶▶▶▶▶▶▶▶▶▶▶▶▶▶

8 October 1912

A poor start to the season by Sunderland is confirmed with a disappointing performance at Chelsea. But one visiting player, Charlie Thomson, the veteran Scotland centre-half, impresses *The Times*, whose football correspondent describes him as 'a great and clean-hearted player'.

16 November 1912

The calm, generous nature of Charlie Thomson was severely tested when the referee adjudges that he handled the ball in his own penalty area against Manchester City. An indignant Thomson says that he 'breasted the ball' – to use the football jargon of the day. The penalty is enough to give City victory. Meanwhile, off the field, Sunderland are losing money; their inconsistent form has led to a decrease in attendances at Roker Park.

27 December 1912

On first glance, a Sunderland supporter examining the Division One table this morning has little to cheer. The Wearsiders are languishing in mid-table. Yet a second look tells a different story: with the top half so congested, Sunderland find themselves only three points adrift of leaders, Aston Villa.

↙

Colour postcard, circa 1909.

27 January 1913

'Wonderland From Sunderland' is the headline in the *Daily Express* above the match report of the 2–1 defeat of Tottenham Hotspur at White Hart Lane two days earlier. 'The Sunderland forwards gave what must have been one of the most astonishing displays of football witnessed in north London,' the paper states. 'Adjectives almost fail one in recalling their play.' Is this the turning point for the Wearsiders?

28 March 1913

A winning vein of form lifts Sunderland into contention in the League. In the FA Cup, they now face Burnley in the semi-finals. On the eve of the game, the Sunderland players are being deluged with letters of encouragement. A number of mascots and good-luck charms are sent to the club, and the gifts include decorated horse-shoes and several black cats.

2 April 1913

It takes a replay, but Sunderland finally overcome Burnley 3–2 at St. Andrew's, to set up a final meeting with Aston Villa at Crystal Palace. 'The game was so cramped in the second half,' the *Daily Express* reports, 'that Sunderland had moments when they were able to play their pretty short-passing game at will.' Thus Burnley join Manchester City, Swindon and Newcastle United as victims of Sunderland in the Cup this season. Now, the double is on – for both Sunderland and Villa.

18 April 1913

On the eve of the final, Peter McWilliam, the Tottenham Hotspur manager, offers Sunderland some advice regarding the 'vastness' of playing conditions at Crystal Palace. 'Sunderland will find the surroundings of the playing pitch so unlike the League grounds to which they have been accustomed, and they may be slightly bewildered at first. The manager, Kyle, could do worse than take his men over the ground once or twice before the final day.'

19 April 1913

A single Aston Villa goal ruins Sunderland's hopes of a famous double. A bigger story, however, is developing off the field. Serious overcrowding within the ground had resulted in several confrontations involving disgruntled spectators. Worse, the absence of terracing created the risk of a 'death-crush', one newspaper charged. Official action is demanded. The days of Crystal Palace as a venue for football's most prestigious fixture are numbered.

Sunderland, 1913.

23 April 1913

Similarly huge numbers of people turn up at Villa Park for the vital League fixture between the Cup finalists and title rivals. The 60,000 people who pack the ground see Sunderland take the lead with a goal from Tinsley, who deputised for Holley. Although Villa equalised, the point strengthens Sunderland's position at the top of the table.

26 April 1913

An outstanding 3–1 win at Bolton Wanderers means Sunderland are champions. Having recovered so ably from their Cup-final disappointment, Sunderland can now boast the highest number of victories for any team in the three Leagues, and the best goal average. 'It is only fitting that Sunderland win one of football's greatest honours,' the *Daily Express* states.

THROUGH THE AGES
EDWARDIAN FOOTBALL

▶▶▶▶▶▶▶▶▶▶▶▶▶▶▶▶▶▶▶▶▶▶▶▶▶▶▶▶▶▶▶

THIS PAGE: **Above** Corinthians, the outstanding amateur side in english football, 1901. **Right** Billy Meredith runs with the ball, 1908.

OPPOSITE: **Left** Sam Hardy, the Liverpool goalkeeper, 1912. **Above right** Alf Common, the first player to command a £1,000 transfer fee. **Below right** FA Cup final at Crystal Palace, 1905.

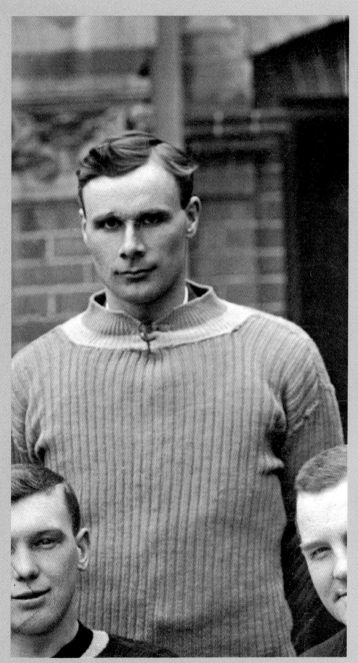

LILY PARR ▶▶▶▶▶▶▶▶▶▶▶▶▶▶▶▶▶▶▶

1905–1978

Lily Parr, 'the most brilliant female player in the world', according to one newspaper, provided the biggest draw card for tens of thousands of supporters who regularly watched women's football at the height of its popularity as a spectator sport.

There was such a clamour to see Parr in action for Dick, Kerr Ladies, the leading women's team in England, that officials had to close the turnstiles at Goodison Park in Liverpool on Boxing Day 1920. The attendance of 53,000 is still a record for the women's game in England.

'Taking sex and age into consideration, there is probably no greater football prodigy in the country than Miss Parr, the outside-left of the famous Dick, Kerr Ladies,' the *Reporter* newspaper stated in 1921.

During the 1920s, when interest in the team peaked, Dick, Kerr Ladies featured on cinema newsreels and their match reports appeared regularly in major newspapers.

In her first season, the then 14-year-old Parr scored 43 goals. She played on until her mid-forties, but throughout her career she was renowned for the strength of her shooting, her 'great kicking power', as one American newspaper put it in 1922.

The previous year, the Preston-based team played 67 games in aid of charity all over Britain, watched by a total of 900,000 people. In its 48-year existence, the team raised £175,000.

The aforementioned game at Everton against St Helens Town generated enormous media interest, with one newspaper stating that thousands of spectators were locked out. 'It was a genuine interest, rather than some kind of novelty,' Gail Newsham, the author of *In a League of Their Own*, said. 'The spectators turned up to watch what they expected to be a good game of football, and Lily was the star attraction.'

Lily Parr heads the ball, 1939.

▶ key match

Dick, Kerr Ladies 4 St Helens Town 0, Goodison Park, 26 December 1920

Lily Parr gave an outstanding performance at outside-left in front of a crowd of 53,000 for this charity match in Liverpool.

Dick, Kerr Ladies were leading 1–0 at half-time when the team made a decisive tactical change, switching Alice Kell, the team captain and full-back, to centre-forward.

It was Parr's job as winger to get as many crosses into the penalty area for the centre-forward to chase. In the second half she did just that, and Kell scored a hat-trick.

Remarkably, more than 10,000 people were locked out, causing so much congestion that the players needed a police escort to reach the changing rooms.

PLAYER • INDUCTED 2002

Dick, Kerr Ladies, 1925.

A Dick, Kerr Ladies medal from the 1930s.

From the start of her career as a teenager, Lily Parr was renowned for having the strongest shot of any female footballer. Although she was praised for her overall play and reading of the game, it was her shooting at goal that excited spectators and earned her newspaper headlines.

There is one story that has become associated with her: while playing a game at Chorley in Lancashire, she was approached by a professional male goalkeeper who challenged her to put the ball past him while he stood in goal. Apparently, the goalkeeper had watched the young Lily shooting at goal during the warm-up before a charity game involving Dick, Kerr Ladies. 'You might look good against other women,' he told her, 'but you would have no chance against a man in goal.'

Never one to shirk a challenge, Lily invited him into the goal. The keeper managed to block her first shot, but at some cost. The force of the ball had broken his arm, so the story went.

Parr was said to have smiled to herself as she heard the man shout to his friends. 'Get me to the hospital as quick as you can, she's gone and broken my flamin' arm!'

Tom Finney, the Preston and England winger, refereed several matches involving Dick, Kerr Ladies during the 1950s. 'Their standard of play was very good,' he said.

At the time there were no organised women's leagues – all the games were friendly fixtures – and the team was in demand for games throughout Britain and the continent. They toured France in 1920 and the United States two years later.

There was such a clamour to see Parr in action for Dick, Kerr ladies, the leading women's team in England, that officials had to close the turnstiles at Goodison Park in Liverpool. The attendance of 53,000 is still a record for the women's game in England.

Results confirmed their status as the best women's team in the country. During the 48 years the team was together, Dick, Kerr Ladies played 828 games, winning 758, drawing 46 and losing only 24 times, an average of one defeat every two years.

'There is probably no greater football prodigy in the country than Miss Parr.' – *Reporter* newspaper, 1921

The boots worn by Lily Parr in 1922.

Parr was made an honorary life member of the amateur club when she retired from football in 1951, at the age of 45. Following her wartime stint as a munitions worker in the Dick, Kerr factory in Preston, she worked as a nurse at a hospital just outside the town. As an amateur footballer, and the most important member of the team, she needed to take a lot of time off work.

'For many years the team enjoyed a fame that has never been equalled by a women's football team since. It is a remarkable story,' Gail Newsham said.

The Football Association had an ambivalent attitude towards women's football when Lily Parr was playing the game.

Dick, Kerr Ladies originally drew players from the women working in a munitions factory during World War One. The team enjoyed universal support for its charitable efforts. The Ladies' first ever game, on Christmas Day in 1917 attracted 10,000 to Deepdale, the home of Preston North End, and raised £600.

At the end of hostilities the team stayed together. Although the side continued to earn money for good causes, there was increasing concern in the men's game that the ongoing popularity of Dick, Kerr Ladies and other women's teams was drawing custom, and potential income, from professional Football League clubs.

In 1921, the Football Association acted, introducing a draconian set of restrictions. Women footballers were no longer allowed to play on any Football League ground and any referee who took control of a women's match would be barred from officiating in the men's game.

In order to carry on, women's teams played some of their matches at the grounds of rugby clubs and the ban from Football League grounds continued to affect the England women's team until 1978.

Despite the ban, the crowds still came. Dick, Kerr Ladies attracted several thousand spectators to some games right up to the mid 1960s, when the team was disbanded.

Dick, Kerr Ladies represent England in an international match against France with music-hall star George Robey kicking-off, 1925.

CLEM STEPHENSON

▶▶▶▶▶▶▶▶▶▶▶▶▶▶▶▶▶▶▶▶▶▶▶▶▶▶▶▶▶▶▶▶▶▶▶▶▶

1890–1961

Clem Stephenson strengthened the reputation of Aston Villa as a major power in English football, and then later played a pivotal role in the emergence of an unlikely dynasty at Huddersfield Town.

During his time at Villa Park, Stephenson was a mainstay in attack in two successful FA Cup campaigns – in 1913 and 1920 – and a third winners' medal followed in 1922. This time, however, he was wearing the blue and white colours of Huddersfield.

It was in the League that this outstanding inside-forward made his greatest contribution, inspiring the Yorkshire club as they secured an unprecedented hat-trick of championship titles, starting in 1923–24.

Former England amateur international Ivan Sharpe wrote: 'A greater club-player and team-maker I have never known.' For his part, Stephenson said: 'Give me teamwork before individualism every time.'

Clem Stephenson, 1928.

PLAYER • INDUCTED 2010 • 1 CAP • 3 DIVISION ONE CHAMPIONSHIPS • 3 FA CUPS

Herbert Chapman built a finely balanced side around Stephenson, and when the game's most innovative manager moved on from Huddersfield Town to Arsenal in 1925, he adopted the same template – with Charles Buchan and, later, Alex James taking over the key role as link/man between defence and attack.

'From his position at inside-left Stephenson has been leader and master-mind in tactics, and the success achieved during the past three years can be traced to his wonderful efforts,' *The Times* stated in 1926. 'For three or four years he has been the general, the man who conceives the tactics to be set in force in a match, and who varies them to meet an emergency, and all the time .... He is still the supreme expert in launching an attack.'

Before his departure to London, Chapman sent Stephenson a letter, in which he wrote: 'I want to thank you personally for your play and wholehearted efforts both on and off the field.

I have never had such confidence in any captain of a team I have been associated with.' That association came about as a consequence of the actions of a group of directors in Birmingham; otherwise, Stephenson would have continued to channel his outstanding ability in the cause of Aston Villa. In what proved ultimately to be a self-defeating action, the Villa board ruled that all their players – including Stephenson – had to live in the local area.

The directors, the *Daily Express* later explained, wanted to guarantee the availability of all their players for daily training, but they only succeeded in alienating several employees, including Stephenson, who refused to relocate from his home in Northumberland. With no sign of a resolution in sight, the directors – no doubt thinking that his best days were behind him, anyway – decided to cash in by transferring him.

Chapman quickly stepped in. He had no

problem with Stephenson living in the north-east, and the player welcomed a move closer to home.

As Villa's fortunes then declined, Huddersfield Town, a club with only a fraction of the resources available at Villa Park, emerged as the greatest power in the country. Decades later, one Villa history described the refusal of the board to compromise with Stephenson and the other dissenting players as 'a disastrous decision for the club'.

In later years, though making fewer appearances than before, on account of his age, Stephenson helped Huddersfield finish runners-up in 1926–27 and 1927–28, the same season they were losing FA Cup finalists.

Clem Stephenson and his Aston Villa teammates are presented to The King, 1920.

CHARLES BUCHAN

▶▶▶▶▶▶▶▶▶▶▶▶▶▶▶▶▶▶

1891–1960

Charles Buchan was the most influential member of the 'Team of All Talents' – the tag given to the powerhouse Sunderland side that invigorated English football during the 1910s.

The mass circulation *Daily Express* once described Buchan as 'the best forward in the world'; years later, that same newspaper identified him as the on-field catalyst behind the rise from mediocrity of The Arsenal, as they were then known, under Herbert Chapman.

The *Express* stated in 1925: '[Buchan] knows so much: when to part with the ball, when to hold it; when to pass or shoot or head. And he gives his knowledge to others. He is player, nurse and coach in one – a past-master in tactics and the maker of a forward line.'

Later still, Buchan became a respected voice for generations of schoolboys who avidly read the popular *Charles Buchan's Football Monthly* journal following its launch in 1951.

↖
Charles Buchan, left, challenges the goalkeeper for a cross, 1927.

PLAYER • INDUCTED 2010 • 6 CAPS • 1 DIVISION ONE CHAMPIONSHIP

'As a footballer, Buchan is clever, immensely clever, in a careful, calculating way.'
– Daily Express, 1925

As a player, his lanky, angular frame – all arms and legs – made him, at times, appear a little awkward in the eyes of some observers, yet, once on the ball, that same appearance belied his skill, the 'feints and stratagems' which, the *Daily Express* informed its readers, 'lead so many half-backs astray'. Newspapers labelled Arsenal's tactics as 'Buchan-ism'.

A Londoner by birth, Buchan joined Sunderland from Leyton in 1911. Two years later, the Wearsiders came agonisingly close to winning the double; after pipping Aston Villa to the title

Charlie Buchan watches a team-mate practise shooting, 1927.

by four points, they lost narrowly against the same opposition in the FA Cup final.

At Roker Park, Buchan was a member of the 'famous triumvirate', along with Mordue, the outside-forward, and Cuggy, the supporting half-back. Years later, David Jack, the former England forward, celebrated a trio 'who thrilled crowds with an artistic, interposing movement'.

During World War One, Buchan served in France with the Grenadier Guards, winning a commission. In a routine examination, Army doctors found an undiagnosed fracture of a small bone in his foot, a handicap that had been bothering him for years.

In a match report in 1925, *The Times* described Buchan's 'head-work' as being 'astonishingly good, even for him. He appears to have either a double-jointed neck or else some

Charles Buchan, left, shakes hands with the Cardiff City captain, 1927.

special neck muscles denied to other men'.

That same year, Sunderland allowed Buchan – by far their most famous player – to leave the club. The decision, seemingly based on a belief that his best days were behind him, provoked widespread outrage and the resignation of one disgruntled director.

'If Mr Chapman's idea of things at Highbury is to build a team around Buchan, he is working on the right lines,' one *Express* football writer declared a year later. 'My own impression is that Buchan will make The Arsenal.'

Although the final breakthrough to success – victory in the 1930 FA Cup final – came two years after Buchan hung up his boots, Chapman later spoke of him as 'a great player and a great captain'.

▶ talking point

The prospect of signing Charles Buchan prompted Arsenal manager Herbert Chapman to move swiftly and with typical boldness and invention.

The transfer terms reflected Chapman's faith in the player. In addition to a £2,000 down-payment, Arsenal would pay £100 every time he scored over the course of the following season, including both games against Sunderland. Twenty-one goals later, Chapman could celebrate his acumen. (Not everyone was best pleased, however: the FA quickly outlawed such terms.)

For his money, Chapman also acquired a trusted advisor on team selection and tactics; in the wake of a revision to the offside law in 1925, it was Buchan who advocated the employment of a strictly defensive centre-half.

TEAM INDUCTEE
HUDDERSFIELD TOWN
▶▶▶▶▶▶▶▶▶▶▶▶▶▶▶▶▶▶▶▶▶▶▶▶▶▶ 1922–1926

28 April 1922

The Chief Constable of Huddersfield says the town previously a stronghold for rugby league, has 'gone football mad' ahead of their appearance in the FA Cup final. 'Large numbers of boys have been summoned to police court for kicking footballs about in the street,' he says.

▶▶▶▶▶▶▶▶▶▶▶▶▶▶▶▶▶▶▶▶

29 April 1922

A penalty by Smith gives Huddersfield Town victory over Preston North End in the last FA Cup final to be played at Stamford Bridge. The decision to rest a host of first-team players before important Cup ties this season has paid dividends. One newspaper describes Town as 'a typical hard, well-trained, professional team of the bulky, bustling variety'.

27 October 1923

A stout defensive display at home against Birmingham City means that a single goal from inside-forward Clem Stephenson gives Huddersfield two points. The result has a wider significance: the Yorkshire side have established themselves at the head of the Division One table. *The Times* rates them the best-balanced side in England.

▶▶▶▶▶▶▶▶▶▶▶▶▶▶▶▶▶▶▶▶

1 March 1924

League leaders Cardiff City visit Huddersfield's Leeds Road, defending an unbeaten run that dates back to early January. They leave for South Wales smarting from a 2–0 defeat in front of a crowd of 25,000. The result marks a turning point for both sides. At the end of the season Huddersfield are crowned champions on goal difference, above runners-up, Cardiff.

15 December 1924

After losing three matches in succession, Huddersfield Town recover their form with a run of five games that yield 11 goals and only one defeat. Their improvement in form is attributed to the signing of Mercer, from Hull City, as replacement for the injured Taylor in goal.

▶▶▶▶▶▶▶▶▶▶▶▶▶▶▶▶▶▶▶▶

2 May 1925

The president of the Football League, Mr John McKenna, presents the championship trophy following a home draw against Liverpool. Huddersfield have lost four fewer games than any of their rivals. Before

↙

Huddersfield Town players, circa mid 1920s.

the start of the following season, the club strengthens its ranks with the signing of Scottish outside-right, Alex Jackson, from Aberdeen. But there is an even more noteworthy departure: Herbert Chapman heads south to take charge of struggling Arsenal.

10 October 1925

Huddersfield remain the only undefeated side in the top division with this 2–1 home win over Burnley. Since 17 January, Town have played 26 matches, winning 15

↘

Huddersfield Town players, clockwise from top left, Clem Stephenson, W.H. Smith, E Davies and G. Slade, 1922.

and drawing 11. This latest victory is all the more remarkable for the injury to Wadsworth, the England left-back, who dislocated his elbow, and then returned at outside right, with his injured arm strapped to his side.

6 March 1926

Huddersfield take an important step nearer a cherished hat-trick of titles with a 2–0 win at St. James' Park. The game is billed beforehand as a battle between rival Scottish centre-forwards – Hughie Gallacher, of Newcastle United, and William Devlin, who was making his debut following a transfer from Cowdenbeath. The goals, however, come from Brown.

26 March 1926

As Huddersfield challenge for an unprecedented hat-trick of titles, their former manager, Ambrose Langley, makes his claim for some of the credit. Langley, who spent two years in charge between 1919 and 1921, says: 'I was responsible for discovering and securing both the present backs – Roy Goodall and Sam Wadsworth. I signed Cawthorne, the right half-back, a Sheffield lad, for nothing. I got Tom Wilson, the famous pivot, for nothing from Sunderland. Those four players only cost us £1,020. What are they worth today?'

10 April 1926

At half-time at Leeds Road, the home side are a goal down against West Ham United. News then filters through to the dressing room that title rivals Arsenal are beating Sunderland. According to one newspaper, the bulletin delivered 'an electric shock' – and within six minutes of the second half, two Huddersfield Town goals have transformed the game. There is only one complaint: a season's wear and tear means there is not a single blade of grass on the pitch.

↗

Huddersfield Town win the FA Cup final at Stamford Bridge, 1922.

3 May 1926

The players enjoy reading the reviews of the 1925–26 season in the national newspapers. 'Their record of winning the championship for a third year in succession is a record that is likely to remain unequalled for a decade or two,' predicts the *Daily Express*. The achievement is a personal triumph for Cecil Potter, the successor to Chapman as manager.

27 August 1926

In the preview of the new season, *The Times* attributes Huddersfield's outstanding run of success to 'their keen fighting spirit', both home and away. 'Other teams are as clever, but they do not possess the same capacity to struggle against the odds. This is seen in their matches away from home, in which they are always specially dangerous.'

ALEX JAMES

▶▶▶▶▶▶▶▶▶▶▶▶▶▶

1901–1953

The owner of the most famous baggy shorts in football, Alex James directed the rise of Arsenal to greatness during the 1930s.

The Highbury honours board confirmed the scale of his contribution: before his arrival in 1929 the club had won nothing, despite heavy recent investment in the transfer market; then, over the ensuing seven years, with James at inside-forward, the Gunners won four titles and reached three FA Cup finals.

'It is impossible to underestimate the contribution made by James to the successful Arsenal side of the 1930s,' the official club history states. 'He was simply the key man.' In 1932, the *Daily Express* described him as 'the most valuable footballer on earth'.

That reputation was confirmed when his obituary was published in *The Times*; notably, for the first time, the august newspaper had marked the death of a working footballer.

Above Alex James holds the FA Cup, 1936.
Below Alex James (left) and Cliff Bastin, 1930.

PLAYER • INDUCTED 2005 • 8 CAPS • 4 DIVISION ONE CHAMPIONSHIPS • 2 FA CUPS

'The skill and bold tactics of James turned the scale in favour of his side.' – *The Times* report on the 1930 FA Cup final

From his deep-lying, roaming position, James initiated counter-attacks of overwhelming speed and directness. Never before had an inside-forward directed play so completely from this part of the field. 'Alex was simply guided by his football instinct and went to the open spaces,' recalled George Allison, the Arsenal manager.

Writing in 1931, David Jack, the former England forward, noted James' gift for 'beating opponents with an artistic dribble, feint or swerve'. What set him apart from other inside-forwards of his era, however, was 'the ability to make the final pass as deadly as circumstances permit', Jack argued.

Those passes were 'usually delivered through the middle for the centre-forward to take in his stride, or to the inside of the opposing right-back for Cliff Bastin, the Arsenal winger, to cut in and collect'.

Rivals soon copied Arsenal's attacking 'W' formation – with a centre-forward and two wingers occupying the most advanced positions. Lacking a player of James' creative ability, however, none could make it work as effectively. Conventional thinking also required an inside-forward to score his share of goals; though previously a prolific marksman for Preston, James now left this task to the other forwards.

Signed from Preston for the then substantial fee of £8,750, James was a conspicuous figure, having developed the habit of wearing over-sized shorts. When newspaper cartoonists caricatured his appearance, probably to accentuate his short stature, the supremely confident James played up to the image, saying: 'They keep my knees warm.' One local lad and Deepdale regular was quick to mimic his hero. 'I began wearing ridiculously baggy

shorts as well,' Tom Finney recalled.

James hated to waste energy. His motto was: 'Let the ball do the work.' George Allison said. 'No one like him ever kicked a ball. He simply left the opposition looking on his departing figure with amazement.'

In 1930, Arsenal won the FA Cup for the first time. Six years later, James lifted the Cup as captain. By now, Arsenal were nursing him through the fixture list more and more, in an effort to prolong his career. As he faded, inevitably, with age, so did Arsenal. Following his retirement in May 1937, the remnants of the side built by Chapman had only one more title left in them. The golden era – the era of Alex James – was over.

Alex James scores in the FA Cup final, 1930.

THROUGH THE AGES
FOOTBALL IN THE 1920s

THIS PAGE: **Above left** Cardiff City players travel by car, 1927. **Below left** Bolton Wanderers captain Joe Smith leads his team out at Wembley, 1926. **Right** Arsenal director and BBC radio commentator George Allison, working at his desk, 1927.

OPPOSITE PAGE: **Above left** Cardiff City captain Fred Keenor shields the FA Cup from the crowd, 1927. **Above right** Bolton Wanderers players and officials pose with the FA Cup, 1926. **Below left** Cardiff City players celebrate victory in the FA Cup final, 1927. **Below right** Arsenal players Alf Baker, Billy Blyth and Jimmy Brain, 1927.

DIXIE DEAN

▶▶▶▶▶▶▶▶▶▶▶▶▶▶▶▶▶▶

1907–1980

William Ralph Dean – the incomparable 'Dixie' – occupies a secure place in the history of English football on the strength of his extraordinary scoring feats during one dramatic season.

In a mere 39 games during the 1927–28 season, Dean scored a record-breaking 60 goals for Everton in the First Division. At the age of 21, he had achieved a degree of recognition and acclaim previously beyond the reach of any footballer – a fame that spread far beyond the reaches of his native Merseyside.

Even members of the Royal family were said to recognise 'Dixie' on account of his sturdy frame, rugged features and mop of thick black hair – features that made his waxwork likeness a popular tourist attraction at Madame Tussauds. For the first time, football had a household name.

Between 1923 and 1939, Dean scored 473 goals in 502 League, FA Cup, representative and international matches. Twice, in 1927–28 and 1931–32, he was leading scorer in Division One. On both occasions, Everton finished the season as champions.

Fittingly, albeit by chance, he was the first player to wear the number nine shirt at Wembley. The Football Association chose the FA Cup final in 1933 for a trial of numbered shirts. Everton were allocated numbers one to eleven. Typically, Dean scored in the 3–0 win over a Manchester City side in shirts numbered 12–22. 'This is the crowning moment of my career,' he told reporters.

In his prime, Dean's value was almost incalculable. An official history of the Football League details how Arsenal offered a blank cheque for his transfer but Everton still said no. Besides, Dixie had no intention of leaving, having turned down a contract tripling his basic wage to play in the United States.

'Dixie was the greatest centre-forward there will ever be,' Bill Shankly once said. 'He belongs to the company of the supremely great, like Beethoven, Shakespeare and Rembrandt.'

Dixie Dean, 1929.

▶ key match

Everton 3 Arsenal 3, Division One, Goodison Park, 5 May 1928

The stage was set for Dixie Dean to achieve greatness. Everton were already confirmed as champions, so only one question remained: could he score the hat-trick he needed to break the League record of 59 goals in a single season.

By five past three, Everton were two-up, and both goals – a trademark header and a penalty – were scored by Dean. It would be another agonising 75 minutes before the dramatic conclusion.

'It came in absolutely perfectly for me from the left,' Dean said, recalling the late Everton corner. 'I ran from outside the area to head it into the net. That was it, the record. I just bowed, but the crowd went wild.'

Recognising the significance of the moment, and forgetting their professional instinct, several Arsenal players shook the hand of the man who had scored against them.

PLAYER • INDUCTED 2002 • 16 CAPS • 2 DIVISION ONE CHAMPIONSHIPS • 1 FA CUP

'I'd have played for Everton for nothing.' – Dixie Dean

At club level Dean shaped the fortunes of Everton for a decade. Put simply, if Dean was fit, the team prospered. The opposite was also true. When Everton were relegated, in 1929–30, Dean missed a large chunk of the season because of injury. He returned the next season, as did Everton.

In a preview of the FA Cup final in 1933, *The Times* noted: 'During recent years the fortunes of the team have risen and fallen with the form of their centre-forward, Dean.'

A year earlier the newspaper offered these words of caution: 'There is always the danger, which has been felt by the club in recent seasons, that, if he loses his form or suffers injury, disaster is piled on disaster and the team falls from great heights to the lowest abyss.'

According to *The Times*, Dean amended his tactics as a centre-forward over the years. 'When Dean first came to Everton he scored goals in every conceivable way, but the great-

est danger to his foes was when he could get his head to the ball anywhere near the goal.

'Gradually other teams found ways and means of holding Dean in check, and the occasions on which he gets a chance to score are now rare indeed. But a remodelling of style and method has imposed the task on the other forwards, and Dean's part now is to make the chances.

'He has a way of getting his head to the ball and with a nod placing it back to a comrade's foot who is just in the right position to bang it through the goal.'

In one game, Manchester City and England goalkeeper Frank Swift noted how Dean 'headed a pass from Cliff Britton, out to the left winger on the touchline. I had never seen any forward do that before'.

Though subject to the then increasingly popular defensive tactic of 'marking', Dean maintained an impressive scoring record in later years. 'Dixie knew a goalkeeper has greater trouble in dealing with a shot on the ground from close range than one in the air so he got well above the ball to head it down,' Swift added. 'On his feet, he was like a ballet dancer and specialised in placing his shots.'

Often times, defenders relied on brute force as a means of trying to stop him, and a succession of injuries was the inevitable result of their rough treatment. His ankles, in particular, took a terrible battering. 'I had 15 operations during my career,' Dean recalled, 'and several of them were to repair bones in my ankle.'

An England cap.

Dixie Dean, (Trevillion).

Psychologically, one of the earliest of those operations was perhaps the most traumatic. In 1924, surgeons removed a damaged testicle – the result, Dean always maintained in later life, of a deliberate kick in the groin by a defender.

Indeed, had it not been for a natural strength developed as a delivery boy lugging milk crates around the streets of his native Birkenhead, Dean may have been lost to the game before he had the chance to achieve greatness.

In 1926, two years before he broke the record, he fractured his skull, jawbone and knee in a motorcycle accident. Initially, doctors feared for his life; they then said he would never play again. However, Dean confounded medical opinion. When, 16 weeks later, he made his comeback for Everton reserves, 30,000 people turned up to see him.

'The greatest player of all for winning games off his own foot, or head, was Bill Dean.' – Charles Buchan

A generous extrovert and larger-than-life character, Bill Dean became an icon on Merseyside at a time of great economic hardship. Before matches, he would often walk the short distance from his clubhouse to the ground in his slippers, chatting to supporters. Once there, he was known to buy tickets for unemployed men out of his own pocket.

Fiercely loyal to a club that he had supported since childhood, Dixie joined Everton from Tranmere Rovers at the age of 17 in 1925, for a fee of £3,000, then a record fee for a Division Three

Dixie Dean in action, 1936.

player. He had already rejected offers from several other leading clubs. 'I'd have played for Everton for nothing,' he said later.

By the early 1930s Dean was the undisputed leader of a team full of experienced internationals. As captain, he assumed much of the responsibility for tactics on the pitch. Off the field, in the absence of a specialist team-manager at Goodison Park, he also advised directors on team-selection.

As the decade progressed, however, Dean began to show the inevitable signs of physical strain following years of rough treatment. As he began to slow, so did his scoring rate. Everton reacted by signing a young Tommy Lawton as his successor.

Even so, there was a sense of deep shock in the city when Everton, suddenly and without warning, sold Dean to Notts County in 1938. He left Everton without fanfare, the victim, he always said, of a club official who saw Dean as a threat to his own ambitions. There wasn't even time to say goodbye to his team-mates; they were not told about the transfer until later.

Three decades later, Everton made some amends for their treatment of a loyal and exceptional club servant when they organised a testimonial in 1964. More than 36,000 people turned out in tribute. In 2001, Everton erected a statue of Dean outside the ground as a permanent memorial.

Bill Dean collapsed and died in the stands at Goodison Park after watching his beloved Everton play Liverpool in March 1980. He was

aged 73. His family believe that Dean wanted those final hours to be spent at his spiritual home – the site of his greatest triumph.

On hearing the news of his friend's death, Joe Mercer, a former team-mate and fellow avid Evertonian, asked the rhetorical question: 'Where else?'

HERBERT CHAPMAN

▶▶▶▶▶▶▶▶▶▶▶▶▶▶▶▶▶

1878–1934

As a result of his achievement in making Arsenal the most famous and celebrated club in the world during the 1930s, Herbert Chapman advanced the role of team manager, creating a legacy that, like his memorial bust, was there for everyone to see at Highbury.

London had yet to celebrate a championship success when Chapman arrived at Arsenal in 1925. Mediocre, debt-ridden and lacking mass support, the Gunners were thought of as unlikely saviours for the capital.

A decade later, however, Arsenal were the dominant power in England, let alone London. At the time of his death, aged 55, from pneumonia in 1934, a second successive title was within sight, to add to an earlier FA Cup win. Furthermore, the team that he built went on to win three more trophies in the 1930s. Meanwhile newspapers noted the addition of a new term to the football lexicon: Arsenal players had begun referring to Chapman as 'the Boss'.

↖
Herbert Chapman, 1931.

MANAGER • INDUCTED 2003 • 4 DIVISION ONE CHAMPIONSHIPS • 2 FA CUPS

'A team can attack for too long. The quicker you get to your opponent's goal, the fewer obstacles you find.'
– Herbert Chapman

His vision and innovative thinking had put Arsenal on the map, literally. In 1932, in a public relations coup, he persuaded the local railway company to re-name the London Underground station close to Highbury after the club.

Remarkably, Chapman won the championship with two different clubs, a feat that would remain unequalled for another four decades, following the securing of successive titles at previously unfashionable Huddersfield Town in the mid-1920s. Determined to lure him south from his native Yorkshire, The Arsenal, as the club was then known,

Herbert Chapman, middle, makes a point to Alex James, 1931.

made Chapman the highest paid manager in football.

From the outset he insisted that selection and all other team matters be left to the professionals – namely, himself. 'Football today is too big a job to be a director's hobby,' he wrote. 'Herbert was definitely the governor,' George Male, the team captain, wrote later.

Tactically, Chapman eventually restricted the role of the centre-half, in response to a revision of the offside law in 1925 that tilted the advantage more in favour of the attacker. From now on, the 'policeman' number five would concentrate almost exclusively on marking the opposition centre-forward, with little thought, unlike before, to forward play. Under this 'third-back' system honed by Chapman, the chief responsibility for initiating attacks now rested with an inside-forward, who dropped deeper to strengthen the link between attack and defence.

In order to realise his tactical vision, Chapman was willing to spend record sums in the transfer market. In 1928 Arsenal paid Bolton Wanderers £11,500 for David Jack, the England inside-forward; the following year Chapman signed Alex James from Preston, for a fee of £8,750.

In another break with custom, Arsenal initiated team meetings during which players were encouraged to speak out. One opinion, above all others commanded Chapman's respect – that of Charles Buchan, the inside-

forward who was routinely consulted about tactics and team matters.

Later, in 1933, the rotund Chapman offered a glimpse of the future when he took charge of the England team, as a one-off, for the international against Italy in Rome. It would be another decade before a manager was appointed on a permanent basis.

Years later, Arsenal's outside-left Cliff Bastin spoke of Chapman's 'aura of greatness', citing his power of inspiration and foresight. 'He should have been prime minister,' Bastin wrote in 1950. 'He might have been but for the lack of opportunities entailed by his position in the social scale.'

JOAN WHALLEY

▶▶▶▶▶▶▶▶▶▶▶▶▶▶▶▶▶▶▶▶▶▶▶▶▶▶▶▶▶▶▶▶▶▶▶▶▶

1921–1998

A skilful right-winger, Joan Whalley was a permanent fixture in the best women's team in England over a period of several decades either side of World War Two.

In the days before officially organised international football, Whalley was selected to play for an England XI against a Scottish select side in a one-off match in 1946.

At club level, for all but a five-year period in the mid-1950s, she played all her football for Dick, Kerr Ladies, the celebrated and almost unbeatable Preston-based side.

In their heyday between the wars, when they were hailed as the best women's team in the world, national newspapers such as the *Daily Herald*, *Daily Mail* and *Daily Sketch* regularly sent photo-graphers and reporters to cover matches and training sessions.

Renowned for her technique, Whalley was an automatic choice for the side throughout her career. Most attacks made by the team were built down her wing.

↗
Joan Whalley (second from left) discusses tactics with her team-mates.

PLAYER • INDUCTED 2007

'Joan was a terrific player.
I enjoyed watching those games
involving Dick, Kerr Ladies.'
– Sir Tom Finney

Born in Preston on 18 December 1921, Whalley was a bit of a tomboy. She loved to play football. At the age of five she received her first pair of football boots as a present from her father, who spotted her potential early.

When Whalley made her debut for the club at the age of 15, she had to take the day off school. The signing of a schoolgirl by the most famous women's team in the country had made headlines; for a while, every time she came home from school there were reporters waiting for her at the front door.

Slim and petite, Whalley made her debut when she travelled with the team to Leeds for a match to commemorate the coronation of King George VI. It was her first taste of playing in front of a large crowd. 'To see thousands of people turn up to watch us was a bit of a

Dick, Kerr Ladies in training, 1939.

shock,' Whalley would recall later.

One of her fellow pupils at school was Tom Finney, the future Preston North End and England winger. Years later, Finney was the celebrity guest at a Dick, Kerr Ladies match, and the two old friends were reunited during the presentation. 'Joan was a terrific player. I enjoyed watching those games involving Dick, Kerr Ladies,' Finney said. 'The standard of play was good.'

In the latter years of her lengthy career, Whalley took on greater responsibility, captaining the side, influencing tactics and delivering team talks in the dressing room. Off the field, Joan entertained team-mates by playing popular songs on a mouth organ.

The highlight of Whalley's time in the game came when Matt Busby watched the team play in Blackpool. After the game the Manchester United manager praised their performance. Busby was then told that the club was short of

Joan Whalley, left, listens to a tactical team-talk given by Lily Parr, 1939.

cash; the following week a package arrived: the gift of a match-ball used by United in a first-team fixture.

Her reputation had been established by now. Immediately after World War Two, the *Daily Express* stated, in reference to Finney and Whalley: 'Preston has the two greatest right-wingers in the world.'

Whalley was an automatic choice for Dick, Kerr Ladies throughout her career. Most attacks made by the team were built down her wing.

▶ key match

Dick, Kerr Ladies 5 Edinburgh Ladies 1, Challenge match, Blackpool, 30 August 1937

The newspapers turned up in force for a match that was billed by the participants as a 'World Championship' between the best two teams in Britain. In issuing the challenge, Edinburgh declared their belief that Scottish craft would prevail over English pace and power.

The previous evening, the players discussed tactics, and those preparations paid off. In the first half, Dick, Kerr Ladies scored five times, with centre-forward Edith 'Ginger' Hutton collecting a hat-trick; Lily Parr and Whalley also found the net.

Fleet Street had its story: unbeaten that season in 27 matches against all-comers, both here and abroad, Dick, Kerr Ladies declared themselves 'champions of the world'.

FRANK SWIFT

▶▶▶▶▶▶▶▶▶▶▶▶▶▶▶▶▶

1913–1958

Who better to describe the qualities of Frank Swift than one of the opponents he frustrated so often – Joe Mercer, the England, Everton and Arsenal player who graced English football during the middle years of the last century?

'He was the best goalkeeper I ever saw,' Mercer wrote in 1964. 'When Frank was in full song, coming out and attacking the ball, he was unbeatable. He would catch shots in one hand, like an apple falling from a tree and then look straight at the opposing forwards contemptuously. It used to break their hearts – he made it look so easy.'

Swift combined extraordinary height and reach with positional sense and courage. 'He was without fear, and he would chill you to the marrow with his blood-curdling roar of "Right!" when he thought that a ball was his.' Tommy Lawton, the England centre-forward, recalled.

A smiling Frank Swift, 1947.

PLAYER • INDUCTED 2009 • 19 CAPS • 1 DIVISION ONE CHAMPIONSHIP • 1 FA CUP

'Frank was the best goalkeeper I ever saw. When Frank was in full song, coming out and attacking the ball, he was unbeatable.' – Joe Mercer, 1964

Though not yet out of his teens – an exceptionally young age for a goalkeeper in the inter-war era – Swift kept goal for Manchester City in their FA Cup final victory over Portsmouth in 1934. He followed up that success with a League championship medal in 1936–37.

Later, in 1948, Swift became the first goalkeeper in the modern era to captain England, in a stunning 4–0 win against Italy in Milan. In the dressing room beforehand, Swift shook the hand of all his team-mates; they, in turn, vowed to run themselves into the ground for their popular team-mate.

↗
Frank Swift saves a low shot, 1941.

'Frank played the game of his life,' Tommy Lawton wrote later. 'One save from Gabetto prompted the number nine to punch the turf in disbelief. We were so determined to make sure that we won the game for Frank.'

'Swifty had an artist's temperament,' Joe Mercer added. 'A good save early on would inspire him. He could also inspire the whole team with his deeds and attitude.'

Tactically, Swift was credited with being the first goalkeeper to use a long throw-out as an attacking weapon. 'He was a creative player, the first really positive goalkeeper,' Mercer wrote. 'He fed the forwards with the ball, throwing it out to the wings and starting positive movements.'

From his earliest days, Swift enjoyed the absolute confidence of his City team-mates. 'Sam Cowan was a dominating captain and defender, and he insisted that I was in command in the penalty area,' Swift recalled.

↖
Frank Swift makes an athletic save, 1934.

'If a back was robbed of the ball because he held it too long, Cowan blamed me for not shouting a warning. I was expected to direct my colleagues when to clear the ball.'

By the late 1940s, Swift was one of the most famous footballers in the world. In Italy, the England team was mobbed by local fans, but it was Swift and Lawton who enjoyed the greatest share of attention.

On and off the field, had there ever been a more popular or entertaining footballer? In tough times economically, his occasional theatrics during games, mischievous sense of humour and generosity of spirit lifted the national mood. To his great friend and Manchester City team-mate of the 1930s, Matt Busby, Swift was simply 'Big Fella'.

▶ key match

Manchester City 2, Portsmouth 1, FA Cup final, Wembley Stadium, 28 April 1934

In one of the most famous incidents in Wembley history, Frank Swift fainted as he walked towards the royal box at the end of the game.

'Swift, a mere lad of nineteen and a bit, falls flat on his face as though struck by a bullet,' reported the *Daily Express*. 'The reaction from a nerve-racking test had stolen all power from his limbs.'

Once revived, Swift needed the help of a City team-mate to guide his faltering steps as he collected his medal.

It had been barely six months since his debut in the City reserves; less than a year later he was challenging for an England call-up.

CLIFF BASTIN

▶▶▶▶▶▶▶▶▶▶▶▶▶▶▶▶

1912–1991

When Cliff Bastin arrived at Highbury for the first time, he was famously refused entry. The doorman, it later transpired, thought that the fresh-faced 17-year-old footballer before him was a young autograph hunter.

Back then, in the late 1920s, it was rare for a teenager to play at the highest level. Yet, within a year or so, the player nicknamed 'Boy' by the newspapers was the youngest ever FA Cup winner.

Switched initially from inside-forward to outside-left by Herbert Chapman, the Arsenal manager, Bastin emerged as an outstanding goalscorer and England international during the Gunners' golden era in the 1930s.

By now, his fame had spread far beyond north London. 'The skilful Bastin has gained for himself a reputation second to none on the Continent,' the *Daily Express* reported in 1933. 'A genius is not too strong a word to describe him.'

Cliff Bastin, 1946.

PLAYER • INDUCTED 2009 • 21 CAPS • 5 LEAGUE CHAMPIONSHIPS • 2 FA CUPS

'Every fan's favourite and one of the world's wonder wingers.' – George Allison

Arsenal revolutionised wing-play: on Chapman's orders, instead of hugging the touchline, Bastin and Joe Hulme cut inside more often, . No longer merely creators of chances for others, the wingers were expected to score goals too.

'Herbert gave his wingers an entirely new concept of their functions,' wrote Bob Wall, the then Arsenal secretary. 'He told them: "Don't go down the line. As soon as you receive the ball, I want you to try to beat your full-back, preferably on the inside, and go for goal. If you get checked, lay it off and let somebody else have a go".'

It was a tactical innovation that changed the face of attacking play in the decade following the change to the offside law in 1925. A dead-ball specialist, Bastin was also danger-ous in the air at the far post – another rare trait for a winger at the time.

Bastin registered 178 goals in almost 400 games for the Gunners, establishing a club goalscoring aggregate record that stood for more than half a century. Those goals helped Bastin amass five championship and two FA Cup medals. At his best, he scored 33 goals in a single season – a record for a winger in the top flight.

In 1936, *The Times* paid this glowing tribute in a match report: 'Bastin was the genius of the England forward line, indeed the team. He managed both to be a force in defence and to be up in every attack that was launched, and to look the most probable scorer.'

Tom Whittaker, the Arsenal trainer, said of Bastin: 'Coupled with his sincerity and his loyalty to all his bosses, he had a trait few of us are blessed with – that is, he had an ice-cold temperament.'

A £2,000 signing from Exeter City, for whom he made only 17 appearances, the ver-satile Bastin was capable of filling in at inside-forward and wing-half. 'The complete footballer,' *The Times* stated. 'He covers an immense amount of ground ... Such was his physical fitness and sense of anticipation that he was always where he needed to be.'

At the height of his fame, Bastin appeared in two movies. A breakfast cereal company also employed him as a spokesman, and a generation of youngsters was encouraged to join 'Cliff Bastin's Football Club', a magazine membership scheme for football-mad teenagers. Having once himself been mistaken for an autograph hunter, the signature of Cliff Bastin came to be highly valued by fans and advertising men alike.

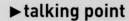

Cliff Bastin, on the ground, in action for Arsenal, 1934.

PETER DOHERTY ▶▶▶▶▶▶▶▶▶

1913–1990

A stylish, inventive and unpredictable inside-forward who enjoyed success with two different clubs either side of World War Two, Peter Doherty was the most valuable footballer of his era – and a champion of the role of player-manager.

'Of all the opponents I faced,' Joe Mercer once wrote, 'I particularly remember Doherty, who was unplayable on his day. He was built like a greyhound, very fast and elusive but with stamina, too. He had a Rolls-Royce engine in him.'

Billy Wright once nicknamed Doherty 'Peter the Great', describing the Northern Ireland international as 'one of the outstanding inside-forwards in the world'. According to the mass-circulation *Daily Express*, he was a forward 'with the hair of auburn and the feet of gold'.

A deep-thinker about the game, Doherty defied convention by ditching the standard football boot – with its heavy leather, reinforced toe-cap and extensive ankle protection – in favour of the lighter and softer boots worn by lacrosse players.

'They give you a grip of the ball, and if you are a forward you can operate much faster,' Doherty wrote in 1950. He was also ahead of his day in that he always packed three different pairs of boots on match-day and then made his choice depending on match-day conditions.

After one outstanding performance for Manchester City in April 1937, the *Express* described Doherty as the 'Intelligent Roamer'. Time and again, a player listed in the programme as an inside-left instigated the switching of positions with other members of the forward line. He was taking this relatively new tactic to a higher level of accomplishment.

'Wandering does not always pay,' the paper stated. 'The Doherty roamings paid 100 per cent because there was thought behind them. He was superb.'

Peter Doherty, 1949.

PLAYER • INDUCTED 2002 • 16 CAPS • 1 DIVISION ONE CHAMPIONSHIP • 1 FA CUP

'His name is already a byword in football, and he is spoken of with respect and admiration by all who know him.'
– Stanley Matthews

When Manchester City won the championship title in 1936–37, the team scored 107 goals – with almost one third of them coming from the boot or head of Doherty.

Almost a decade later, he orchestrated the Derby County attack in the first post-war FA Cup final. Working in partnership with fellow veteran, Raich Carter, Doherty scored one of the goals as Derby ran out 4–1 winners against Charlton Athletic at Wembley.

Either side of these successes Doherty played for Blackpool, Huddersfield Town and Doncaster Rovers, where he won promotion to Division Two as player-manager in 1949–50. 'I've had five clubs during my career,' Doherty said. 'Four of them senior English clubs, and the sum total of fees paid on my transfer is greater than that paid for any other first-class player.'

His enthusiasm for the game never wavered, as Harry Johnston, the Blackpool and England centre-half, observed when he likened Doherty's attitude to that of a young lad 'playing his heart out in a cobbled back-street as though his life depended on it'.

'Peter darted round the field like an enthusiastic colt,' Johnston wrote. 'He was leggy, awkward to tackle; he had a body swerve, keen football brain and a non-stop energy which made him want to be where the ball was.'

Lauded for his talent for spotting an opening in attack, Peter Doherty was a visionary off the field, too. A vociferous advocate of coaching, he railed against orthodox training methods.

Instead of running endless laps of the pitch, as was the norm at the time, Doherty suggested volleyball, 'to promote jumping, timing and judgement'; basketball, 'to encourage split-second decision-making and finding space'; and walking-football, 'to build up calf muscles'.

It was revolutionary thinking at the time. 'Most training at clubs is a slow form of torture,' he wrote. 'We need more variation.'

Doherty was equally forthright – and, at times, confrontational – in his lobbying on the issue of working conditions for professional footballers. In this case, his actions were shaped by bitter experience – the decision by Blackpool to sell him against his will in 1933.

'My personal feelings counted for next to nothing in the transaction,' he wrote later,

The cap awarded to Peter Doherty in recognition of his participation in the internationals against England and Scotland, 1936–37.

Peter Doherty in Huddersfield Town kit, 1946.

referring to the registration system that allowed clubs to buy and sell players at will. 'I might as well have been a bale of merchandise.'

Then, at the outbreak of World War Two and the consequent cancellation of League fixtures, Football League clubs collectively agreed to rip up the contracts of players in order to save money. 'Without a scrap of consideration or sentiment, our means of livelihood were simply jettisoned,' he said.

Under the existing rules, Manchester City, as holders of his registration, could still dictate when and where he played even though the contract between them was no longer honoured. The club repeatedly used this power to prevent him playing as a guest for

Peter Doherty playing for Manchester City, 1936.

promptly played a crucial part in saving the proud Yorkshire club from relegation from the top flight.

In a final move in April 1949, Doherty was appointed player-manager at Doncaster Rovers. This combined role had come back into fashion somewhat since the end of the war, and the success Doherty achieved in winning promotion at the end of his first season added substance to the belief that it was possible for an individual to fulfil it.

Doherty was always prepared to try something new. In those days the number on the

another club, denying him a match fee. 'I bitterly resented City dictating to me in this way,' he said. It was a system governing football's labour market that Doherty railed against for many years.

In December 1945, when City decided to cash in on their asset, the 31-year-old Doherty was sold to Derby County for a fee of £3,500. Remarkably, one year and one FA Cup winner's medal later, his value had risen three-fold.

Significantly, both his previous clubs – Blackpool and Manchester City – were prepared to pay £10,000 for his transfer. Derby, however, honoured an earlier promise to give Huddersfield Town first option – and Doherty

back of the shirt always related to a set position: number two was the right-back, number three the left-back, and so on. On a number of occasions the player-manager sent out his team-mates with the 'wrong' numbers on the shirts. Even such a simple play confused opponents. But that was Doherty – always thinking one step ahead.

The FA Cup trophy.

THROUGH THE AGES
FOOTBALL IN THE 1930s

THIS PAGE: **Above left** Goalmouth action in the FA Cup final, 1938. **Below left** Huddersfield Town players inspect the pitch at Wembley, 1938. **Right** Liverpool goalkeeper Elisha Scott clears the ball, 1933.

OPPOSITE PAGE: **Above left** The Duke of York is presented to Manchester City players, 1933. **Above right** The son of Eddie Hapgood kicks the ball, with his father, left, and Alex James looking on, 1934. **Below left** Action from the FA Cup final, 1937. **Below right** Raich Carter carries the FA Cup into Roker Park, 1937.

TOMMY LAWTON

▶▶▶▶▶▶▶▶▶▶▶▶▶▶▶▶▶

1919–1996

Tommy Lawton, the owner of arguably the most distinctive head of hair in post-war football, was an automatic choice in the England side for a decade – a centre-forward described by Joe Mercer as 'technically, surely the greatest number nine of all time'.

At his peak in the late 1940s, Lawton was the central figure in the most celebrated of all England forward lines: Stanley Matthews, Wilf Mannion, Stan Mortensen and Tom Finney supplied the chances, but Lawton was the undisputed leader – the fulcrum – of the attack.

It was his job to score the lion's share of the goals, a task requiring power, courage and skill. 'Tom was the lightest mover of any big man who played football,' Alex James said.

Throughout his career Lawton kept in mind some early advice about shooting: 'As soon as you see the white lines of the penalty area, son,' the Burnley trainer told him, 'hit the bloody thing. Hard.'

↖
Tommy Lawton, 1947.

Tommy Lawton, right, jokes with Everton team-mate Joe Mercer, 1939.

Lawton, whose slicked-back black hair and centre parting made him an instantly recognisable figure, was rated by many of his contemporaries as the greatest ever practitioner of the art of heading, surpassing even Dixie Dean.

At the height of his career, Lawton earned in the region of £3,000 a year, making him, it was claimed, the first ever footballer to pay the top rate of income tax. Sadly, though, he would end his life a lonely, impoverished figure.

A football prodigy, Lawton began a career of rich promise at the age of 16 years and 174 days, when he became the youngest centre-forward, it was reported, ever to play League football. The day after signing professional in 1936, Lawton scored a hat-trick against Tottenham Hotspur, outwitting Arthur Rowe, the Spurs and England centre-half.

Everton had seen enough. They invested £6,500 – a record fee for a teenager – to bring him to Goodison Park the following December. The veteran Dean immediately took the newcomer under his wing. 'You'll be no good at this heading lark 'til you move your feet more,' instructed Dean, a mentor whom Lawton idolised. 'Tommy soon learned,' Dean said later, 'and he had just the right build for a centre-forward.'

The following season, his first full campaign at Goodison Park, Lawton was the leading scorer in the First Division, with a total of 28 goals. As leading scorer again in 1938–39, his tally of 35 goals helped Everton lift the title. 'It was easily the best club side I ever played in,' Lawton recalled.

In 1945, Lawton left Everton for Chelsea, a decision he later regretted. Having already lost six years of his career to the war, Lawton then became something of a footballing nomad, with stints at Notts County, Brentford and Arsenal.

He stayed only one full season at Stamford Bridge before making the most controversial move of his career, to Third Division Notts County, who paid a record transfer fee of £20,000. He was also promised a job outside

Tommy Lawton, centre, signs for Brentford, 1952.

▶ key match

Chelsea 3 Moscow Dynamos 3, Friendly, Stamford Bridge, 13 November 1945

Moscow Dynamos rated Tommy Lawton so highly that they assumed his transfer to Chelsea was ordered by the English authorities in order to ensure a home victory in this prestigious friendly.

By chance, Lawton arrived from Everton for a record fee shortly before the Soviets, a wartime ally, opened their tour of Britain.

A vast crowd watched Lawton score for Chelsea, who led 2–0 at half-time. In the second half, the tourists 'flashed the ball from man to man and waited for the opening', the new signing recalled.

Years later, Lawton insisted that the Russians' third goal was blatantly offside. 'I screamed at the referee, but he told me he had to give it for diplomatic reasons.'

football to augment his income. The transfer caused a sensation. It was certainly good business for County: the club won promotion and crowds rose almost four-fold.

At 28 years of age, Lawton was in his prime. However, the following season Lawton made his last appearance for England, despite being assured that a drop down the divisions would not harm his international prospects. Both Billy Wright and Stanley Matthews thought that he was omitted prematurely. 'It was a huge mistake,' Matthews said later.

STANLEY MATTHEWS ▶▶▶▶

1915–2000

During the middle decades of the last century Stanley Matthews stood alone as the most famous and revered footballer in the world – a degree of pre-eminence beyond the scope of any other individual, either before or since.

Year after year, record crowds flocked to grounds in England and overseas for a glimpse of the 'Wizard of the Dribble' weaving his way down the right wing for England, Blackpool or Stoke City. Indeed, he was so famous that they gave him another nickname: 'The King of Football'.

Matthews played for England over a longer period than anyone else in history. Twenty-three years after he made his international debut, he collected the last of his 54 caps at the age of 42, in 1957. Even then, Billy Wright was convinced that Matthews still had something to offer his country. 'The selectors dropped him too soon,' the England captain said. 'Just his name on the team sheet had given us a psychological advantage.'

By that time, Matthews was revered throughout the world. Recalling his excitement before playing against him at Wembley, in 1953, Ferenc Puskas, the Hungary captain, said, 'We were in awe of him and England. Matthews was a giant in our eyes.'

In 1956, Brazil were mesmerised and then demoralised by his skill. At the end of the game at Wembley, Nilton Santos, the great full-back and World Cup winner in Sweden two years later, shook his hand. 'Mr. Matthews, you are still the great master,' he said.

In the middle of an international against Belgium, the other 21 players on the field stood and clapped in rhythm as Matthews jogged back into position following yet another dazzling run that resulted in a rare goal for the England outside-right.

Matthews was the first Footballer of the Year in 1948, the first European Footballer of the Year in 1958 and, in 1965, he became the first active footballer to be knighted.

Stanley Matthews examines his FA Cup winners' medal, 1953.

PLAYER • INDUCTED 2002 • 54 CAPS • 1 FA CUP

'He will run defenders into the ground. He makes them look like fumbling children, and the more they curse him the more he will do it.' – Joe Mercer

'Fitness is confidence,' the son of boxer Jack Matthews, the 'Fighting Barber of Hanley', once said. Matthews junior neither drank nor smoked. Famously, he was fit enough to play Division One football at the age of 50.

No matter the weather or the time of year, the daily routine was the same: up at dawn, a cup of tea, then the short drive to the beach. Once there, he did his breathing exercises,

↗
Stanley Matthews dribbles past his full-back, 1959.

stretching and sprints. It might last anything between 30 minutes and an hour and a half; his body told him when he'd done enough. Later in the day, there was a four-mile run.

'If I needed to find Stanley, the first port of call was South Shore beach at 8.00 a.m.,' Jimmy Armfield, the Blackpool full-back said. 'There he'd be, in his windcheater and flat cap, training alone.'

Once back home, Matthews had a cold shower. Breakfast was toast and cereal. For lunch it was salad and crispbread. On Mondays, he ate nothing, to 'detoxify my body'. All his training was geared to developing and maintaining his renowned acceleration over 20 yards. In his forties, he still had the speed off the mark to get away from defenders half his age.

His dedication and self-discipline set him apart. 'Stanley trained religiously,' Alf Ramsey, his England team-mate said. 'No youngster fighting to gain a place in a League side would have worked harder.'

Overseas, Matthews was idolised. 'He is one of the great examples in the world of an intelligent player,' said Didi, the Brazil forward. 'The Englishman knows himself absolutely, and how to use his strength at the right moment for positive objectives.'

Several years later, Pelé described Matthews as 'the man who taught us the way football should be played'. In Europe, in the immediate post-war era, when the Russians determined to become a major soccer power,

↖
The Blackpool shirt worn by Stanley Matthews in the FA Cup final, 1953.

they studied the methods and movement of one man – Matthews: 'the greatest footballer in the world'.

No player before or since has commanded such drawing power. In 1947–48, Arsenal, Sunderland, Manchester United and Aston Villa had all recorded their highest attendances of the season against Blackpool. At Everton, 72,000 turned up, with nothing more than the two points at stake; the masses came out to see the great man.

Matthews also possessed a rare strength of character. In the era of the maximum wage, minimal employment rights for players, and bruising defenders, the 'Ageless Wonder' took control of his own destiny in the game.

'His mental courage is the greatest I have known,' England team-mate Joe Mercer said. 'If full-backs upset him – and dozens have tried, using all kinds of methods – he will run them into the ground. He makes them look like fumbling children, and the more they curse him, the more he will do it, absolutely mercilessly.'

Unusually for his time, Matthews made the game work for him. During the war he decided that he wanted to live by the sea. He made his home in Blackpool, buying a small seaside hotel. Training at Bloomfield Road, he only travelled to Stoke on match days. In 1947, he persuaded the Stoke board to agree a transfer to Blackpool.

He was equally single-minded when it came to negotiating contracts for his media work and endorsements. His business

Stanley Matthews, (Trevillion).

acumen reputedly made him the highest-earning player in the country.

In 1961 Matthews returned to Stoke City, at the age of 46, for a nominal fee. It was money well spent: home gates trebled during his second stint at the Victoria ground.

▶ talking point

Joe Mercer knew exactly what to expect when Stanley Matthews ran at him with the ball at his feet; yet, more often than not, the knowledge made not the slightest difference.

In one game Mercer was beaten 10 times by his England team-mate. 'Stan would bring the ball squarely to me so that I would never know whether he would go inside or outside,' Mercer said. 'He would lean so far that it was obvious that he had to go that way, but his balance is so perfect he could then sway away and go the other way.'

Johnny Carey, the Manchester United full-back likened the experience of marking Matthews to 'playing against a ghost'.

He developed those skills as a young boy, placing the kitchen chairs in a row in the back-yard and then dribbling with the ball back and fourth in-between them for hour after hour, perfecting his skill and body swerve.

In the mid 1930s, when he first broke into League football, it was the custom for the winger to wait for the defender to come on to him. Only then would he try to jink round his opponent. 'In a reserve game, I bucked the trend. I ran straight at him,' Matthews said. 'The full-back looked absolutely dumfounded.'

They were witnessing a Stoke revival, culminating in promotion to Division One in 1962–63. Fittingly, Matthews scored the goal that ensured they went up as champions.

The end finally came in 1965: a player who made his debut in 1932 as a contemporary of Dixie Dean was bowing out in the age of George Best.

Stanley Matthews trains alone on Blackpool sands, 1961.

WILF MANNION

▶▶▶▶▶▶▶▶▶▶▶▶▶▶▶▶▶▶▶

1918–2000

Wilf Mannion, the inside-forward nicknamed 'Golden Boy' during the 1940s on account of his mop of blond hair and precocious talent, was once described by England team-mate Alf Ramsey as the 'greatest soccer brain in modern football'.

Idolised by the supporters of Middlesbrough, his hometown club, Mannion was a member of the celebrated post-war England forward line, alongside Stanley Matthews, Tommy Lawton, Stan Mortensen and Tom Finney.

Matthews once said of Mannion, the winner of 26 caps between 1946 and 1951, and team-mate in a post-war representative Great Britain XI: 'Wilf is my idea of a perfect inside partner.' When England were struggling for form during the 1958 World Cup in Sweden, Walter Winterbottom told journalists: 'I would give a lot for another Wilf Mannion right now.'

Meanwhile, Alf Ramsey said: 'He was in a class of his own as a skilful strategist.'

Wilf Mannion, 1947.

PLAYER • INDUCTED 2004 • 26 CAPS

**'Wilf played football the way Fred Astaire danced.'
– Brian Clough**

Middlesbrough held him in equally high esteem. But after returning from wartime service in the Army, Mannion fell into dispute with the club. However, his determination to play elsewhere was matched by the club's insistence that he must stay. 'Even if we were given a cheque for £50,000 we would not transfer Mannion,' the Boro manager said. 'Why should we let the best player in Britain go?' A sum of £50,000 would have smashed the record transfer fee.

It was Middlesbrough's choice; the rules then governing the registration of players allowed clubs to retain an out-of-contract player against his wishes. 'Against this soccer

serfdom, even the Army seemed to be a haven of freedom,' Mannion recalled.

Relations deteriorated, and in 1948 Mannion staged a one-man strike in a bid to force the issue, refusing to sign a new contract. It meant that he was ineligible to play for England. Even so, the directors still refused to budge. Mannion was now idle, a football outcast. Boro had made their ultimatum: either play for us or don't play at all. The stand-off dragged on, sapping his resolve. Eventually, Mannion backed down.

Playing for England also had its problems. After a game against Scotland, Mannion was forced to stand all the way between Glasgow and Darlington. The train was full, and the FA hadn't bothered to book him a seat.

On the pitch, at least, he was highly valued. In the late 1950s Winterbottom rated Mannion as the 'greatest of our inside-forwards since

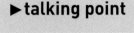
▶ talking point

A front-line soldier in France and Italy during World War Two, Wilf Mannion was weakened and traumatised by his experiences in combat.

In Sicily, his company was pinned down by incessant enemy fire. 'We lost half of our men that day,' he recalled. Physically, Mannion suffered jaundice and then malaria during his time in the Army, and he endured 10 relapses. The prolonged illnesses sapped his energy, and only gradually did he regain sufficient stamina to play football – initially with the Wanderers, the Army team that entertained troops on active service. But the strain on the mind and body of a professional footballer had been enormous.

the end of the war in 1945, an artist reliant exclusively on sheer skill.'

'The most notable partnership over the past dozen years for England has been that of Wilf Mannion and Tom Finney, reaching its sublimation in the famous 10–0 win against Portugal in 1947,' Winterbottom said. 'Wilf had stunning ball-control and high deftness of touch.'

'He was always prepared to fit in with Finney, a clear indication of his greatness. When a super player in his own right is prepared to subordinate himself to the optimum needs of the team, he puts severe stresses on his own inclinations. But in doing it he confirms his own greatness.'

Left and right: Wilf Mannion shoots, 1947.

BILLY WRIGHT ▶▶▶▶▶▶▶▶▶▶▶▶▶▶

1924–1994

Billy Wright, a player described as 'a national treasure' by *The Times* in 1959, offered a reassuring authority and stability in the heart of the England team – qualities that earned him a then record total of 105 caps.

Over a period of eight years, starting in 1951, England did not once take to the field without Wright in their ranks – a record run of 70 consecutive appearances. Ninety times the Wolverhampton Wanderers half-back captained his country, setting another record. In football terms, he was something of an institution.

'Billy had a heart of oak and was the most reliable of men,' Walter Winterbottom, the England manager said. 'I considered myself lucky to have him to call on so often.'

Between 1946 and 1959 Wright experienced defeat with England only 21 times and went six years before enduring defeat at Wembley. In character and temperament he represented 'the spirit of the English game: sporting and vigorous, tolerant and determined, confident and self-effacing', as one football writer put it. Moreover, in 541 League and Cup games for Wolves, at wing-half and centre-half, he was never booked or sent off.

'Essentially a team player who never tried to seek personal glory, Billy turned simplicity into an art form,' Winterbottom said. After one England international, *The Times* wrote: 'Billy Wright had a rare day off. He only played like one man.'

Footballer of the Year in 1952, Wright was still the captain of both England and Wolves, the then champions, when he retired from football seven years later. In recognition of his long service to the game, the Football Association made him a Life Member. He was the first professional player to be awarded the honour.

Billy Wright leads out the England team, 1950.

PLAYER • INDUCTED 2002 • 105 CAPS • 3 DIVISION ONE CHAMPIONSHIPS • 1 FA CUP

As a youngster, Billy Wright collected the autographs of Stanley Matthews and Tommy Lawton, little realising that one day he would line up alongside them in the same England team.

Barely five feet tall when he joined the Molineux staff as a teenager in 1938, there was no indication that Wright would enjoy such a long and distinguished career. It was not long before he was summoned to see Major Frank Buckley, the Wolves manager. 'Sonny, you're far too small to ever make the grade,' Buckley told him. 'I'm sending you home.'

Only the intervention of the training staff persuaded Buckley to change his mind. Within half an hour Wright was back in the manager's office: 'The Major pushed his finger at my chest and said: "I'm assured that you're big where it really matters: in the heart. You can stay."'

↙
An England shirt, 1948.

Wright played at wing-half for club and country until the summer of 1954. He had not thought of switching position until circumstances intervened.

At the World Cup in Switzerland, Wright was asked to cover when the regular England centre-half was ruled out by injury. A few games into the following season, the same situation occurred at Wolves. Wright found the new role less demanding physically and he wore the number five shirt for the rest of his career.

The change, albeit unplanned, prolonged his career by several seasons. Eventually, however, at the age of 35, Wright realised it was time to bow out. A young Jimmy Greaves gave Wright the first hint by running rings around him in a fixture at Chelsea. Then, during pre-season training, Wright was running up a hill when he realised his legs had 'gone'. 'At that moment I decided to retire while I was still at the top in the game.'

At five-feet-eight-inches tall, Wright was a little on the short side for a central defender. He worked hard in training to make good this potential shortcoming in the air. Jumping over

**'He was essentially a team player. You never saw him trying to seek personal glory. He wanted everyone to share the success.'
– Walter Winterbottom**

↗
Billy Wright holds the League trophy, 1959.

hurdles from a standing position improved his spring, as did weight training to strengthen his leg muscles. A tenacious tackler despite his slight frame, Wright never shirked physical confrontation. 'I only had two things on my mind as a player: to win the ball and then to give the simplest pass I could to the nearest team-mate,' Wright once said.

Writing in 1958, Tom Finney praised his captain's reliability, rating him a better centre-half than wing-half. 'He must be challenging for the honour of the most consistent centre-half ever to play for England. Billy fully deserves the nickname Mr Dynamo. He never stops running.'

On one of the rare occasions that Wright was unable to play for England because of injury, Alf Ramsey led the side. Before his first international as captain, Ramsey received a telegram from Wright congratulating him on the honour and wishing him well.

'As a captain Billy gets results by the "human touch", Ramsey wrote in 1952. 'He has the knack of setting an example to the rest of the team, and his tackling cannot be surpassed for its accuracy and perfect timing.'

Opponents praised his sportsmanship. An hour after Hungary thrashed England 6–3 at Wembley in 1953, Wright rushed from the dressing room, still dripping with water, when he spotted one of the Hungary officials. 'He shook me by the hand and told me that it had been a wonderful match and that he enjoyed it very much,' Sandor Barcs recalled. 'He then said, "I congratulate you. You have a wonderful team." I was so moved. What a fantastic gesture.'

On his retirement, *The Times* wrote of Billy Wright: 'There were more talented and more skilful players, but what he embroidered into the fabric of our lives were the values of loyalty and industry, attributes which helped pull us as a nation through those difficult years immediately after the war. Billy Wright, the man, is a human being of exemplary character. Billy Wright, the footballer, was a national treasure.'

'I only had two things on my mind as a player: to win the ball and then to give the simplest pass I could to the nearest team-mate.' – Billy Wright

Billy Wright leads out the England team versus Italy, 1949.

THROUGH THE AGES
FOOTBALL IN THE 1940s

THIS PAGE: **Above left** Billy Wright, far right, looks on as the ball flies out of play, 1949. **Below left** Stoke City players walk off a packed Burnden Park, 1946. **Right** Nat Lofthouse works as a miner as part of his National Service, 1946.

OPPOSITE PAGE: **Above left** Arsenal and Moscow Dynamo play in fog at Highbury, 1945. **Above right** Neil Franklin, the Stoke City and England centre-half, makes a diving header, 1947. **Below left** Southampton players listen to a tactical team-talk, 1949. **Below right** Stanley Matthews joins a ball-juggling double-act at Blackpool Tower Circus, 1949.

▶▶▶▶▶▶▶▶▶▶▶▶▶▶▶▶▶▶▶▶▶▶▶▶▶▶▶▶▶▶▶▶

TOM FINNEY ▶▶▶▶▶▶▶▶▶▶▶▶▶▶▶▶▶

1922–

Tom Finney, a man described by Bill Shankly as 'the greatest player I ever saw, bar none', was the toast of international football during an illustrious England career that spanned a dozen years.

'No better player than Tom has ever worn an England shirt,' wrote Billy Wright, his captain, in 1956. 'He is such an astute footballer, and his ability to produce a surprise move has often shocked me.'

A remarkably versatile forward, Finney played on both wings for his country, before making a brief switch to centre-forward in the latter stages of his career. Soon, he was wearing the England number nine shirt for England, too.

Thirty goals – a record tally – in 76 international appearances highlighted his worth; at the time, only Wright had amassed more. 'I could never imagine an England team without him in it in those days,' recalled England manager Walter Winterbottom. 'Tom is a gentleman footballer,' Winterbottom added. 'A darting player with immensely powerful legs who can get round defenders both ways, inside and outside.'

The first player to be twice voted Footballer of the Year, in 1953–54 and 1956–57, the Preston North End stalwart Finney was revered throughout Europe.

His performances on tour with England in 1952 prompted an Italian millionaire to offer him a fortune to join Palermo. In addition to promising him a free car and seaside villa, the Sicilian club was prepared to pay Preston substantial compensation in return for a two-year loan. Alternatively, Preston could bank £30,000 for his permanent transfer. North End refused to sell, even for a record fee; Finney was irreplaceable.

Tom Finney re-studs his boots, 1960.

PLAYER • INDUCTED 2002 • 76 CAPS

'Three of four Arsenal defenders dithered like old women on a zebra crossing every time Finney had the ball.' – *The Times*

Tom Finney played for Preston for 14 years between 1946 and 1960. North End were a decent side during the 1950s, losing an FA Cup final and twice finishing runners-up in Division One.

The team relied heavily on the versatile Finney, who at one time or another occupied all five forward positions for the club. One national newspaper said he 'was half the Preston team' and, as if to prove the point,

North End were relegated from Division One the season following his retirement.

If Finney didn't perform, more often than not nor did Preston. Their defeat against West Bromwich Albion in the FA Cup final at Wembley in 1954 was Finney's greatest disappointment in the game. Nerves and a mass of defenders got the better of him. 'My legs felt heavy and I was running around like I had a sandbag across my shoulders,' he said.

Finney was an established England player when Preston were relegated in 1948–49. Had he agitated for a transfer, Blackpool and Manchester United were ready to pay a record fee for his signature.

Finney had a quiet word with the chairman. Assured that the club had the means and

↗
An England cap.

ambition to recover, he was happy to stay. Two years later, Preston won promotion as champions of Division Two. It was the only medal he won in his career.

His loyalty to the club and the town was rewarded later in life. In 1972, he was made a Freeman of Preston. Knighted in 1998 for his work as a footballer, magistrate and civil servant, Finney's name will forever be associated with Preston North End. In recognition of his contribution to the club, a statue was erected at Deepdale in 1998. Following a name change, the ground itself can now be found on Sir Tom Finney Way.

The great 'Who's the best – Matthews or Finney?' debate divided football opinion for the best part of a decade. Spectators may have preferred the sight of Matthews in full flow; within the game, though, opinion was divided,

↙
A teamsheet for the England vs Ireland international in the 1946–47 season, signed by the players involved.

with Finney, the all-rounder, often getting the nod. It was not for them to decide who played for England, however. The people who did, the members of the FA selection committee, tended to favour Matthews, particularly during the decade following the war.

The national debate arose inevitably out of competition; both men played on the right wing for their respective clubs, and both wanted to wear the number seven shirt for England. Faced with a dilemma, and loath to leave one of them out, the selectors switched Finney to the opposite wing, a solution he always maintained was unfair. 'Why is it that I should always be the one to play out of position?' he once asked. The England selectors weren't listening; they picked Finney at outside-left in 33 of his 76 internationals for England.

On the Continent opponents both feared and revered him. At the official banquet following England's 5–3 victory over Portugal at Goodison Park in 1951, all 11 Portuguese players stood in salute. The captain made a toast: 'To Mr Finney – the Master.' Four years earlier Finney had been the outstanding England player in a 10–0 rout of Portugal in Lisbon.

Late in his career, he also won three caps at centre-forward. 'Finney is the greatest club centre-forward I have ever seen or played against,' Bill Dodgin, the Arsenal centre-half, wrote in 1957.

Although left-footed, Finney always preferred playing on the right wing. From there, he was able to cut in for a shot on goal. If he went the other way, on the outside, he could also cross the ball accurately with his right foot.

Tom Finney crosses the ball for England, 1954.

The opposition had no idea which way he would go. 'Three or four Arsenal defenders dithered like old women on a zebra crossing every time Finney had the ball,' one newspaper wrote.

Comparing Finney to fellow winger Stanley Matthews, Johnny Haynes said: 'Tom is the more complete footballer. He can do more things. Also, he never flinched no matter what hard knocks he took. His skill was quite exceptional.'

Walter Winterbottom, the England manager, said that Finney averaged one goal or one 'assist' per match, a remarkable record for a winger. 'When the chips were truly down he would try and try and then try a little bit

▶ **talking point**

The emotion of the day got the better of Tom Finney when he made his 433rd and final League appearance for Preston North End, his only club, on the last day of the 1959–60 season.

'Don Bradman was out for a duck in his last Test match because he said he couldn't see the ball for tears in his eyes. Well, that's the way I felt for the whole of the game. It was so hard to concentrate,' Finney later recalled.

Before the kick-off at Deepdale, the Preston North End and Luton Town players formed a circle in the middle of the pitch. As a tribute to Finney they sang 'Auld Lang Syne' and 'For He's a Jolly Good Fellow', accompanied by the large home crowd numbering twice the season average.

Choked with emotion, his voice trembling, Finney addressed the crowd by microphone after the game. He concluded his speech by saying: 'It is sad, but today is a day I will remember forever and thank you all for making it so grand.'

Cliff Britton, the Preston manager, had been playing Finney at centre-forward. However, for this game Britton invited his senior player to choose his own position, in recognition of his service to the club. Finney opted for outside-right – the same role that he performed on his debut.

harder. He was the complete team man,' Winterbottom said.

Bill Shankly once joked that Finney, his Preston team-mate, could beat his marker 'wearing an overcoat'. Having seen Finney practise his skills, with both feet, against a wall at Deepdale, Shankly introduced similar drills when he took over at Liverpool in 1959.

STAN MORTENSEN

▶▶▶▶▶▶▶▶▶▶▶▶▶▶▶▶

1921–1991

Stan Mortensen, the England forward nicknamed 'Electric Heels' on account of his lightning pace, was the first player to score a hat-trick in an FA Cup final at Wembley Stadium.

Respected within the game for his courage, enthusiasm, work ethic, good humour and sportsmanship, Mortensen was once described as 'a lionheart' by England manager Walter Winterbottom.

'England owes much to Stan Mortensen, for his spirit, for his biting at the most meagre morsel thrown up by an attack, for his sheer invincibility,' Winterbottom said.

Stanley Matthews, a team-mate with both club and country, said: 'Morty treated opponents, referees, media, and supporters as he did the club's directors – with the greatest of respect. When decisions went against him he simply shrugged his shoulders, and he never retaliated, no matter how rough the treatment from defenders.'

↖
Stan Mortensen practises heading the ball, 1952.

PLAYER • INDUCTED 2003 • 25 CAPS • 1 FA CUP

A Tynesider by birth, Mortensen arrived in Blackpool at the age of 16, and chose to stay once his career was over, running a postcard shop on the resort's famous Golden Mile. A loyal servant of the Seasiders, he played 395 games, scoring 225 goals.

The scorer of a then record 30 FA Cup goals, his most celebrated performance in a tangerine shirt turned the 1953 FA Cup final against Bolton Wanderers on its head. From 3–1 down, Blackpool completed a remarkable comeback with a winning goal in injury time.

With his side losing at half-time that day, Mortensen walked over to congratulate Nat Lofthouse, the Bolton centre-forward, for his feat in scoring in every round of the competition, as the two England internationals walked back to the dressing room.

Such good-natured sportsmanship was nothing new. In 1948, at the end of another thrilling FA Cup final, a game won 4–2 by Manchester United, Mortensen praised his opponents: 'It was a privilege to have been part of the game even though we lost.'

Originally considered too slow to make the

Stan Mortensen, right, goes up for a header, 1955.

grade, Mortensen trained intensively to improve his speed after being grounded by the RAF after his bomber crashed on landing during World War Two. It was a narrow escape: Mortensen suffered serious head injuries that caused him blinding headaches, and doctors told him he would not play football again.

When official competition resumed, the indefatigable Mortensen made his full England debut in 1947, scoring four goals against Portugal, followed by a hat-trick against Sweden later in the year.

Perhaps his finest moment in international football came in 1948 when England travelled to Turin to face a powerful Italy side. Running onto a Matthews pass, Mortensen beat two defenders, then cut back, before shooting into the roof of the net from a narrow angle. England went on to record a famous 4–0 win. 'I've never known a stadium fall so silent,'

Stan Mortensen, middle, trains alongside Stanley Matthews and Harry Johnston, 1948.

Winterbottom said. 'The Italians were stunned by Stan's goal.'

Between 1947 and 1953, Mortensen made 25 appearances for England, many of them alongside Matthews, his more famous Blackpool team-mate, scoring 23 goals.

'Mortie was barrel-chested, and he had cornflake-box shoulders and legs like bags of concrete,' Matthews said. 'I can't ever recall him being knocked off the ball and when he went after it, he did so with demonic enthusiasm. His change in direction and speed threw his markers. He had great ability to swivel and turn his body, and that helped him shield the ball. Although not the tallest forward, he seemed able to defy gravity and hang in the air for ages when heading the ball.'

WALTER WINTERBOTTOM

▶▶▶▶▶▶▶▶▶▶▶▶▶▶▶▶▶▶▶▶▶▶▶▶▶▶▶▶▶▶▶▶▶▶▶▶▶

1913–2002

A pioneering coach and football theorist, Walter Winterbottom worked tirelessly in his efforts to drag English football into the modern era, encouraging players, clubs and administrators to change the way they thought about the game.

'Nobody believed in coaches at first,' Winterbottom later recalled. 'I wanted to change the whole attitude to coaching in this country.'

It was a monumental task that occupied all of his 16 years as FA director of coaching and England manager, following his appointment in the dual role in 1946.

Ron Greenwood, for one, believed football owed Winterbottom a debt of thanks: 'He launched our coaching system and gave it impetus and status.' Bobby Robson described Winterbottom as 'a prophet', adding: 'As England manager, Walter always believed in positive, attacking football. He set high standards, on and off the field.'

Walter Winterbottom, 1962.

MANAGER • INDUCTED 2005

Founder of the national coaching centre at Lilleshall in Shropshire, the studious, bespectacled Winterbottom wrote a groundbreaking coaching manual in 1952.

Gradually, Winterbottom brought about radical change within the national team set-up, whilst all the time chipping away against the widespread indifference and scepticism, expressed at both professional and amateur level, concerning the value of coaching.

He campaigned in tandem with his mentor, Stanley Rous, Secretary of the FA and later FIFA President. 'Walter brought entirely new ways of thinking to the game, achieving remarkable success in changing attitudes.' Rous said.

'His combination of the scholarly and practical opened up new horizons for the likes of Ron Greenwood, Dave Sexton, Jimmy Armfield, Bobby Robson and Alf Ramsey,' Rous added. 'Inspired by him, they developed into a new breed of manager.'

Winterbottom encouraged players to analyse the game more deeply, and change the 'slapdash, unrealistic and haphazard' habits of many in terms of fitness, training, diet and match-preparation.

Players had to take on greater responsibility, he argued. As late as 1960, Winterbottom defied a Football Association regulation when

'Many people in the game now have no idea how much English football owes Walter.'
– Ron Greenwood

Walter Winterbottom walks to the dressing room with Warren Bradley, 1959.

he permitted his players to talk to the media. England blazers were also handed out, in order, he stressed, 'to encourage a team mentality'.

But perhaps his greatest battle was waged against the England selectors, whose influence and power he gradually weakened, paving the way for Alf Ramsey to assume full responsibility for team selection – a legacy Ramsey readily acknowledged. 'I have the greatest respect for Walter,' he said.

During the 1950s, England were coming to terms with their decline as a football power. Embarrassed by the United States and humiliated by Hungary, they did not get beyond the quarter-finals at four successive World Cups, between 1950 and 1962.

An astute politician, Winterbottom used these setbacks as justification for his campaign for change. He argued that in order to compete at the highest level, the England set-up had to be more professional in its preparations. For instance, no more cooking the food for the players as the over-worked manager had done in Brazil in 1950.

Those defeats also highlighted the necessity of squad training sessions ahead of

international fixtures. Tactically, Winterbottom changed England's formation from the orthodox 2-3-5 to a 4-2-4 system. He also formed an Under-23 side, in order to improve continuity in the selection process. All told, the foundations were being laid for Ramsey.

'There cannot be many men in the game who see the theory, practice and politics of football as clearly as Walter does,' Bobby Charlton wrote in 1967. Jimmy Greaves concurred, saying that Winterbottom had 'the shrewdest football brain in the country'.

▶talking point

A generation of young managers transformed English football in the early 1960s, and they readily acknowledged the debt that they owed to Walter Winterbottom.

As they neared the end of their playing careers, Bobby Robson, Ron Greenwood, Bill Nicholson, Jimmy Hill and Billy Wright were all encouraged by Winterbottom to attend coaching courses organised by the Football Association.

Winterbottom also opened doors, using his contacts to secure coaching work at university level with either Cambridge or Oxford, or a job on the FA coaching staff – all vital experience. Later, Greenwood was recommended for the manager's job at West Ham United. 'Walter spotted my potential, and he was an inspired teacher,' Greenwood said.

ALF RAMSEY

1920–1999

From his position at right-half for England, Billy Wright observed at close hand the way in which Alf Ramsey 'brought something entirely new to the full-back art'.

A permanent fixture in defence at a time when England were widely regarded as the best team in the world, Ramsey made his international debut in 1948 – alongside the likes of Wright, Tom Finney, Stanley Matthews and Tommy Lawton.

Over the ensuing five years, the reliable and consistent Tottenham Hotspur right-back won 32 caps, including a run of 29 consecutive appearances – a remarkable achievement at a time when selectors routinely chopped and changed the side.

When Wright – another England stalwart – lost his place briefly, the selectors handed the captaincy to 'The General', as Ramsey was nicknamed, on account of his commanding presence in the dressing room and on the field.

Alf Ramsey trains at The Dell, 1948.

PLAYER • INDUCTED 2010 • 32 CAPS • 1 DIVISION ONE CHAMPIONSHIP

**'Alf's special brand of constructive defence, which entailed holding on to the ball until good use could be made of it, appealed to everyone.'
- Billy Wright**

After serving with the Army during the war, Ramsey made up for lost time at club level and established himself as a regular at Southampton in his mid-twenties. When Tottenham then paid £21,000 for his transfer in 1949, Ramsey became the most expensive full-back in English football, and it would be another 15 years before that record fee was broken.

For their money, Spurs acquired a squat but powerful full-back whose excellent positional sense and astute reading of the game compensated for his weakness: a lack of pace. A firm believer in the adage about practice making perfect, Ramsey would put himself through endless sprinting drills – often alone – in order to improve his speed off-the-mark.

At White Hart Lane, Ramsey came under the wing of Arthur Rowe, an innovative manager who guided Spurs to the title in 1950–51. Going forward, Ramsey did much to set the pattern and tempo of Tottenham's 'push and run' tactics, with the emphasis on short, accurate passes to feet and movement off the ball.

In doing so, Ramsey and Rowe were challenging orthodox thinking. Not for them the safety-first 'get rid' mentality then so prevalent in English football. Above all, Alf Ramsey advocated the importance of keeping hold of the ball. In 1953 he wrote: 'By retaining possession of the ball you are always poised

for an attack …. If you retain possession, how can the other side attack and get goals?'

At international level, Ramsey enjoyed many highlights, including a 5–3 win in Portugal and a celebrated 3–2 victory over Austria in Vienna. On the downside, there was the shock humiliation by the United States and subsequent early exit from the 1950 World Cup, and the landmark 6–3 defeat by Hungary at Wembley – a loss which precipitated the end of his England career.

Throughout it all, Ramsey enjoyed the respect of his peers, including Billy Wright, who devoted a chapter of an early autobiography to England's specialist penalty-taker, and the footballer with a temperament 'as cool as an ice-soda'.

Alf Ramsey, middle, watches England goalkeeper Gil Merrick catch the ball, 1953.

NAT LOFTHOUSE ▶▶▶▶▶▶▶▶▶▶

1925–2011

Nat Lofthouse was the last great champion of a celebrated company: the traditional English centre-forward – embodying the qualities of courage, physical power and skill.

An inspirational talisman, Lofthouse – 'The Lion of Vienna' – embraced the responsibility for leading the attack as a spearhead, taking more than his fair share of the knocks, and scoring most of the goals. When he advanced, his team-mates followed – as others in the past had followed Dixie Dean and Tom Lawton.

Over a period of eight years, the tough, immensely strong Lofthouse scored 30 times in 33 internationals. Since then, only Jimmy Greaves has matched that strike rate for England over a prolonged period.

Modestly, Lofthouse once described himself as little more than a human 'battering ram'. But there was far more to his game than simple brute strength, as Tom Finney noted. 'Nat has the qualities of speed, fearlessness, a hard shot in either foot, and good heading ability,' his team-mate wrote, 'and a robust form to stand up to all the physical stuff.'

His performance in the 1953 FA Cup final was typical: Lofthouse scored one goal, hit the post, harassed opponents and was knocked out briefly – then carried on regardless. At the end of the game, in defeat, he shook the hands of the celebrating Blackpool players.

Such acts of sportsmanship added to his popular appeal. Voted Footballer of the Year in 1953, he was elated when his conduct on the field was praised as highly as his scoring prowess by the judging football writers.

After making his debut in 1951, Lofthouse began a run of 18 successive games for England the following year. For six years, England made a point of aiming everything at his head.

Nat Lofthouse holds aloft the FA Cup, 1958.

▶ key match

Austria 2 England 3, International Friendly, Vienna, 25 May 1952

Nat Lofthouse earned the nickname 'Lion of Vienna' for his bravery in scoring a crucial goal that also prompted a rare display of emotion from Alf Ramsey.

With the score at 2–2, Lofthouse chased a through-ball from Tom Finney. Now he had only the keeper to beat, as Billy Wright looked on. 'It was obvious there was going to be a collision,' Wright said. 'Nat just kept going. It was unbelievable bravery.'

Lofthouse was knocked unconscious briefly, but insisted on returning to the action despite a knee injury also sustained in the collision.

'It was one of the few occasions in my football life I really did feel like shouting out with joy,' said Alf Ramsey, normally the most phlegmatic of full-backs. 'The players all but kissed him for what we felt would be the winning goal. Nat's example made us re-double our efforts to keep the Austrians out.'

PLAYER • INDUCTED 2002 • 33 CAPS • 1 FA CUP

'Nat was a leader. He had fantastic ability in the air. If you were a centre-forward you had to do more than score goals. You had to lead.'
– Bobby Charlton

Nat Lofthouse was born and bred in Bolton. He signed for Wanderers as a 14-year-old amateur in 1939, and he played his last game for them 21 years later. During that time he played 503 games for the club, scoring 285 goals. The total number of appearances would have been higher but for the loss of several seasons of first-class football as a result of World War Two. Consequently, his League debut

was delayed until 1946, when he turned 21.

The conflict shaped him as a player. 'My war-time experience toughened me up, physically and mentally,' Lofthouse recalled. Too young for military service, he worked in a coal mine. On Saturdays he awoke at 3.30 a.m. in order to catch the tram to work an hour later. His shift below ground lasted eight hours, pushing tubs of coal. At the end of it, the team coach was waiting for him at the gate. Only then did he play 90 minutes of football.

His fitness level was rising but his form remained stubbornly flat. At the age of 19, Lofthouse became so disillusioned with his own performances, and demoralised by the criticism of supporters, that he considered giving up the game. 'I was very limited at this time,' he recalled.

↗
The programme for the 1953 FA Cup final between Bolton Wanderers and Blackpool.

Then, suddenly, it all came together. 'Just like that,' Lofthouse recalled. 'One day you go up for the ball and, bang, it's in the net. You've been doing the same thing for months and getting nothing for it. That's how it was. No one was more surprised than me.' On the resumption of League football in 1946, he was a first-team regular.

Nat Lofthouse served Bolton Wanderers as a player, manager, executive club manager and club president. His association with the club lasted a lifetime. Blackpool, Plymouth

↖
Nat Lofthouse scores against Belgium, 1952.

Argyle and Arsenal all tried, and failed, to sign him, Lofthouse said. There was also an offer from 'a foreign team' in 1952. 'I was tempted, but now I'm really and truly glad that I didn't take it up and stayed put,' he added.

The huge physical demands of playing centre-forward eventually had their effect. Injured during a summer tour to South Africa, he missed the whole of the 1959–60 season. He made his final appearance in December 1960. During the match he damaged cruciate ligaments, an injury that effectively ended his career. There was a brief attempt at a comeback but it ended in resignation.

Football was changing. Lofthouse and the rest of the 'old guard' had played a simpler game tactically, with the centre-forward as the 'pivot' of the attack. Len Shackleton

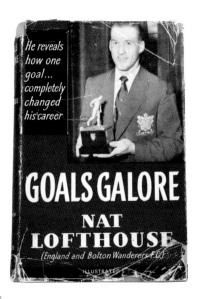

↗
Nat Lofthouse's book *Goals Galore*, published in 1954.

explained it this way: 'Billy Wright won the ball and passed it to me. I gave it to Stan Matthews who ran down the wing and centred for Nat Lofthouse, who scored.'

A new 4–2–4 formation was being adopted. There would still be burly, robust forwards in the game – Bobby Smith of Spurs, for instance – but the responsibility was now being shared between twin forwards. The playing career of Nat Lofthouse was ending, as was the golden age of the centre-forward.

His international career appeared over in 1956 when he was dropped by the selectors, despite scoring 32 goals in 36 games for Bolton that season.

↖
Nat Lofthouse runs onto the pitch, 1955.

▶ **talking point**

Nat Lofthouse had the misfortune of playing in two of the most emotionally charged FA Cup finals in history. It seemed every neutral in the country wanted his team, Bolton Wanderers, to lose at Wembley in 1953 and 1958.

Lofthouse gave his side the lead in 1953 but the nation celebrated the result it wanted when Blackpool staged a late comeback to win 4–3. Stanley Matthews, the most famous man in football, had his winner's medal at last.

Five years later, in the wake of the Munich air disaster, the tide of public feeling against Bolton was even stronger. Against the odds, Manchester United, a club in mourning, had battled their way to the final.

It was all a little unfair on Bolton who had their own romantic story: all 11 of their players were local lads, and none of them had cost more than the £10 signing-on fee. This time, Bolton and Lofthouse ripped up the script. Lofthouse scored twice, bundling the ball into the net with a shoulder charge against Harry Gregg, the Manchester United goalkeeper, for one of his goals.

'Bolton was an island surrounded by the opposition,' he recalled. 'It was unlucky, really having everybody supporting the other side on the two times we went to Wembley. In the second, God forbid, it was after Munich. If I hadn't been a Bolton player, I would have wanted them [Manchester United] to win as well.'

In the wake of England's disappointing performance in the World Cup in 1958, Lofthouse was briefly recalled the following winter. 'It made no sense that Nat was left out for the World Cup in the first place,' Billy Wright, the England captain recalled. 'The old guard was gradually being stood down.'

STAN CULLIS

▶▶▶▶▶▶▶▶▶▶▶▶▶▶▶▶▶

1916–2001

Stan Cullis was the 'Iron Manager' who forged Wolverhampton Wanderers into a commanding power in English and European football during the 1950s.

On his orders the Wolves players increased the tempo of their play. 'Fast, direct attack', was the Cullis mantra. The ball had to be played forward quickly. To pass the ball sideways, let alone backwards, he argued, was to shirk responsibility. Their positive, energetic play carried Wolves to three championship titles in the space of five years, successes sandwiched between FA Cups triumphs in 1949 and 1960.

A strict disciplinarian, his frequent dressing-room tirades made him unpopular at times with some of his players, but those uncompromising, often abrasive methods were undoubtedly effective: only once in nine consecutive seasons did Wolves finish outside the top three, a record of consistency that no other side came close to matching.

↖
Stan Cullis works out moves on a
miniature pitch in his office, 1948.

MANAGER • INDUCTED 2003 • 3 DIVISION ONE CHAMPIONSHIPS • 2 FA CUPS

'Wolves in those days stood for everything that was good about British football.' – Matt Busby

There were plenty of highlights: in the middle of the decade Wolves beat several of the leading club sides of Europe, including Honved and Spartak Moscow in prestigious midweek friendlies under newly installed floodlights at Molineux.

Standing in the dressing room after watching a thrilling 3–2 victory over Honved in December 1954, Cullis motioned the newspapermen towards the exhausted Wolves players. 'There they are,' Cullis told the journalists, 'the champions of the world.'

Their stirring comeback did much to restore confidence and belief, coming as it did only 13 months after England were humiliated 6–3 at Wembley by Hungary. 'The legend of Hungarian invincibility perished forever in the Molineux quagmire,' one newspaper reported under the headline 'Hail Mighty Wolves.'

On the domestic front, only Manchester United rivalled them during the 1950s. For many youngsters, Wolves were the most glamorous club in the country. As a boy growing up in Belfast, George Best dreamt about playing at Molineux, not Old Trafford. Matt Busby commented that Wolves 'played with great power, spirit and style'.

Famously described as the 'Passionate Puritan' by the sportswriter John Arlott, Cullis watched games with the same intensity he expected his men to play them. Agitated, arms flying, he could not keep still. Those sitting next to him often ended up with a few bruises. 'He got carried away in games completely,' said Billy Wright, the Wolves captain.

Cullis railed against the charge that he discouraged individualism. In 1959 he wrote: 'I will never condemn any player for an act of individuality or for taking a calculated risk, whether pre-planned or spontaneous, merely because it fails.' Rather, it was wasteful, unnecessary embellishment that bothered him.

Intensely loyal to the club, having previ

Stan Cullis signs paperwork, 1964.

ously worn the famous gold shirt with such distinction as captain, Cullis, like the rest of football, was shocked when Wolves sacked him in 1964, after several mediocre seasons. The decision shattered him, and an equally mystified Matt Busby sent him a warm letter of sympathy.

At their best, in the late 1950s, Wolves scored more than 100 goals in four successive seasons. Though praised by many coaches here and abroad – indeed, Juventus once offered Cullis four times his Wolves salary to work for the Turin club – some critics decried their flat-out, relentless long-ball football as 'kick and rush'. Cullis did not care. 'They can say all they like. Our supporters get more entertainment from watching Wolves than any other two teams put together.'

LEN SHACKLETON

▶▶▶▶▶▶▶▶▶▶▶▶▶▶▶▶▶▶▶▶▶▶▶▶▶▶▶▶▶▶▶▶▶▶▶▶▶▶

1922–2000

In describing Len Shackleton as a great showman and entertainer, Jimmy Greaves was celebrating the 'Clown Prince of Soccer' who put a smile back on the face of English football at a time of economic hardship and austerity.

Shackleton played football 'with the aplomb of an artist', according to Billy Murray, his manager at Sunderland in the 1950s. A stint at Newcastle United made him an idol there, too.

Once the most valuable footballer in England, Shackleton was not one for theory and over-elaborate tactics. Instead, he revelled in his individualism and trickery, often embellishing his play deliberately for the entertainment of the crowd.

On one occasion he deliberately stood still on the ball in the penalty area and mimed the act of combing his hair. '"Shack! Shack!" roared the Sunderland crowd in the most terrific, sustained hysterical roar ever heard on a football field,' the *Daily Express* reported in 1955. 'It was their tribute to Len Shackleton.'

Len Shackleton is charged by a defender, 1947.

PLAYER • INDUCTED 2009 • 5 CAPS

**'I have seen Len Shackleton do things with a football that would be beyond the power of even Puskas. Shack is a genius.'
– Jimmy Hogan**

However, behind all the showmanship, wit and humour existed an astute football mind. For Shackleton there was a point to all the jokes and tricks, including a habit of playing one-twos with the corner flag. Not only did they lift the crowd, he argued, they also created a psychological advantage over the opposition.

Similarly strong-minded off the field, Shackleton railed against authority, describing the contract binding a player to the club that held his registration as 'an evil document', and the transfer market as 'public auctions with human beings under the hammer'.

Indeed, he is perhaps best remembered today for the blank page he included in his 1955 autobiography, under the chapter heading: 'The average director's knowledge of

Len Shackleton makes a point, 1955.

football'. During his time at Newcastle United, he once staged a one-man strike in protest of his treatment.

Publicly ridiculing club directors, some of whom sat on the England selection committee, hardly enhanced his prospects, and he ended his career with only a handful of caps to his name, despite the repeated demands of some football writers for his inclusion.

Rejected as a teenager by Arsenal, Shackleton played for Bradford Park Avenue during the war, before being transferred to Newcastle United, then a Second Division club, for a fee of £13,000. On his debut he scored six times against Newport County.

Len Shackleton shoots at goal, 1948.

After that his career stalled, and the following season he moved on to Sunderland, 'the grandest club' – as Shackleton described them – for a record fee of £20,500. Though infuriated at times by Shackleton's reluctance to play 'straight-forward football', Sunderland manager Alan Brown recognised his talents. Throughout his career, Shackleton railed against the coaching fraternity, whom he argued were stifling talent and damaging the game as a spectacle. Plenty of people agreed with him, and for many fans the sight of Shackleton at work engendered a deep and enduring affection for the game that transcended the result of any particular match. Win or lose, they loved 'Shack'.

MATT BUSBY ▶▶▶▶▶▶▶▶▶▶▶▶▶▶

1909–1994

Matt Busby, the visionary, charismatic manager who almost lost his life in the Munich air disaster in 1958, created an aura of style and quality around Old Trafford – transforming the popular image of both the club and his profession in the process.

On the field, the former Scotland half-back created two revered sides during more than two decades as manager: the 'Busby Babes' of the mid 1950s; and the European Cup-winning side of the 1960s – the celebrated team of Bobby Charlton, Denis Law and George Best.

As his career progressed, Busby exercised an increasing degree of control over the day-to-day running of the club – from the boot-room to the boardroom, where Busby shaped long-term strategy in his role as a director.

Put simply, Busby re-wrote the job description for the role of football club manager. Never before had a manager wielded this level of authority. Herbert Chapman had advanced the cause of the manager; now Busby was re-writing the job description again.

An advocate of flair and adventure, Busby outlined his football philosophy in a speech delivered in 1967, when he was made a freeman of the City of Manchester: 'There is nothing wrong with trying to win, so long as you don't set the prize above the game,' he told the audience. 'There is no dishonour in defeat, so long as you play to the limit of your strength and skill.

What matters above all is that the game should be played in the right spirit, with the utmost resource of skill and courage, with fair play and no favour, with every man playing as a member of the team, the result accepted without bitterness or conceit.'

Nobby Stiles, the Manchester United and England midfield player, wrote: 'Matt urged us to give expression to all our talent. "Regimenting isn't coaching; inspiring is coaching," he used to say.'

Matt Busby prepares to give a speech at Manchester Town Hall, 1968.

MANAGER • INDUCTED 2002 • 1 EUROPEAN CUP • 5 DIVISION ONE CHAMPIONSHIPS • 2 FA CUPS

'Regimenting isn't coaching; inspiring is coaching.'
– Matt Busby

In 1945, at the age of 35, Matt Busby was appointed manager of Manchester United. The situation he confronted appeared desperate: the club had an overdraft of £15,000, a sum then equivalent to a record transfer fee; a bomb-damaged Old Trafford was unavailable for home games; and the only place for the players to train was the car park.

Worse still, the club had a poor reputation. Mediocre and overly physical, United were seen by many observers as an unsophisticated provincial side of little interest outside Manchester. 'United played the kind of football that makes a man stay at home and dig his garden,' one newspaper noted during the pre-war era.

The arrival of Busby changed everything. Within three years the club had captured its first major honour since 1911, following victory over Blackpool in the FA Cup final. Moreover, his team was celebrated for its style and attacking flair.

As one of the first 'tracksuit' managers, Busby challenged the existing equilibrium by insisting on absolute control of all team affairs. 'Matt will seek the board's advice, ponder over it and then go away and do precisely what he wants to,' Harold Hardman, the club chairman, said years later.

'I wanted a different kind of football club from the norm at the time,' Busby recalled. 'I wanted to manage a team the way I thought the players wanted it. The atmosphere was bad at

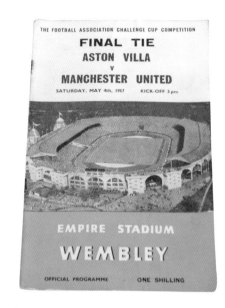

↗
The programme for the FA Cup final, 1957.

clubs. The manager would sit at his desk and the players would only see him once a week.'

Another project was soon embarked upon: to find, recruit and then train the best young players from all across Britain, as a means of building a team. His network of scouts found Duncan Edwards in Dudley, under the noses of rivals Wolverhampton Wanderers. Meanwhile, north-east schoolboy star Bobby Charlton rejected the overtures of Newcastle United and a host of other leading clubs.

In 1951–52 the club won the championship. Busby then made another bold decision: he broke up a successful, experienced side to make way for youth. By the

↖
Matt Busby celebrates with his players after clinching the championship title, 1957.

middle of the decade, the team's average age was 22. The legend of the 'Busby Babes' had been born.

Winners of successive titles in 1956 and 1957, United were also the first English club to compete in Europe. The club was on the rise. When eight players, including Edwards, died in the Munich air crash in February 1958, the team was chasing an unprecedented treble: League championship, FA Cup and European Cup.

Busby was the only passenger facing the front of the plane at the time of impact who survived. His injuries, however, were terrible. 'I wanted to die,' he recalled. 'Lung punctures, broken-bone manipulation, torn-flesh repairs

↗
A shirt worn by Alex Stepney in the European Cup final, 1968

▶ talking point

Matt Busby always argued that 'challenges should be met, not avoided', and he followed his own advice when he persuaded Manchester United to enter the European Cup in 1956.

The Manchester United board had been strongly advised by the Football League against entering the competition, then in its second season. The Old Trafford club was reminded that its first duty was to the League.

'Matt was eager to enter,' said Stanley Rous, Secretary of the Football Association at the time. 'He had been to Europe and come back telling everyone that we had to get involved or fall behind. He deserves a lot of credit for his vision.'

Chelsea had been eligible to enter the previous season but the club had agreed with the League's argument that domestic football must be paramount.

After seeking the advice of Rous, Busby successfully argued that the money raised could be spent on installing floodlights at Old Trafford and that football was increasingly an international game.

without anaesthetics were a regular drill of undiminished horror.'

It took time before Busby was able to gather all his energy for the task of rebuilding the club. Denis Law, Pat Crerand and Alex Stepney were bought, George Best was unearthed, and Bobby Charlton found his niche in midfield. By the mid 1960s Manchester United were finally ready for another crack at the European Cup.

↖
Matt Busby smiles as Denis Law signs for Manchester United, 1962.

BERT TRAUTMANN

▸▸▸

1923–

The remarkable rise of Bernhard Trautmann to the top was cemented in 1956 when he displayed great courage in the FA Cup final and was voted Footballer of the Year. The man everyone called 'Bert' was a national hero.

With almost a quarter-of-an-hour to go at Wembley, the Manchester City keeper fractured a bone in his neck. Unaware of the true nature of the injury, and despite the obvious pain, Trautmann played on.

In showing such courage and good humour, the former German paratrooper, prisoner-of-war camp escapee, and one-time hate-figure secured not only a winners' medal but also the respect of his adopted nation.

'Trautmann is one of the great sportsmen of our time,' wrote Mervyn Griffiths, a leading referee. Tactically, the City keeper introduced new methods of play. 'His push-throw could send the ball 40 yards to great effect,' Bobby Charlton said. 'Most goalkeepers have now copied this technique.'

Bert Trautmann, 1955.

PLAYER • INDUCTED 2005 • 1 FA CUP

'To be selected as captain of the Football League representative side is the greatest achievement of my career.' – Bert Trautmann

'I've never seen a goalkeeper who compares with Trautmann in the form he was in for two or three seasons before 1956,' Bobby Charlton wrote a decade later. 'The man was inhuman.'

In his prime, Trautmann was the only goalkeeper ever to figure in the team-talks given by Matt Busby. 'Don't stop to think where you're going to hit it,' the Manchester United manager implored his players. 'Hit it first and think afterwards. If you look up, he will read your thoughts and stop it.'

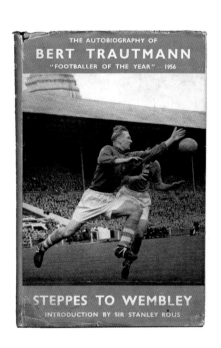

↖
Bert Trautmann's autobiography, 1956.

Pressures off the field made his performances on it all the more impressive. Trautmann had fought for four years against the Allies, making the former Hitler Youth member an obvious target for Britons who harboured lingering hostilities. 'The Nazi indoctrination began when I was nine years old,' he wrote later.

One game at Fulham in 1950 began to the sound of incessant chants of 'Kraut' and 'Nazi'; by the end, however, rival players and supporters alike were applauding him. At Sunderland the crowd yelled 'Sieg Heil' when he kicked the ball away in frustration after the referee ordered a penalty Trautmann had saved to be re-taken. Undeterred, he saved the second shot as well.

Following his capture in 1945, Trautmann spent time in a prisoner-of-war camp in Lancashire, and it was only then that he began playing football, adapting skills that he'd developed playing handball as a boy.

After being released from internment, he signed for Manchester City from non-League St Helens Town. It was to be a tough baptism at Maine Road: there were protests from fans and misgivings in the dressing room; on the field, City conceded 68 goals in 42 games and were relegated.

Promoted at the first attempt, City then relied heavily on Trautmann to keep them up in each of the following three seasons, making him by far the club's most popular player.

Off the field, he worked diligently on behalf of his club and city, escorting visiting German trade delegations and acting as an interpreter. He also made a point of assisting Jewish youth clubs.

Tactically, his ability to throw the ball quickly and accurately over distance, cutting out several opponents, was vital to City's attacking play. 'That was my handball experience,' Trautmann wrote later.

Confirmation of his acceptance came when the Football League broke with normal practice in selecting him – a foreigner – in their representative side.

Years later, when asked to name two world-class goalkeepers, the great Russian keeper Lev Yashin rather immodestly named himself and 'the German boy who played in Manchester'.

JOHN CHARLES ▶▶▶▶▶▶▶▶▶▶▶

1931–2004

The most valuable and versatile footballer of the post-war era, John Charles was English football's greatest export – and his success overseas had important, and far-reaching ramifications for the domestic game.

In 1957 Juventus paid Leeds United a world record fee of £65,000 for the statuesque 25-year-old Welshman. They had effectively bought two players for the price of one.

'To this day, John remains a mythological character in Italy,' Bruno Garzena, a Juventus team-mate said. 'He wasn't a normal footballer; he was an extraordinary one. Even now, he is still considered a god in Turin.'

In his first season in Italy, Charles led Juventus to the championship, scoring 28 goals in 34 games. Over the next four seasons, Juventus added two more League titles and two Italian Cups. In 150 appearances, he registered 93 goals; twice he was voted Footballer of the Year in Italy.

As always, success led to imitation, with rival clubs soon copying the Juventus model. Suddenly, thanks to Charles, the demand for British attacking talent soared. Before long, Denis Law, Jimmy Greaves and Gerry Hitchens had all been lured south by the greater riches on offer.

The Charles-inspired player-drain alerted Football League bosses, who feared the appeal of English football was being denuded by the loss of its most exciting players. In 1961, a few days after Johnny Haynes became the latest target for the Italians, the ruling body acted. It was announced that the maximum wage – then universally fixed at £20 per week basic – was to be abolished.

None of the other British exports of the day came close to equalling the feats of the footballing hero whom the worshipful football folk of Turin nicknamed 'The Gentle Giant'.

John Charles, 1964.

▶ key match

Wales 2 Hungary 1, World Cup group game, Solna, Sweden, 17 June 1958

John Charles needed all of his renowned self-discipline when he took a battering as Wales achieved their finest moment in international football by reaching the last eight.

Released at the last moment for the tournament in Sweden by his Italian club Juventus, Charles attracted the attention of the Hungary defenders.

'John had scored with a header in an earlier pool game and the Hungarians had clearly prepared their tactics with him in mind. During the game he was subjected to some savage treatment by the Hungarians,' said Ivor Allchurch, the Wales inside-forward.

By half-time Charles had been virtually kicked out of the game. 'We refused to lie down,' Allchurch recalled. 'John was magnificent in the example he set.'

PLAYER • INDUCTED 2002 • 38 CAPS

'John shook off an opponent like a dog shakes water off its back. He was a mountain of a man, hard but with an inordinate amount of self-control.' – Stanley Matthews

Equally effective in defence or attack, Charles was rated the best centre-half in Europe by both Denis Law and Tom Finney. 'Mind you,' Law said, 'when he plays up front, he's also one of the top three centre-forwards I've ever seen.'

John Charles posed a dilemma for managers. They had to choose where to play him: centre-forward or centre-half.

John Charles signs for Cardiff City, 1963.

His record in attack for Leeds United was impressive: Charles scored 164 goals in 318 games, yet it was not until his fifth season at the club that he switched to centre-forward from centre-half. In 1956–57, in only his second season up front, he scored 38 goals, making him the leading goalscorer in Division One. Sunderland, Arsenal and Manchester United all offered huge sums for his transfer, but the decisive move came from Italy.

After they had signed him, Juventus adopted their tactics to make best use of his versatility. Charles often played in both attack and defence in the same match. Once Juventus went ahead – often the result of a Charles goal – he usually would drop back to help protect the lead.

Juventus wanted him to extend his stay in Italy beyond five years. 'I could have stayed, playing centre-half, which is the easiest job in football,' Charles said. 'But I didn't want to overstay my welcome.'

Charles signed as a professional at the age of 17. He owed much of his versatility as a footballer to his early education at Elland Road. Major Frank Buckley, the manager, played him at left-half, right-back, centre-half, inside-forward and, finally, centre-forward. The Major also insisted that all players, Charles included, were two-footed.

Short of money, Leeds refused to release Charles to a rival English club when they were forced to sell him in 1957. He did not agitate

A Wales international cap, 1908.

for a transfer. 'Leeds was my team,' Charles said. 'I loved the place.'

Tall and muscular, John Charles was renowned for his immense physical strength – and exemplary behaviour. For good reason, he was nicknamed 'The Gentle Giant'.

'You had no fear of playing against him because you knew that it was going to be a fair game,' Denis Law recalled. Others agreed. 'Whoever came out on top, well, that was it. It was fair.' Jack Charlton said: 'John never, ever did anything nasty.'

In his Leeds days, when an opposition centre-forward broke Jack Charlton's nose in an aerial challenge, Charles dropped back to centre-half as cover. 'The same forward just bounced off John when they went up for a header,' Norman Hunter, a team-mate that day, recalled.

Bruno Garzena was taken aback when 'this giant of a man' walked into the dressing room at Juventus. 'A defender would grab his shirt,'

↗
John Charles shoots for goal, 1956.

↖
John Charles, (Trevillion).

▶ talking point

John Charles wrote a guide for British footballers on how to survive as a foreign 'import' in Italian football, but many of the players who followed in his footsteps ignored his advice.

'In England, footballers were ordinary working men; in Italy they're royalty,' he said. 'I'd been a half-pint-of-shandy man; now I was drinking the finest red wines and eating pasta, which I'd never tasted before.'

It was a culture shock. The football was much more defensive, the rewards for winning were much higher and discipline was stricter. Italian clubs fined players heavily for breaking rules and demanded more of their time.

On the strength of his own experience, Charles advised ex-pat British players who came to Italy to 'toe the line'. Protesting about the defensive style of the football and the restrictive club rules, as Jimmy Greaves and Denis Law did during their brief stints in Italy, was a waste of energy, he said.

'Playing in Italy is just like going into one of the Services. If you try to kick against everything then you are in for a miserable time. You must tell yourself you are getting well paid and put up with the strictness and soul-destroying defensive football. Then you will have a fine time.'

he recalled, 'and John would just drag him along like a tow-truck.'

Even rival Torino fans liked him for his character and sportsmanship. 'In a derby match I bumped into a fellow and hurt him accidentally,' Charles said. 'I was on my way to goal. I stopped and kicked the ball out so he could get treatment.' The home crowd cheered his action.

Gordon Banks never forgot his first meeting with the Wales centre-forward.

Chesterfield Reserves were playing Leeds. Banks had only a handful of games behind him; Charles was returning from injury. 'He walked up to me, and he said, "Now, don't worry, son. You do your best out here today. I won't hurt you."

As a 16-year-old I would have been a pushover for him, but he played it fair and he played it straight.'

JACKIE MILBURN

▶▶▶▶▶▶▶▶▶▶▶▶▶▶▶▶▶▶▶

1924–1988

Jackie Milburn has been idolised by generations of Geordies on the strength of his goalscoring exploits in the black and white of Newcastle United.

The name of Milburn is now synonymous with the city; United were the only English club he played for, and his tally of 177 goals in League football is a club-record that stands to this day.

Importantly, 'Wor Jackie' was one of them: a local, working-class lad who came up from the mines to play for his beloved United, the team he supported as a boy. More than five decades on, there are two statues standing in his honour: one in Newcastle, the other in nearby Ashington, the place of his birth in 1924.

Originally an outside-right, Milburn was ordered to switch positions by his manager. 'I will never make a centre-forward,' he responded. Within a year later, he was wearing the England number nine shirt.

↖
Jackie Milburn heads the ball, 1950.

PLAYER • INDUCTED 2006 • 13 CAPS • 3 FA CUPS

'As a boy watching him from the terraces, I liked his energy and character. He was a taker of chances.' – Sir Bobby Robson

In his heyday, the darting, effervescent Milburn inspired United to three FA Cup final wins in the space of five seasons during the club's golden era in the 1950s.

Some stories surrounding Milburn are now part of Geordie folklore: how he turned up for a trial as a schoolboy carrying borrowed boots in a paper bag; how he scoffed a meat

pie before every home game; and how he travelled to St. James' Park on the bus, surrounded by supporters.

Once, early in his career, he played in front of 50,000 people, only seven hours after completing a nightshift underground, wedged on his back in a tunnel only 18 inches high.

In the late 1940s, a young Bobby Charlton was one of the multitude on the terraces who watched Milburn help Newcastle win promotion. 'He used to remind me of a wave breaking,' Charlton recalled. 'He would just surge past defenders with his incredible pace. Everybody loved watching him.'

A lightning-quick raider, the former professional sprinter scored 10 goals in 13 appearances for England. His team-mate, Tom Finney, said that Milburn was hampered by a mystifying lack of confidence. 'He simply didn't realise how good he was,' Finney once said.

That self-doubt surfaced again in 1967, when, characteristically, Milburn worried that no one would turn up for his testimonial. On the day, 45,404 people packed the ground.

In 1951, Milburn scored both goals in the 2–0 defeat of Blackpool in the FA Cup final. In celebration, he famously dived headfirst into the communal bath in full kit, boots and all.

A year later, Milburn and Newcastle were back at Wembley Stadium, with Prime Minister Winston Churchill as guest of honour. During the presentations Britain's wartime leader, spoke to Milburn: 'Are you going to

Jackie Milburns shoots at goal, 1955.

▶ key match

Newcastle United 2 Blackpool 0, FA Cup final, Wembley Stadium, 28 April 1951

Jackie Milburn was so nervous before kick-off that he sneaked into the showers for a quick smoke in order to calm his nerves, only to find four team-mates already there doing the same thing.

After a goalless first half, trainer Norman Smith switched tactics, instructing the wing-halves and inside-forwards to play more of a long-ball game. 'They're terrified of Jackie's pace,' he said.

Within minutes of the re-start, Milburn raced clear, before firing a shot into the bottom corner. Soon after, Milburn scored a spectacular second: this time, a left-foot shot from distance. Elated, his first thought was to jump into the crowd to celebrate with his fellow Geordies.

grab the headlines again this year, Jackie?'

Milburn didn't score that day, but his tricky play helped Newcastle defeat Arsenal 1–0. A third winners' medal followed in 1955, with Milburn scoring the opener in a 3–1 victory over Manchester City.

Three decades later, on the day of his funeral in 1988, the people of Newcastle lined the streets in their thousands in tribute. As a lasting memorial, the club named the new West Stand after their famous number nine. 'The stories surrounding Jackie are passed on, generation to generation, by Newcastle fans,' Sir Bobby Robson once said. 'Now for that to happen says something very special about him as a footballer.'

TEAM INDUCTEE
MANCHESTER UNITED
▶▶▶▶▶▶▶▶▶▶▶▶▶▶▶▶▶▶▶▶▶▶ 1955–1958

30 November 1953
Five days after Hungary humiliate England at Wembley, the *Daily Express* puts forward its suggestion as to the remedy for England's soccer woes: 'England need the Busby Plan – the plan introduced by the Manchester United manager to discover and groom young footballers for stardom.'

1 September 1955
For all their obvious potential, the inexperience of youth inevitably comes to the fore on occasion. After the narrow away win at Spurs, Busby asks his players: 'What do you think you were doing in the second half? You fooled about like learners and it nearly cost you the game.'

30 March 1956
There are nearly 59,000 crammed inside Old Trafford to watch the 5–0 thrashing of Newcastle United. With five games to go, Busby's side are six points clear at the top. The title race is all but over. Indeed, United extend their advantage to a massive 11 points by the end of the season.

5 September 1956
United go top of the League after defeating Chelsea 2–1 at Stamford Bridge – a fixture billed as 'Busby's Babes v Drake's Infants'. Like Busby, Ted Drake, the Chelsea manager, has overhauled a championship-winning side. Busby, then, is not alone in putting his faith in youth. However, judged on results he is the philosophy's most successful exponent. Man-of-the-match is Duncan Edwards, 'the 20-year-old with the confidence of a veteran', as one newspaper puts it.

5 October 1956
'Another Busby Babe rolls off the Manchester United assembly line,' reports the *Daily Express*. 'He is Bobby Charlton, the 18-year-old forward brother of Leeds centre-half Jack. He stands in for Taylor, who is on England duty.'

6 October 1956
After watching the 4–2 defeat of Charlton Athletic at Old Trafford, the *Express* correspondent fears for the rest of the First Division. However, he has a suggestion: 'Make the League championship a handicap, with United scratch and the rest getting a six-point start.'

20 December 1956
Newspaper reports suggest that Ferenc Puskas, the great Hungary inside-forward, wants to play in England. 'You can count me out,' says Matt Busby. 'I'm building a team. The last thing I would dream of doing is to sign any Continental player, however big his reputation. In a year or two's time, some of my young ones will be as good as, if not better than, any players in the world.'

Duncan Edwards in action, 1957.

28 December 1956

Billy Wright, the England and Wolves captain, is asked to nominate the team of the year. He replies: 'That's easy – Manchester United.'

11 February 1957

With Manchester United advancing in Europe and accelerating towards another seemingly inevitable championship triumph, Busby is asked the secret behind this success. 'Team spirit,' he replies. 'Right through the club. The entire staff – senior players, reserves, juniors – share these values. It's a happiness that flows right through the club, a sense of wanting to serve Manchester United, a feeling that it is an honour to do so.'

25 April 1957

Manchester United are knocked out of the European Cup by Real Madrid. The more experienced Spaniards are, on average, seven years the senior. 'It was a contest between two great teams – a mature side and a young side, and, of course, experience told. But our time will come,' Busby says afterwards. The average age of the United players is 21.

Roger Byrne collects the League championship trophy, 1956.

27 April 1957

When the final whistle blows on the League season, Manchester United are champions again, by a margin of eight points. It turns out that, even if the *Daily Express*' idea of a six-point handicap had been introduced, Busby's side would still have finished two points clear of the rest.

4 May 1957

A bad-tempered FA Cup final ends in a 2–1 defeat against Aston Villa. Controversy rages when Peter Mc-Parland, the Villa forward, charges goalkeeper Ray Wood, who sustains a fractured cheekbone. Press photographs also suggest that one of the Villa goals was offside. By such slim margins is a League and Cup double lost.

Manchester United players prepare to fly to Madrid, 1957.

1 February 1958

Eight months later United are again chasing honours. For a second season in succession the treble – League championship, FA Cup and European Cup – is on. After a rousing 5–4 victory at Arsenal, the *Express* enthuses: 'Manchester United are mighty near to being the best soccer machine ever created.'

6 February 1958

The plane carrying the United party crashes in Munich. Eight players – Duncan Edwards, Tommy Taylor, Roger Byrne, David Pegg, Bill Whelan, Geoff Bent, Eddie Coleman and Mark Jones – die as a consequence of the tragedy. Two years later, Frank Taylor, the only journalist on board who survived, details his account of the crash in a book, *The Day A Team Died*.

JOHNNY HAYNES ▶▶▶▶▶▶▶▶▶

1934–2005

Johnny Haynes, a perfectionist inside-forward whom Jimmy Greaves hailed as 'the greatest passer of the ball I've ever seen', left the nation stunned when he became the first player in English football to be paid a basic salary of £100 a week.

'I would sooner have the job of marking any other footballer in the world than Johnny Haynes,' said Dave Mackay of Tottenham Hotspur and Scotland. 'I've tried close-marking him and getting in quick tackles, but that didn't stop him. In one match, I decided to lay off in the hope of anticipating his next move, but he was even more deadly.'

As a youngster finding his way in the game in the early 1960s, Johnny Giles made a point of studying Haynes. 'Johnny redefined the job of inside-forward,' the future Leeds United stalwart wrote. 'He rewrote the rules on positional discipline by roving around the pitch to dictate play. He played in a way I had never seen before, freeing himself to go wherever he could get possession of the ball. For the first time, a player was making the ball come to him.'

Fulham made the offer of a five-fold pay rise as a means of keeping Haynes – the 'King of Craven Cottage' – at the club, in the face of determined efforts by Milan to lure the England captain to Italy in 1961. Advertisers were equally covetous, and it was his face that famously adorned adverts for Brylcreem.

In 1955, the England selection committee decided to build the team around the then 21-year-old Haynes. 'He represents a wonderful future,' one selector said. The following year, the Football Association identified him as a future England captain, and he remained an automatic choice until 1962, when Walter Winterbottom stood down as manager.

'There has rarely been such a dominant figure as Johnny for England,' Jimmy Greaves wrote later. 'Nearly every forward move was masterminded by him.'

Johnny Haynes juggles the ball, 1965.

▶ key match

England 9 Scotland 3, Home International Championship, Wembley Stadium, 15 April 1961

Johnny Haynes was chaired off the field on the shoulders of his team-mates after orchestrating the most comprehensive defeat of Scotland in history.

'We paraded the great Haynesic around the Wembley pitch as if he was the FA Cup at the end of the match in which he touched perfection,' recalled Jimmy Greaves, the scorer of a hat-trick that day.

This match marked a pinnacle in international football for Haynes, whose appreciation of the instinctive, off-the-cuff play of Greaves was fundamental to England's attacking play.

'Sometimes I didn't even have to look up when I hit a long pass,' recalled Haynes, who scored twice himself from inside-left. 'I just knew that Jimmy would be on the end of it.'

PLAYER • INDUCTED 2002 • 56 CAPS

'I went out of my way to watch Haynes play for Fulham at Maine Road, and he gave the greatest display of inside-forward play I have ever seen.' – Jimmy Murphy, Manchester United assistant manager

As a young boy growing up in north London, the diminutive Johnny Haynes always knew what present to expect at Christmas. 'My father would buy me a brand new football,' he recalled. 'I was so small but, because it was my ball, the other boys always gave me a game. I don't think that would have happened otherwise.'

He still stood only five-foot-one-inch tall in 1950 when he gave an outstanding display in

the schoolboy international against Scotland in front of 60,000 people at Wembley, and a television audience of millions. 'I became a national figure overnight,' Haynes recalled.

At the time, Haynes was identified by the newspapers as the first product of the 'Postwar Memorandum' – the FA plan that established a national coaching system and youth and intermediate national sides. His progression was seen as the way forward, although some critics did not take to his habit of excessive self-criticism during games.

When, four years later, Haynes made his senior debut, he immediately impressed Billy Wright, the England captain. 'Johnny was just 19, and it was unusual at that time for the selectors to put their faith in youth,' Wright recalled. 'But he already looked an assured and confident player, someone who could hit accurate 40-yard passes with either foot.'

'By the mid 1950s, there was no question that he was the most accurate passer of a football in the League,' Wright later wrote. 'I almost used to purr when watching Johnny play his beautifully disguised reverse passes with either foot. He was a footballing master.'

For the next seven years, Walter Winterbottom devised his tactics with Haynes as the pivot in midfield. 'Basically, if Johnny was fit during my time in charge, he played,' the England manager recalled.

By the time England arrived in Chile for what proved to a disappointing World Cup campaign in 1962, Winterbottom's reliance

Johnny Haynes, 1961.

A poster for the 1962 World Cup finals tournament in Chile.

on Haynes was obvious to all, including the opposition.

Asked how his team would play against England in their group game, Hungary coach Baroti told reporters: 'Simple: number 10 takes the corners; number 10 takes the throwins; number 10 does everything. So what do we do? We put a man on number 10. Goodbye England.' And so it proved. England lost.

That summer, Haynes – now aged 28 – was involved in a serious car accident that put him out of the game for almost a year and effectively ended his international career. He had captained his country 22 times.

However, Haynes was still the highest paid

footballer in England by some way. Only the year before, in April 1961, Milan made a bid of £100,000 for his signature. Fulham turned it down: 'He is not for sale,' said Tommy Trinder, the club chairman.

During the winter of 1960, as rumours circulated about the Italians' interest, Trinder, a famous comedian, said: 'Haynes is an entertainer like I am, and if the maximum wage is ever abolished, I will pay him what he is worth, which is £100 a week.'

A few days after Milan lodged their offer, the wage restrictions in English football were lifted. Trinder had little option but to offer his captain

what was a five-fold increase in salary. 'I signed the contract straight away,' Haynes said.

'I love London, I am captain of England and I feel I owe the game something,' Haynes said at the time. Milan had offered a salary of £10,000 a year plus bonuses.

But there was one more twist to the story: 'I was the first player to be paid £100 a week, but Fulham did not increase my wages by a penny to the day I retired in 1970,' Haynes recalled.

In April 1969, more than 24,000 Fulham supporters watched Haynes' testimonial at Craven Cottage – an attendance that con-

▶ talking point

During the early stages of the 1956–57 season, rumours surrounding the future of Johnny Haynes as a Fulham player began to circulate in London.

In response, the then club chairman Charles Dean issued the now familiar 'Hands Off!' warning to rival clubs through the columns of the mass circulation *Daily Express*. His words illustrated the importance of Haynes to the club and its supporters, many of whom had telephoned the ground in protest.

'If Johnny leaves Craven Cottage, then I follow him,' Dean said. 'That's the end – we shut up shop.'

What would happen if Haynes wanted to leave? Dean was asked.

'It would be a disastrous blow to morale,' he replied. 'His colleagues look up to him. They are not playing very well right now but they are fighting their way out of it with an England player to lead them.'

Dean need not have worried. In the same story, Haynes responded to the speculation by saying: 'The only reason I would dream of leaving Fulham is if it were in the club's interest for me to go. I have been worried about our bad start to the season, but that is the only worry I have. I got my first break at Craven Cottage and will never forget it.'

firmed the measure of their appreciation and affection for this loyal one-club man. It was higher than any of Fulham's home League gates that season.

↖
Johnny Haynes evades a Burnley defender to cross the ball during a match at Craven Cottage, 1961.

THROUGH THE AGES
FOOTBALL IN THE 1950s

▶▶▶▶▶▶▶▶▶▶▶▶▶▶▶▶▶▶▶▶▶▶▶▶▶▶▶▶▶▶▶

THIS PAGE: **Above** Manchester City and Birmingham City players wait in the tunnel at Wembley, 1956. **Right** Tom Finney, far left, stands alongside Billy Wright as the England players dress after training, 1952.

OPPOSITE: **Above left** Frank Mountford, the Stoke City centre-half, heads the ball clear, 1951. **Above right** Billy Wright is met by his girlfriend, Joy, of The Beverley Sisters singing group, 1958. **Below left** Denis Law eats his daily steak, as ordered by Huddersfield Town manager Bill Shankly, 1957. **Below right** John Bond leads Bobby Moore in a West Ham United training exercise, 1958.

DUNCAN EDWARDS ▶▶▶▶▶▶

1936–1958

The emergence of Duncan Edwards in his teens as an automatic choice for England broke down a long-held prejudice that age and experience were prerequisites at the highest level – ushering in a period of optimism for the future of the domestic game.

'What football needs today is still more young men with the Duncan Edwards spirit and determination,' Billy Wright wrote in 1957. 'He has the talent to attract large crowds to our soccer grounds, just as film stars lure people to the cinema.'

When the Manchester United half-back made his international debut at the age of 18 against Scotland in 1955, he established himself as the youngest player to represent England that century. After the game, Walter Winterbottom had a quiet word with Wright. 'I think we've uncovered a gem with this one, Billy,' the England manager said.

Stanley Matthews, a team-mate that day, was equally impressed, describing Edwards as 'the most complete footballer of the post-war era', before adding: 'When the going gets rough, Duncan is like a rock in a raging sea.'

A month before Edwards died, at the age of 21, from injuries sustained in the Munich air crash of February 1958, Matt Busby described him as 'the best all-round player in Britain, if not the world'.

Physically, Edwards was an imposing figure. At the age of 16, Edwards was six feet tall and weighed more than 13 stone – and a regular in the recently established England Under-23 side.

His favourite position was left-half, as it allowed him the freedom both to attack and defend. Exceptionally versatile, he also played at inside-forward and centre-forward. After one emergency appearance at centre-forward, the *Daily Express* posed the rhetorical question : 'Is young Edwards the best number nine in the country?'

Duncan Edwards, 1953.

▶ key match

West Germany 1 England 3, International Friendly, Berlin, 26 May 1956

The German newspapers nick-named Duncan Edwards 'Mr Boom Boom' after watching his barnstorming display – and memorable individual goal – against the World Cup holders. 'He has a Big Bertha shot in his boots,' the papers said.

'Duncan was phenomenal,' Billy Wright said. 'There have been few individual perform-ances to match what he pro-duced in Germany. He tackled like a lion, attacked at every opportunity and topped it all off with a cracking goal.'

His surging run took him past several defenders, and he then unleashed a shot from 25 yards, some distance out, given the heavier footballs of the day.

Hugo Meisl, the manager of Austria, watched Edwards in action against West Germany. 'Duncan could win a match alone, and won many games that way,' he said.

PLAYER • INDUCTED 2002 • 18 CAPS • 2 DIVISION ONE CHAMPIONSHIPS

'When I think of Duncan, I feel the rest of us were like pygmies. He was terrific. A professional through and through.'
– Bobby Charlton

Few players in history have exerted as much influence on the development of the domestic game as Duncan Edwards.

For years, there had been a reluctance to throw youngsters into the fray for fear that they would be overwhelmed by the weight of expectation and responsibility.

The success of young Edwards at club and international level offered convincing evidence against such long-held prejudice. A shift in emphasis towards youth had been gathering momentum since the early 1950s; now it developed into something of a craze.

More and more time and energy was being devoted to the scouting and coaching of young talent, and it was Manchester United who stole a march on their rivals when the much-heralded 'Busby Babes' won back-to-back titles between 1955 and 1957.

'Duncan Edwards – 20 today – held his rattled Babes together,' the *Daily Express* reported in its account of the 2–1 defeat of Arsenal at Highbury in October 1956. 'He is mature, magnificent, the supreme wing-half by any standards.'

The following year the same newspaper

A football signed by Manchester United players, 1957.

reported that the rich Italian clubs were prepared to pay a world record transfer fee to secure his signature. 'John Charles has been a sensation in Italy since his transfer to Juventus,' the *Express* reported, 'but they rated Edwards even more highly.'

'When Duncan first came to Old Trafford I tried to find fault with him,' Busby recalled in 1974, 'but I couldn't find one. He was never really a boy; in football terms, he was always a man.'

At international level, Walter Winterbottom was looking forward to the 1958 World Cup in Sweden. 'Duncan was vital to England,' he recalled, 'and other young players were coming through, like Johnny Haynes, Ron

Duncan Edwards in training, 1954.

Clayton and Bobby Charlton.' In May 1957, the *Daily Express* stated: 'Edwards must be England's left-half for the next 10 years.'

Tragically, all that optimism evaporated in the aftermath of the Munich air disaster in February 1958. Fifteen days after the crash that claimed the lives of England team-mates Roger Byrne and Tommy Taylor, Edwards died in a German hospital.

Though he fought for his life with the same tenacity with which he played his football, Edwards could not overcome the massive internal injuries he sustained on impact. Had he survived, a badly broken thigh would almost certainly have ended his playing career.

Football had been his life. 'Duncan would have played every day of the week if he

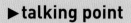

↗
Duncan Edwards, Mark Jones, Roger Byrne and David Pegg adorn the front cover of a 1957 edition of *Red Devils* magazine.

could,' said Jimmy Murphy, the Manchester United assistant manager. 'There was no stopping him.'

Two of his friends – Bobby Charlton and Billy Wright – later revealed other aspects of Edwards' character.

'We were sharing digs in the early days, and money was tight for me,' Charlton wrote. 'Once, Duncan gave me a new shirt which he said was too small for him. I don't think it was really, but it was a very welcome addition to my sparse wardrobe.'

Wright, meanwhile, remembered the practical joker who enjoyed playing tricks on

↖

Duncan Edwards heads the ball.

the senior England players. 'A leg-pulling rascal off the pitch, but everyone loved him,' he said. 'Duncan always had this infectious boyish enthusiasm as he ran down the tunnel before games.'

At the funeral, 5,000 people stood outside the church in his native Dudley. More than three decades later, in 1993, his then 83-year-old mother, Anne, said, 'People still haven't forgotten. Strangers come up and tell me: "He were a real good 'un was your Duncan."'

DANNY BLANCHFLOWER

▶▶▶▶▶▶▶▶▶▶▶▶▶▶▶▶▶▶▶▶▶▶▶▶▶▶▶▶▶▶▶▶▶▶▶▶

1926–1998

'Football is not really about winning, or goals, or saves or supporters,' said Danny Blanchflower. 'It's about glory. It's about doing things in style, doing them with a flourish. It's about going out to beat the other lot, not waiting for them to die of boredom. It's about dreaming of the glory of the double.'

Blanchflower convinced his Tottenham Hotspur team-mates that it was their destiny to win the League and FA Cup double, a feat many pundits at the time considered to be beyond any football team. Famously, in 1960–61, Spurs proved otherwise.

When the title had been secured, supporters invaded the pitch at White Hart Lane in celebration. Once there, they saluted the Spurs captain, chanting: 'We want Danny! We want Danny!' before the presentation of the trophy.

It was a triumph that had been achieved in the grand manner Blanchflower so fervently advocated.

Danny Blanchflower holds aloft the FA Cup, 1961.

PLAYER • INDUCTED 2003 • 56 CAPS • 1 DIVISION ONE CHAMPIONSHIP

2 FA CUPS • 1 EUROPEAN CUP WINNERS' CUP

'He has a nimble brain, fanatical enthusiasm and the ability to take the right decision practically every time.' – Arthur Rowe, Tottenham Hotspur manager

The previous summer, Blanchflower had predicted 'a season of destiny' for Spurs. 'At pre-season training I was impressed with the team: its individual ability, its teamwork and its whole personality,' he said later. 'But I knew that it couldn't be done with a weak heart. The team would really have to believe.'

At the age of 34, Blanchflower was ever-present in the League in 1960–61. 'Danny has great balance and passing ability,' said Cliff Jones, the Spurs winger. 'He was always on his feet. He was never on his backside unless someone put him there.'

Danny Blanchflower, Johnny Haynes and Les Allen, 1960.

In later years, Jimmy Greaves attributed much of his success as a goalscorer to the creative talent of the team's right-half. 'Danny always looks for the gap for a 30-yard pass down the middle,' he said at the time. 'It's just the kind of pass I like, giving me the chance of a quick dash on goal.'

An eloquent, effusive and lyrical speaker, Danny Blanchflower was typically forthright when it came to the subject of captaincy. 'You cannot lead from the middle of a pack,' he always argued. 'I believe in trying the unorthodox when the orthodox isn't working.'

The opinionated Blanchflower was equally outspoken in his frequent criticism of authority. As the decade progressed he also railed against the 'cold', negative and defensive football he'd witnessed on the Continent.

The Northern Irishman began his career in England at Barnsley, before making a move to Aston Villa. Frustrated at what he believed to be old-fashioned thinking and outdated training methods at Villa Park, he moved on again, to Spurs, in 1954, for a club record fee of £30,000.

At White Hart Lane, Blanchflower found his spiritual home; he was voted Footballer of the Year in 1958, the year Bill Nicholson took over as manager. After some early setbacks – including a relegation fight and loss of personal form that led to Blanchflower being dropped briefly – their partnership gelled. With Blanchflower restored as captain, Spurs were on the rise, and a second Footballer of

the Year award followed in 1961.

'I had never seen a captain so ready to face up to his responsibility,' Greaves recalled. 'It takes common sense to see what's wrong and then courage to change it. That is great captaincy.'

In April 1964, when Blanchflower announced his retirement, the sense of loss was immediate. 'A light has gone out at White Hart Lane,' Greaves said.

'He's got the lot. Danny is the greatest character and greatest captain I have met in 30 years in football.' – Arthur Rowe

BOBBY CHARLTON ▶▶▶▶▶▶▶

1937-

A player of both graceful menace and destructive power, Bobby Charlton was an inspirational and pivotal figure for England and Manchester United in the two most important finals ever staged at Wembley Stadium.

In victory, Charlton shed tears at the end of both games. First in joy, choked with patriotic pride and gratification, following the World Cup final in 1966. Then, when Manchester United won the European Cup two years later, he cried again, this time in memory of the eight team-mates who perished in the Munich air disaster in 1958 – a tragedy that he miraculously survived on a physical level with barely a scratch.

Wearing the number nine shirt for both club and country, Charlton generated a mix of fear and respect in his opponents. 'He is the central figure of every match he plays in,' Helmut Schöen, the West Germany manager said. 'A truly great player.'

Over the years United received many world-record bids for his transfer. 'Never would we have sold him. Never,' Matt Busby said in 1973. When told of the offers Charlton always replied: 'I am a Manchester United player. I don't want to play anywhere else.'

No other Englishman has completed the prized quartet of honours: World Cup, European Cup, League championship and FA Cup. In 1966 he was voted Footballer of the Year, to be followed by the European individual honour the following season. All told, between 1958 and 1970, Charlton made a then record 106 England appearances. 'I keep all my caps in plastic bags, so that they don't lose their colour,' he once said.

Overseas, Charlton was a popular figure who earned widespread admiration, as Harold Shepherdson, the England trainer, observed on their travels together. 'As soon as Bobby steps off a plane or bus, they just start clapping.'

Bobby Charlton, 1961.

▶key match

England 2 Portugal 1, World Cup semi-final, Wembley Stadium, 26 July 1966

After Bobby Charlton scored the second of his two goals of the game, a Portugal player walked up to shake the hand of the player who had just deprived him and his team-mates of a place in the final.

The Portugal team respected Charlton to the point of reverence. Earlier in the season he played in Manchester United's famous 5–1 win against Benfica in the European Cup, and they also remembered his two outstanding goals for England against Portugal in 1958.

'After the second goal at Wembley in the semi-final, Augusto ran over and shook my hand. I was very touched by this gesture and often think about it,' Charlton said.

PLAYER • INDUCTED 2002 • 106 CAPS • 1 WORLD CUP • 1 EUROPEAN CUP •

3 DIVISION ONE CHAMPIONSHIPS • 1 FA CUP

'Trouble is, although you know that Bobby intends to shoot, you're never quite sure when. Until ... whoosh! It's in the back of the net.' – Tony Waiters, Blackpool and England goalkeeper

Matt Busby was taken aback by the powerful play of the 15-year-old schoolboy international who chose Manchester United over the other 17 clubs desperate to sign him in the summer of 1953.

'Bobby had exceptional timing,' Busby later recalled. 'Even with the heavier ball we used in those days he could hit a corner beyond the far post with either foot and with scarcely any back-lift. A lot of senior players couldn't do that.'

Busby advised Charlton to alter the mix of his passing 'with a touch of the short stuff as

Bobby Charlton celebrates a goal at Old Trafford, 1963.

well as the long passes' that had made him stand out in schoolboy games.

He was ordered to do individual training sessions, often on Sunday mornings at a deserted Old Trafford, with Jimmy Murphy, the Manchester United assistant manager. 'He used to drive this message into me about movement and making myself available for the return pass until I was sick of it,' Charlton recalled. 'Jimmy would say, "You've got to learn to do it instinctively", and eventually I did.'

The hard, one-on-one work with Murphy paid off. Five days before his 19th birthday, Charlton made his first-team debut in October 1956. In 1958 he was playing for his country.

Years later, as a mark of his respect for Murphy, Charlton made an England shirt available for auction. As a rule, he guarded all his memorabilia – his 'England stuff', as he called it – because of its personal value. Now Charlton made an exception. 'That was for Jimmy Murphy,' he said. 'It was a thank-you, because I learned more from him than anyone else at Old Trafford.'

From his deep-lying position in midfield, Bobby Charlton was the irreplaceable lynch-pin of both the Manchester United and England attacks. In the early years of his career Charlton had played at inside-forward or winger for both his club and country, without ever settling in either role.

The turning point came in 1964, when Matt Busby brought him infield in order to make the most of his exceptional shooting power. Within

Bobby Charlton in action for the Reds, 1968.

A poster for the World Cup, 1966.

a year Alf Ramsey had made the same positional change; Charlton was installed as the creative pivot of the England attack for the World Cup in 1966.

He had long been the central figure at Manchester United. In the wake of the Munich

air disaster in 1958, Charlton became 'the foundation on which we had to rebuild over the ruins', Busby said. 'He is as near perfection as a man and player as it is possible to be.' In total, Charlton played 606 League games for United, scoring 199 goals. When he staged a testimonial in September 1972, 60,000 people packed into Old Trafford to acclaim him. It was the biggest-ever benefit game played in Britain. He retired the following April.

Charlton was also important to the England manager. 'I knew months, even years before the World Cup that Bobby Charlton would have a number nine on his back,' Ramsey said.

Ramsey always liked to have specialist cover for each position in his team. That way the team could stick to the same tactics if injury ruled out a first-team player. Charlton was the key. His ability to break from deep

A European Cup final winners' medal, 1968.

positions and threaten goal was vital to England's strategy in 1966.

Asked several years later if he had looked for a substitute in a similar mould in case injury sidelined Charlton before the tournament, Ramsey said: 'No, there wasn't one. Bobby was one of a kind.'

Bobby Charlton shoots at the Scotland goal, 1967.

BILL NICHOLSON

▶▶▶▶▶▶▶▶▶▶▶▶▶▶▶▶▶▶

1919–2004

Bill Nicholson built one of the most celebrated sides in the history of English football – the 'Super Spurs' team that secured the double in such thrilling style in 1961.

A gruff, avuncular Yorkshireman who devoted his professional life to the club as both player and manager, Nicholson was respected throughout the game as a pioneering coach and tactician who positively shaped the development of English football.

Under his leadership Tottenham Hotspur became the first English club to win a European trophy – the European Cup-Winners' Cup – in 1963, following on from their defence of the FA Cup the previous season.

In 1971 Nicholson was asked the secret of his success in management. 'In a word, work,' he replied. 'Just damned hard work.'

↖
Bill Nicholson and Danny Blanchflower hold aloft the FA Cup, 1962.

MANAGER • INDUCTED 2003 • 1 DIVISION ONE CHAMPIONSHIP • 3 FA CUPS • 1 UEFA CUP

1 EUROPEAN CUP-WINNERS' CUP • 2 LEAGUE CUPS

'Spurs are the finest English club team I've ever seen.' – Wolves manager Stan Cullis, 1960

As one of the leading figures in the vanguard of young managers preaching the new gospel of coaching in the late 1950s, Nicholson shifted the emphasis away from the traditional high-tempo, direct, long-ball game employed by Wolverhampton Wanderers. Instead, Spurs perfected a more deliberate, short-passing style.

'Spurs were a brilliant side, full of light and shade, a team of individual brilliance and collective excellence,' wrote Brian Butler, the respected BBC commentator, in his official history of the Football Association, published in 1991.

A second side built by Nicholson enjoyed more success; this time, however, the triumphs were restricted to cup competitions – the FA Cup in 1967, League Cup in 1971 and 1973, and the UEFA Cup in 1972.

Bill Nicholson with the Spurs squad, 1968.

Bill Nicholson supervises training, 1967.

Although frustrated in his great ambition to win a second League title, Nicholson achieved outstanding consistency for the times: only once during the 1960s did Spurs finish outside the top eight in the top flight.

Following his appointment in 1958, Nicholson spent three years introducing new methods in training, devising new tactics and investing heavily in the transfer market.

All the tactical preparations were done pre-season. Set pieces and patterns of play were devised and practised. This was 'ghost football': training games in which the players went through set moves without a ball. 'I introduced the best training schedules, the sort of organised training which all clubs brought in during the 1960s and 1970s,' Nicholson said.

While instructing individuals on particular aspects of the game, Nicholson also worked on the group-mentality, rejecting the 'flat-out for 90 minutes' approach then prevalent. 'The intense pressure must come in spells,' he said. 'My players are intelligent enough to know now when just such a spell is on. It is then that they should score enough goals to win.'

Tragically, by the middle of the decade, the creative and physical engine room of the 1961 side had been struck down by the death of John White, injury to Dave Mackay and Maurice Norman, and the retirement of captain Danny Blanchflower. As Jimmy Greaves said: 'The heart was ripped out of Spurs in a painful way, and a black cloud of despondency enveloped us.'

That side reached its zenith in the autumn of 1960 when they crushed Wolves, the FA Cup winners and League runners-up the previous season, 4–0 at Molineux.

Summing up his philosophy, Nicholson once said: 'It is better to fail aiming high than to succeed aiming low.'

▶ talking point

Bill Nicholson lived almost all of his adult life in a modest terraced house close to White Hart Lane. It meant a shorter journey to work, allowing more time for his obsession: managing Tottenham Hotspur.

Over a period of 38 years, as player and then manager, Nicholson set an example in dedication. 'Bill is the one who turns on the lights in the morning and turns them off at night,' joked one rival manager.

'No matter how hard you might work or how many hours you put in, you know that Bill is doing a lot more than you for the club,' said his captain Danny Blanchflower.

JIMMY ARMFIELD

▶▶▶▶▶▶▶▶▶▶▶▶▶▶▶▶

1935–

An adventurous full-back who collected 43 caps, Jimmy Armfield earned the respect of his peers as England captain under successive managers during the 1960s.

The Blackpool defender, a loyal one-club man and pioneering 'overlapping' full-back, had already led his country with distinction during the 1962 World Cup in Chile. Walter Winterbottom, the then England manager, encouraged Armfield's dashing 'sixth forward play'. By this time his international reputation was firmly established; in 1959, after a friendly in Rio, Brazil winger Julhino said: 'He was so strong in the second half, I would not like to play against him every week.'

Then, in 1964, Helmut Schoen, the manager of rivals West Germany, identified Armfield as one of the best players in England, a status reinforced when Armfield was one of three Englishmen nominated by the Football Association for selection in an all-star Europe XI for a prestigious friendly.

Jimmy Armfield ties his boot laces, 1966.

PLAYER • INDUCTED 2008 • 43 CAPS • 1 WORLD CUP

**'Jimmy Armfield takes the game with fierce, professional seriousness.'
– *Daily Express*, 1962**

Two years later, Armfield – a transfer target of Spurs, Arsenal, Wolves and Liverpool at one time – was recalled after a long absence by Alf Ramsey in the run up to the World Cup. Moreover, Armfield was named captain for two vital warm-up games.

In the event of Bobby Moore suffering an injury or being dropped because of poor form, Armfield had emerged as a serious candidate for the captaincy. Unfortunately, his prospects of retaining a place in the side were effectively dashed when he sustained a toe injury during a warm-up match. His chance had gone.

Jimmy Armfield is chased by Geoff Hurst, with Alf Ramsey looking on, 1966.

During the tournament, the immensely popular Armfield assumed the role of unofficial leader of the reserve players, a 'link man', as he put it, 'between them and the manager'. Tellingly, Ramsey regularly invited his opinion on playing matters.

'To retain his speed, Armfield does ten 30-yard sprints each day, in conjunction with routine training,' the *Daily Express* reported in 1962. 'He takes the game with fierce, professional seriousness.'

As a boy, Armfield attended a rugby-playing school before joining Blackpool. In 1955, Joe Smith, the manager, publicly stated: 'This boy will play for England.' Armfield proved him right after only 22 first-team games when he was selected for the Under-23 side.

An unfortunate turning point in his career occurred during the game against Ipswich Town on 25 April 1964. From his seat in the

Jimmy Armfield (right) and Jimmy Greaves, 1962.

stands Alf Ramsey saw Armfield sustain a severely torn groin muscle. It was, Armfield said, 'the most painful moment of my career'. In his absence, his England rival George Cohen seized his opportunity.

It didn't help either that Blackpool were entering into a period of decline. A top-flight club for all but one of Armfield's seasons at Bloomfield Road, the Seasiders' results had gradually deteriorated, culminating in relegation in 1971, the year of his retirement.

Armfield had been captain for 13 years. 'People used to call me Gentlemen Jim, probably because I was never sent off in 626 games for Blackpool and 43 England appearances.' He had played more than 500 games before his first booking. 'The referee was almost apologetic,' he said.

ALF RAMSEY ▶▶▶▶▶▶▶▶▶▶▶▶▶▶▶▶

1920–1999

Gordon Banks spoke for all his team-mates in the England team of 1966 when he said: 'Without Alf Ramsey we would never have won the World Cup.'

'Alf was an excellent coach,' the England goalkeeper wrote. 'His motivation and man-management skills were also outstanding. He was always fair to his players and scrupulously honest. A man of unyielding integrity and absolute loyalty, and his loyalty was reciprocated by the players,' said Banks. 'He was devoted to the team ethic, and yet he always stressed that no one was indispensable. He bore no grudges and had no favourites. His knowledge was unrivalled, complemented by superb tactical acumen, yet his instructions were clear and simple.'

Above all, Ramsey made the players believe in themselves – both as individuals and collectively. He'd managed the feat on a shoestring budget at Ipswich Town, guiding them to the most remarkable championship success of the modern era. Then he repeated the trick with England.

At the peak of his powers, Ramsey instilled in his players an abiding and absolute faith in English football. In his opinion, the domestic game was the best in the world, and he made the players believe that too. 'Alf made us proud to wear the England shirt,' Alan Ball wrote later.

Bobby Charlton valued Ramsey's professionalism and integrity. 'He gave you the confidence that you'd been picked because you were a good player, not because your club team was doing particularly well or because of anyone else's say-so, or because the press had been clamouring for your inclusion.

'He found a formula that made England consistent for the first time ever. Up until Alf came along anybody could beat us abroad. He stopped us being frightened of anybody, and he made us believe we were better than anybody else.'

Sir Alf Ramsey, 1973.

▶ key match

England 4 West Germany 2 (aet), World Cup final, Wembley Stadium, 30 July 1966

The professionalism that underpinned everything Alf Ramsey stood for as a manager did not desert him when he faced his greatest challenge.

The stoical Ramsey remained calm and focused following Germany's last-gasp equaliser – a goal that stunned the crowd and devastated his players. It was now that Ramsey delivered his best-remembered line – the perfectly timed and inspiring rallying cry: 'Now go out and win it again.'

Urging his exhausted men to stay on their feet, so as not to display any weakness to the opposition, Ramsey then rallied each player individually. 'When he came to me,' recalled Alan Ball, 'he said: "Attack, attack, every time you can, attack."'

Victory secured, and having declined all appeals to join the lap of honour, the manager strode, smiling and composed, to the dressing room with the chant 'Ramsey! Ramsey!' echoing around Wembley.

MANAGER • INDUCTED 2002 • 1 WORLD CUP • 1 DIVISION ONE CHAMPIONSHIP

In May 1966 the top five teams in the FIFA rankings were Portugal, Brazil, England, West Germany and Argentina. In July, England beat three of them within the space of seven days to win the World Cup.

Soon after his appointment by the Football Association in 1962, Ramsey made an unequivocal statement about England's prospects four years hence. 'We will win the World Cup,' Ramsey said, without qualification. 'We have the players, the ability, the strength of character and temperament to win the title in 1966.'

Two years after England's subsequent triumph over West Germany at Wembley, a journalist interviewed Ramsey.

'You were sticking your neck out a bit, weren't you?' the reporter asked. 'No one expected you to commit yourself to that extent.' In reply Ramsey stated: 'It was what I believed. I couldn't have taken the job if I didn't think we would win.'

A methodical, practical man, Ramsey built his team from the back. In only his second match in charge he handed Gordon Banks his first cap. Once established, Banks remained an automatic choice in goal until the loss of an eye in a car accident nine years later.

The defensive formation was settled one year before the start of the tournament with the introduction of both Jack Charlton and Nobby Stiles against Scotland. They would play, respectively, alongside and in front of Bobby Moore, the captain and sweeper. Either side of them, George Cohen and Ray Wilson were established as a full-back pairing

These six players stayed together as a stable unit throughout the World Cup, conceding only one goal on their way to the final, a record for the tournament.

Ramsey was now able to concentrate on attacking formations and tactics. Over the following months he experimented with several systems, all pivoting around Bobby Charlton, the deep-lying number nine, and the one player deemed irreplaceable. In selecting the other forwards, Ramsey put the emphasis on hard work and flexibility.

The first former England player to manage the national team, Ramsey was also the first professional club manager to be put in charge. The appointment marked a

↖
Sir Alf Ramsey, (Trevillion).

An official badge issued to the press in 1966.

turning point in English football.

His predecessor, Walter Winterbottom, though an outstanding coach and administrator, had no experience at club level. From the outset, Ramsey – a professional football man 'with mud on his boots', as Bobby Charlton put it – insisted on picking the team. In return for this transfer of power away from the 'amateur' selection committee, Ramsey took responsibility for results.

After watching England lose twice following his appointment, Ramsey then experienced defeat only four times in 44 internationals, culminating in the World Cup final in 1966. Overall, his record as England manager read: played 113; won 69; drawn 27; lost 17; goals for 224; goals against 99.

Only when those results began to turn against him in the early 1970s, with successive disappointments in major competitions, did he become vulnerable. With the Press now largely hostile he was sacked, abruptly, in May 1974.

Under Ramsey, England regained international respect as a football power. He believed England's rightful place was at the top of the

↗
Sir Alf Ramsey with Bobby Charlton, 1970.

world game. Thus, when England finished third in the European Nations Cup in 1968, Ramsey was dissatisfied. This, he argued, was not good enough for England. 'England are still the world champions and third place in Europe is not our place,' he said.

Two years later England defended the World Cup in Mexico as joint favourites, even though they had never before gone past the quarter-finals stage of the tournament on

↖
An official replica of the World Cup trophy.

► **talking point**

In May 1962, two days after Ipswich Town clinched the First Division championship, Alf Ramsey gave an interview to a mass-circulation national newspaper.

'Football is a simple game, and we have never tried to embroider it,' he told the *Daily Express*. 'Football is also a team game, and we have been steadfast to the conception of the 11-man unit.'

The newspaper noted the additional, arduous administrative responsibility Ramsey assumed as club-secretary, in addition to his role as team-manager. Ramsey, however, played down his contribution. 'I do not seek personal publicity,' he said. 'The championship has been won by the players of Ipswich, not the manager.'

Almost half the Ipswich side had been with Ramsey since their days in the Third Division five years earlier – a time when they were considered little more than club-journeymen. Never before had a footballer won Third, Second and First Division medals with one club. Now five of them had done it.

Such was the level of amazement surrounding their success that the *Express* devoted an editorial to 'this glorious achievement' of the underdog and outsider.

foreign soil. Beforehand Brazil regarded them as their most serious threat; other nations also feared Ramsey's side.

Following his dismissal as England manager, the FA put on record its 'deep appreciation of all that Sir Alf Ramsey has accomplished'. English football, they said, owed him a debt 'for his unbending loyalty and dedication and the high level of integrity that he brought to world football.'

GEORGE COHEN

▶▶▶▶▶▶▶▶▶▶▶▶▶▶▶▶▶

1939–

Dedication, strength and a sprinter's raw speed: these were the qualities that George Cohen supplied for Alf Ramsey and the England team of 1966.

At his peak, Cohen could cover 100 yards in 10.3 seconds, and it was this searing pace at right-back that ideally complimented the height of Jack Charlton, the poise of Bobby Moore and the tenacity of Ray Wilson in the England defence.

Three of the greatest post-war managers – Bill Nicholson of Spurs, Everton's Harry Catterick and Stan Cullis of Wolves – all tried to sign this fitness fanatic and boyhood boxer, but Fulham – Cohen's only club – always refused to let him go.

In 1967, Vic Buckingham, the Fulham manager, declared Cohen the best right-back in Europe. That same year, Cohen came second in the voting behind Bobby Charlton for the Footballer of the Year award. 'That was my best year in football,' Cohen later recalled.

George Cohen trains at Craven Cottage, 1963.

PLAYER • INDUCTED 2009 • 37 CAPS • 1 WORLD CUP

'We knew that no winger could get the better of George on the outside. His pace was amazing.' – Jack Charlton

During the World Cup Cohen was assigned the task of nullifying two of the most exciting and dangerous forwards in the world – the tricky and nippy Oscar Mas of Argentina and West Germany's Lothar Emmerich, a dynamic winger with one of the most powerful shots in international football. Neither of them could get the better of Cohen.

The watching international press rated England the best defence in the tournament. 'As a four-man unit, we played 37 matches,

↗

George Cohen turns to watch the flight of the ball, 1966.

including the World Cup, and lost only three times,' Cohen recalled.

Writing in 1967, Jack Charlton detailed Cohen's contribution: 'The defence worked so well because I knew nobody could out-run him on the outside. If they came inside he might be in trouble and it would be up to me to help out. If they went the other way George could give anybody two or three yards start and still beat them to the goal line. He was so fast it was barely believable at times.'

In the aftermath of victory, both Wilson and Bobby Charlton rated Cohen the most likely of all the 1966 heroes to keep his place for the 1970 World Cup in Mexico. Sadly, though, at the age of 29, a career-ending knee injury put paid to that ambition. 'England,' as Sir Alf Ramsey said at the time, 'have lost a great player in his prime.'

Fulham fans responded by generating

↖

George Cohen, 1965.

more money for his testimonial than they would for Johnny Haynes, the other great servant of the club. Many of his World Cup colleagues, including Bobby Moore and Jimmy Greaves, turned out in support of Cohen, whom *The Times* described as 'a great-hearted player'. That evening, Sir Alf told reporters: 'George had all the qualities required of an international player, particularly in defence. He was a serious-minded young man, dedicated to his task.'

Nobby Stiles was another England stalwart who turned up for Cohen's testimonial, and he told reporters afterwards: 'I would have been here tonight for George's sake, even if that meant getting here on crutches.'

> **▶ key match**
>
> **England 1 Poland 1, Friendly, Goodison Park, 5 January 1966**
>
> George Cohen produced what he considered to be his best performance in an England shirt in this vital warm-up match ahead of the World Cup.
>
> Playing on his favourite away ground, Cohen set up a rare goal for Bobby Moore, the England captain, and 'did not put a foot wrong in defence', according to the *Daily Express*.
>
> 'It happened that I always played well at Goodison,' Cohen said later. Perhaps that explains why Harry Catterick, the Everton manager, made strenuous efforts to sign him on several occasions.
>
> 'Defensively, England gave a very strong display, with George Cohen always willing and able to help out the attack.' the *Express* noted.

DAVE MACKAY ▶▶▶▶▶▶▶▶▶▶▶▶▶

1934–

'Dave Mackay was the physical leader of the double-winning Tottenham Hotspur side,' Jimmy Greaves once wrote. 'He went into games as if he was a warrior going into battle.'

Describing Mackay as 'the greatest player in that great side', Greaves added: 'He had just about everything: power, skill, stamina and enthusiasm. He was the best professional I ever played alongside. When his name was missing from the team-sheet we all had to work twice as hard.'

Cliff Jones, a member of the double team of 1960–61, said: 'Once Dave Mackay settled into that number six shirt at left-half, he turned a good side into a great one.'

Bill Nicholson paid Heart of Midlothian £30,000, then a British record fee for a wing-half, to bring Mackay to White Hart Lane in 1958. He stayed for a decade, a period during which Spurs won the Division One title once and the FA Cup three times – in 1961, 1962 and 1967.

By the time Mackay captained Spurs to victory at Wembley in 1967 he had, by his own admission, slowed considerably. Struggling to keep up with the pace in midfield, he was deployed in a more defensive role in the final against Chelsea. The following year he was made available for transfer.

On hearing the news, Brian Clough raced down to London, unannounced. Risking rejection, Clough subjected himself to the indignity of being kept waiting at White Hart Lane for several hours – all for the chance to persuade the veteran Scot to sign for Derby County.

Clough regarded the experienced Mackay as a potential mentor for his young side – and he was prepared to meet Mackay's high wage demands. At the end of his first season at the Baseball Ground, Derby were promoted to the top flight as champions, and Mackay was voted Footballer of the Year.

Dave Mackay is restrained by Mike Summerbee of Manchester City.

PLAYER • INDUCTED 2002 • 22 CAPS • 1 DIVISION ONE CHAMPIONSHIP • 3 FA CUPS

'In Dave Mackay – the finest wing-half in the world today – Spurs have a magnificent tackler and a chap who can take care of himself in any situation.' – Joe Mercer, 1961

'I can't overstate the impact and influence Mackay had at the Baseball Ground,' Clough said. 'David was Derby – the cornerstone. Our self-confidence soared because of him. He was the consummate, complete professional, a man of immense talent.'

The big English clubs were surprised when Hearts suddenly put their best player up for sale in 1958. Dave Mackay, the lynchpin of the Scotland half-back line, had recently fractured a bone in his foot. The newspapers were suspicious: reporters asked whether fitness concerns were prompting the sale. Bill Nicholson ignored all the rumours and tabled a bid.

In fact, Hearts had simply wanted the money, Mackay said later. A foot injury had been troubling him, but a regime of treatment and weight training at Spurs soon corrected the problem.

Mackay was bought to strengthen the defence, and his arrival freed the creative talent of Danny Blanchflower, his half-back partner, and Cliff Jones, the Spurs winger. 'With Dave behind him, I knew Cliff would be able to show his full potential,' Blanchflower said.

After watching his Aston Villa side lose at home in an FA Cup tie in February 1961, Joe Mercer described Tottenham as 'the finest post-war club in Great Britain'.

'In my opinion, the whole side revolves around Danny Blanchflower and Dave

Ticket for the international between England and Scotland, 1951.

Mackay,' Mercer wrote. 'Stop this pair, and you stop Tottenham, you might say, but then tell me how in the name of football you stop such genius. You see, Spurs' most valuable attacking asset is their incredible ability to improvise or, shall I say, play it off the cuff. It shows in their confidence and thoughtfulness.'

The turning point for this great Spurs side occurred on a bitterly cold night at Old Trafford in December 1963. When Mackay suffered a broken leg his first reaction was one of surprise. He had expected to feel sharp pain; instead he just felt sick.

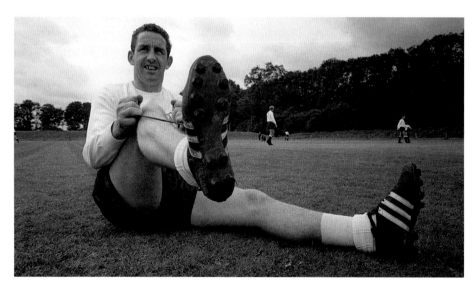

Dave Mackay ties his laces before training, 1966.

It was a serious injury. Mackay would be sidelined for more than a season. 'When Dave was carried off, the heart of the double side went with him,' Jimmy Greaves said. 'We were never the same again.'

The following September Mackay sustained a second fracture of his leg on his comeback for the reserves. 'It plunged all of us at the club into a mood of gloom,' Greaves said. Bill Nicholson 'was absolutely choked' on hearing the news.

'Dave was critical to the double side,' Greaves added. 'Looking back, it was as if the team died overnight at Old Trafford. It took more than a season for its complete break-up but somehow the magic was gone.'

Dave Mackay helped Derby County reach the top, first as a player and then as a

Dave Mackay, (Trevillion).

manager at the Baseball Ground.

Brian Clough needed all his powers of persuasion to bring Mackay to the Midlands. The player looked set to quit England altogether. He had set his mind on the job of assistant manager at Hearts.

When all else failed, Clough offered to make Mackay one of the highest paid footballers in the country. 'Done,' Mackay said immediately. Clough described the deal as 'the best bit of business I did in my entire career'.

Instead of playing in midfield, Mackay was told to drop back as sweeper, the ideal position from which to bark out his orders.

Dave Mackay jumps over bench, 1965.

'Brian went out of his way to build me up as a superman,' Mackay said. 'Even when I had a bad game others were criticised. It was good psychology, though, because I could only make the young players believe in themselves if they believed in me.'

Soon after the club won promotion Mackay left to begin his management career. In October 1973 he returned to Derby County as manager. Under his leadership Derby won the Division One title in 1974–75.

RAY WILSON

▶▶▶▶▶▶▶▶▶▶▶▶▶▶▶

1934–

Ray Wilson was the senior professional in the England side that won the World Cup in 1966 and an accomplished defender whom Alf Ramsey rated as 'the finest left-back I have ever seen'.

An automatic choice for his country during successive World Cup campaigns, the unflappable Wilson gained the respect of colleagues for his calming presence and good sense in the England dressing room and outstanding reliability on the field.

A proud, circumspect Derbyshireman, Wilson chose his words carefully. But when he did speak, others listened, as Nobby Stiles would recall. 'Ray Wilson carried a lot of influence with the players, and although Alf always basically knew what he wanted to do, I did notice that he tended to prick up his ears when Ray had something to say.'

Ray Wilson walks onto the pitch at Wembley, 1963.

PLAYER • INDUCTED 2008 • 63 CAPS • 1 WORLD CUP • 1 FA CUP

'The finest left-back I have ever seen.' – Sir Alf Ramsey

Jack Charlton summed up Wilson's qualities as a defender. 'If he missed a tackle, he was remarkably quick in his recovery, and the rest of us always had the greatest confidence in him.' Charlton said.

At club level, Wilson enjoyed success relatively late in his career as a member of Everton's FA Cup-winning side in 1966 – two years after joining the club from Huddersfield Town for a fee of £40,000, a record for a full-back at the time.

'Ray is worth double the sum Everton paid for him,' wrote Alan Ball, a team-mate at Goodison Park. 'No winger who played against him in the World Cup can claim to have broken even in the exchange, let alone come out on top.'

After winning his first representative honour in 1959, Wilson was an established

↗
Ray Wilson, right, and Roger Hunt parade the World Cup at the Charity Shield at Goodison Park, 1966.

international when England took part in the World Cup in Chile three years later.

In 1964 Huddersfield finally decided to cash in, perhaps convinced that his best days were behind him. On joining Everton, Wilson prospered under a more rigorous training regime, shedding almost a stone in weight and building his stamina.

By the time Everton won the title in 1969–70, Wilson had been moved on to Oldham Athletic, having been sidelined as a first-team regular at Goodison Park due to serious injury.

Over a career spanning more than 400 appearances, Wilson never had his name

↖
Ray Wilson guards his post during the FA Cup final, 1966.

▶ talking point

A late developer, Ray Wilson struggled to make an impact at Huddersfield Town, the club for whom he signed after leaving school.

In his first two years at Leeds Road, Wilson did not make a single appearance, even in the reserves, in his favoured position of wing-half. National Service then took him out of the game completely for two years. On being demobbed from the Army in 1955, his career prospects looked bleak.

Then came the breakthrough: on Wilson's first day back at training, Andy Beattie, the Huddersfield Town manager, told him to play left-back. It was the first time he had ever worn the number three shirt.

taken in a Football League match for committing a foul. His first booking, in September 1966, was for dissent. 'I don't think I ever gave away many fouls,' Wilson would recall.

He will, of course, be best remembered for his performances for England earlier that summer. After barely putting a foot wrong throughout the tournament, Wilson made a rare mistake in the final when his weak defensive header opened the way for West Germany's opening goal. However, his reaction was vital to England's recovery and eventual victory, as Nobby Stiles would recall later. 'On a rare occasion Ray made a mistake – and I can't remember another one he made in the 1966 World Cup – he would never hide, and it was the same now. Ray had moral courage to burn,' Stiles added. 'He never blinked or flinched at a moment of heavy pressure. He was an inspiration to us all.'

TEAM INDUCTEE
TOTTENHAM HOTSPUR
▶▶▶▶▶▶▶▶▶▶▶▶▶▶▶▶▶▶▶▶▶▶ 1960–1961

July 1960

On their return for pre-season training, the players begin work on a new 'Stop-Start Plan'. Pre-planned attacking moves are run through over and over again, with Bill Nicholson repeatedly stopping play to make his point. 'We try to make training progressive,' he says. The season opens with a 2–0 home win over Everton.

The Spurs team in March 1961.

September 1960

Bill Nicholson explains his football philosophy: 'When the obvious is "on", I like them to do the obvious. When it's "not on", then they have to find alternatives, and have enough faith in their own skills to carry them through.'

▶▶▶▶▶▶▶▶▶▶▶▶▶▶▶▶▶▶▶▶▶▶

3 September 1960

After four successive wins, Spurs face Manchester United. The result: a 4–1 home win. 'You gave my lads an education,' Matt Busby tells the Tottenham players. 'Our toughest game yet,' responds Danny Blanchflower.

24 September 1960

After a sparkling 6–2 home win against Aston Villa one national newspaper states: 'Spurs are the best-loved side the game has known. Their success is not resented by others.'

October 1960

The Football League is thinking about selecting 11 Spurs players for their prestigious fixture against the Italian League. Meanwhile, Real Madrid want to play Spurs in a friendly at Wembley. Neither plan materialises.

1 October 1960

The away fixture against Wolves is billed as the biggest game of the season so far. These are the country's two most powerful sides – and Tottenham assert their pre-eminence with a 4–0 win. 'With this team I could play until I was 64,' Danny Blanchflower says. 'They make football a pleasure.'

10 October 1960

After 11 successive victories, Spurs are held by Manchester City. Bert Trautmann, 'the greatest goalkeeper in Britain, performed miracles', one newspaper reports. Defeat at Sheffield Wednesday follows.

November 1960

'If we don't win anything it doesn't matter,' says Fred Bearman, the 88-year-old Spurs chairman. 'Playing football and making people happy – that's all that matters.'

19 December 1960

Final score: Everton 1 Spurs 3. In the Goodison Park boardroom afterwards, Johnny Carey, the Everton manager, tells his directors: 'Gentlemen, we've been beaten by a great side.' The *Daily Express* states: 'Spurs can start planning their title celebration.'

4 February 1961

As the pitches turn increasingly to mud, Spurs fall to their first home defeat – a 2–3 setback against Leicester City. Newspapers are asking: is doubt creeping in?

11 February 1961

'This was the match of Danny Blanchflower's life,' one newspaper reports after Spurs restore morale with a 2–1 win at Villa Park. The captain leads by example.

18 February 1961

The Cup draw takes Spurs straight back to Villa Park. Reflecting on their first highly physical encounter, Nicholson says: 'Our victory gives us the psychological advantage.' Tottenham win 2–0. 'Their most valuable attacking asset is their incredible ability to improvise,' says Joe Mercer, the Villa manager. 'It shows their confidence. Any team playing against Spurs can so easily develop an inferiority complex.'

22 February 1961

Their rivals are not giving up, however. After watching Wolves take a point with only 10 men, manager Stan Cullis says: 'Spurs can crack.'

25 February 1961

Tottenham respond by winning at Manchester City. 'What impresses one about Spurs is that everyone is moving, everyone is way ahead, thinking about the next move,' says Denis Law, the City forward.

8 March 1961

Sunderland fans queue up all night for Cup tickets. After a draw at Roker Park, Spurs win the replay 5–0, prompting the headline: 'Super-Duper Spurs.'

11 March 1961

After defeat in the League against Cardiff, Nicholson

Danny Blanchflower interviewed by reporters.

The victory parade in 1961.

gets tough. 'There has been a lack of desire for action,' he says. A once commanding 10-point lead has been cut to three points – with nearest rivals Sheffield Wednesday still to play. 'This is now a test of character,' Nicholson tells his players.

17 April 1961

Their nerve holds. By defeating their nearest rivals, Spurs complete the first half of the double – the championship title – with several weeks to spare.

6 May 1961

At the end of the FA Cup final, the exhausted Leicester City players line up at the tunnel entrance at Wembley in a guard of honour for the double-winners. Afterwards the City manager Matt Gillies tells Nicholson: 'You are worthy of the double, and you will be a credit to English football in the European Cup.'

BOBBY MOORE ▶▶▶▶▶▶▶▶▶▶▶

1941–1993

Bobby Moore, the only Englishman to lift the World Cup, inspired his team-mates through the example of his own unshakeable composure and self-belief. Ninety times he captained his country, equalling the record established by Billy Wright.

'He did not know the meaning of the word panic,' Alan Ball recalled. 'He put the rest of the players at ease. He was the best defender, the best reader of play and a superlative captain.'

His positive influence was evident before a ball had been kicked in the World Cup final against West Germany in 1966. 'He carried out the match ball, resting on his hip with the kind of panache that no other captain could manage,' Geoff Hurst recalled.

Alf Ramsey once described Moore as 'my general on the field who translates our strategy into reality'. One of Ramsey's earliest decisions as England manager was to promote Moore to captain; he was 22 at the time. The following year, 1964, Moore was voted Footballer of the Year, the youngest ever recipient of the award.

Ramsey told Moore: 'Whatever you do, whatever decisions you think are necessary during a game, you will have my full backing.' The two men had made a professional bond that would shape their country's footballing fortunes for a decade, at the end of which Moore had amassed a then record 108 England caps.

'I was thrilled,' Moore said. 'I like being captain. I like the feeling of responsibility, that if something happens on the field I have to make a decision.'

In three successive seasons, Moore led his side up the steps to the Royal Box at Wembley to collect a trophy: the FA Cup in 1964, the European Cup-Winners' Cup in 1965 and the World Cup in 1966.

Bobby Moore leads out the England team, 1971.

▶key match

West Ham United 2 TSV Munich 1860 0, European Cup-Winners' Cup final, Wembley Stadium, 19 May 1965

Early in his career, Bobby Moore was taken to one side by Ron Greenwood for a quiet chat. 'Bobby,' the West Ham manager said, 'I'm going to build this team around you.' The fruition of that work was seen in this match of high quality and sportsmanship.

'This was Bobby's greatest game for the club,' Greenwood wrote later. 'It was technical perfection.' Moore had contributed fully to a fluid, attacking team performance that in later years Greenwood highlighted as the ultimate expression of his values as a coach.

In earlier rounds of the competition Greenwood made a crucial tactical change, switching Moore into a deeper, more defensive sweeper role for away legs.

'You don't have to go around kicking people up in the air to be a good tackler,' Moore wrote later. 'The art is to deny a forward space and force him to knock the ball away.'

PLAYER • INDUCTED 2002 • 108 CAPS • 1 WORLD CUP • 1 FA CUP • 1 EUROPEAN CUP-WINNERS' CUP

'The England player with the best temperament is undoubtedly Bobby Moore, the skipper.' – Harold Shepherdson, England trainer, 1971

In 1970, after England had played Brazil in the World Cup, Pelé described Bobby Moore as 'the greatest defender I ever faced.' One Mexican newspaper called him 'The King of World Football'.

In the game against Brazil, Moore dispossessed Jairzinho with a perfectly timed challenge as the Brazil winger bore down on goal. Alan Hansen, the Liverpool defender, has since described it as the best tackle he has ever seen.

A World Cup winners' medal, 1966.

Bobby Moore on England duty, 1970.

Yet Moore was not particularly quick, nor the hardest of tacklers. Worse still, especially for a central defender, he did not like to head the ball, preferring to control it on his chest or foot instead. 'I don't think he wanted to spoil his hair,' Ron Greenwood, the West Ham manager, once joked.

None of this mattered. His abundant composure and technical skill, allied to an unrivalled ability to read the play, made Moore great. 'A cool, calculating footballer I could trust with my life,' Ramsey said. Jock Stein, the Scotland manager, once argued jokingly: 'There should be a law against him. He knows what's happening 20 minutes before anyone else.'

As a teenager, Moore became the youngest holder of a full coaching badge; and added to theory had a willingness to graft. 'Bobby had a fanatical dedication,' Greenwood said. 'He made himself into a great player. He wanted to know everything.'

Bobby never let me know but I knew that when the bugle sounded he would always find

Bobby Moore holds aloft the European Cup-Winners' Cup, 1965.

'Bobby knows exactly when and how to switch the play to suit each tactical situation. The way he makes use of his experience is fantastic.' – Martin Peters

another 20 per cent. He grew to meet the challenge. This is what being a top international player is all about.'

Bobby Moore won the respect and admiration of his manager and team-mates as a leader whose presence was considered essential to England's success.

At Wembley in 1966, Ramsey demonstrated his regard for Moore to the world in a single gesture. As Moore walked towards the steps to collect the trophy, the normally reserved manager rose from the bench, smiling, approached his captain and then gave him a warm victory embrace.

The players unquestioningly accepted Moore as their spokesman. The day after the final, Ramsey wanted to know how they thought the £22,000 win bonus should be divided up. Moore spoke up immediately: 'It should be divided equally between every member of the squad, Alf.' The others nodded their approval.

The number six shirt worn by Bobby Moore in the World Cup group game against Brazil, 1970.

By 1970 Moore had assumed an even more integral role as the team's talisman and figurehead. After being falsely accused of stealing and briefly locked up in a Colombian jail, Moore finally arrived in Mexico alone, just before the start of the tournament. Ramsey met him at the airport in Guadalajara.

Ramsey, a man rarely given to displays of emotion, scampered across the tarmac to greet Moore. 'How are you, my old son?' Ramsey asked, telling him that seeing him again was the most wonderful sight he had

Bobby Moore chats to a group of schoolboys, 1962.

▶ **talking point**

The pass Bobby Moore made in the dying moments of the World Cup final at Wembley encapsulated him as a footballer.

As West Germany pressed for an equaliser, the ball fell to the England captain just outside his own penalty area. Jack Charlton, his central defensive partner, screamed at him to 'hoof it into the stands'. Instead, Moore controlled the ball, drawing a couple of German players. To Moore's left stood Ray Wilson but giving a short pass would only shift the responsibility and pressure to the England full-back. Looking up, Moore saw the run made by Geoff Hurst. He then delivered an inch-perfect pass over 40 yards into space for his West Ham team-mate to collect, whose shot made the score 4–2.

'It's always been in my manner to try and play, whereas others with another type of make-up might have just tried to hit the corner flag ball in that type of situation,' Moore said later. 'The pass gave us the opportunity to get in behind them. It was the best way of finishing the game as it turned out.'

had since watching him lift the World Cup. 'I feel 10 years younger just putting my arms round this lad,' Ramsey told 'the waiting reporters.

Later, when Moore arrived at the team hotel, the entire England squad lined up outside to applaud him. 'His clothes were completely unruffled, as was the man himself,' recalled Gordon Banks.

In 2007, a statue of Moore was unveiled outside Wembley Stadium in a ceremony attended by the then Prime Minister, Tony Blair.

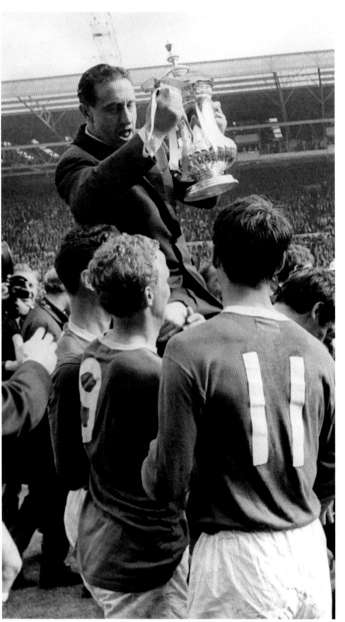

HARRY CATTERICK

▶▶▶▶▶▶▶▶▶▶▶▶▶▶▶▶▶

1919–1985

In the 1960s, a decade during which English football was served by several of the most famous managers in history, one man stood out for his ability to 'get a result', as the modern parlance goes, and that man was Harry Catterick.

Over that 10-year period, teams under Catterick's control amassed a total of 535 points in the top flight – a greater return than any of his rivals; more than Matt Busby, Bill Shankly, Don Revie and Bill Nicholson.

After starting the decade in charge of Sheffield Wednesday – the runners-up to champions Tottenham Hotspur in 1960–61 – Catterick spent the remainder of the 1960s at Everton, winning two championship titles in 1962–63 and 1969–70 and the FA Cup in 1966.

Throughout it all, Catterick exercised firm control. 'It's no accident I can see both full-size training pitches from my office merely by turning in my seat,' he once remarked.

↖

Harry Catterick holds aloft the FA Cup, 1966.

MANAGER • INDUCTED 2010 • 2 DIVISION ONE CHAMPIONSHIPS • 1 FA CUP

**'Standards are important. There is no shame in defeat if the game has been well played and the effort sustained.'
– Harry Catterick**

In many ways, Catterick was a prototype for the modern manager. Inside Goodison Park, the former Everton centre-forward was assigned full responsibility for spending the large sums of money invested by club chairman John Moores, the Littlewoods pools tycoon.

With the money, however, came heightened expectations. Moores had raised the stakes. He left Catterick alone to do the job. However, in return the chairman had identified in advance the employee to blame if success was not achieved. 'Catterick is the man who

Harry Catterick and Alan Ball leave Goodison Park, 1966.

does it,' Moores said in the immediate aftermath of their first title triumph. 'He decides the football strategy. I just make it possible.'

A shrewd and often stealthy operator in the transfer market, Catterick honed a knack for hijacking deals at the last moment. In 1963, for instance, negotiations had advanced so far that Alex Scott agreed to sell his story – 'Why I signed for Spurs' – to one national newspaper, only for the Rangers winger to end up at Everton. 'It's all about timing your move right,' Catterick said.

Similarly, in 1967, Bill Shankly was infuriated when his efforts to sign Howard Kendall from Preston North End were thwarted by Catterick, again at the last moment.

The rivalry between the two managers – 'The Catt' and 'Shanks' – engrossed Merseyside, such was the contrast in character: introvert versus extrovert; aloof Englishman versus populist Scot. Though differing so sharply in approach, the two men were level, at 3–3 in terms of honours, as listed in the summer of 1970, with two titles and one FA Cup each.

Behind the scenes at Everton, Catterick also established a youth system and oversaw the construction of Bellefield, then widely regarded as the finest, most modern training facility in English football.

A fierce disciplinarian in his dealings with players, Catterick often cut an intimidating figure. Famously, he insisted that his players

sign a register every morning before training; anyone who turned up late was fined.

At the outset of the 1970s, Bobby Charlton was not alone in predicting a prolonged period of success for Everton. History, however, proved otherwise. Catterick watched his side suffer a sharp decline, and as Everton fell, rivals Liverpool, under Shankly, rose again to the summit.

As results continued to deteriorate the strain took its toll on Catterick's health. In January 1972 he suffered a heart attack; a year later he was moved upstairs to a director's role. Then, after a period of recuperation, Catterick spent two years at Preston in a last throw at management.

A loyal club-man, Catterick died, aged 65, in March 1985, after collapsing at Goodison Park on a match day.

GORDON BANKS ▶▶▶▶▶▶▶▶▶▶

1937–

'If anyone had to be ill, why did it have to be him?' With those few despairing words, uttered in the aftermath of England's elimination from the 1970 World Cup in Mexico, Alf Ramsey encapsulated the importance of Gordon Banks to the cause of the national team.

Only days earlier Ramsey had abandoned his normal reticence on the subject of individual footballers in order to identify Banks as 'the greatest goalkeeper in the world, no doubt about it' following his performance in the group game against Brazil.

At the previous World Cup, on home soil in 1966, Banks kept a clean sheet in each of England's first four matches. He remained unbeaten for a total of 443 minutes, and even then it took a penalty by the great Eusebio of Portugal in the semi-final to beat him.

In open play, Banks did not concede a goal during the tournament until the final itself – a record of consistency and dependability that in time led to the reworking of a popular simile to read: As Safe as the Banks of England. An investment in Banks – as both Leicester City and Stoke City appreciated – offered a guaranteed and generous return.

Four years later a stomach bug had flattened Banks before the quarter-final against West Germany in Mexico. Ramsey was prepared to risk playing his number one keeper half-fit. Barely able to run or dive, only hours before kick-off, Banks passed a ridiculously easy fitness test. Ramsey was pinning his hopes on a dramatic recovery. However, a relapse left Banks too weak and ill to play.

After making his international debut in 1963, Banks remained an automatic choice for 10 years until the loss of an eye in a car accident forced his retirement from English football. Footballer of the Year only the season before, he had won the last of his 73 caps.

Gordon Banks makes a save for Stoke City against Derby County, 1970.

PLAYER • INDUCTED 2002 • 73 CAPS • 1 WORLD CUP • 2 LEAGUE CUPS

'If you put the ball on the D in training, provided that Banksie could see it, you would never score – and people said I had one of the hardest shots in the game.' – Francis Lee

A glutton for training, Banks often asked his England team-mates to stay behind to take shots at him. 'He would never let anything in,' Alan Ball recalled, 'so finally we told him that he was shattering our confidence. The next time he asked us, we just walked off. At times, Gordon was simply unbeatable.'

There were no instruction manuals for goalkeepers and clubs did not employ specialist coaches when Gordon Banks was building

his career at Leicester City in the late 1950s. So Banks set out to teach himself through a process of experiment and trial and error. 'I thought of goalkeeping as more of a science,' he recalled. 'It was all about practice, and there was definitely an element of hit and miss. It was, in the main, uncharted territory.'

On Sunday mornings he reported for extra training. 'I devised my own training schedules, working on agility, positioning, strength, reactions and focus,' he said.

In match situations he made a concerted effort to improve his reading of situations. 'I wanted to be able to anticipate my opponent's intended cross or pass by adjusting my position quickly, so making him think again,' he said.

Banks had the ideal physique for a goalkeeper: six-feet-one, 13 ½ stone and strong upper body strength, the inadvertent result of

his time as a lad lugging bags of coal around for a job.

He began his career inauspiciously, conceding 122 goals in the Chesterfield reserves in the 1954–55 season. Against players his own age his record was more impressive: in 1956–57 lowly Chesterfield surprised the bigger clubs by progressing to an FA Youth Cup final against the 'Busby Babes' of Manchester United. Banks could not prevent his team losing but his fine performance alerted several bigger clubs, including Leicester City.

After making the first team at Filbert Street, the number of goals the team conceded fell sharply – from 75 in season 1959–60, to 53 in 1962–63. His hard work paid dividends. By the end of this run he was an England player. The following season he won a League Cup winners' medal with Leicester.

In 1977, at the age of 39, Gordon Banks was voted the best goalkeeper playing in the United States soccer league. In 26 games for Fort Lauderdale Strikers, he conceded 29 goals. He was nearing the veteran stage now, though it wasn't his age that made his performance so remarkable, but the physical handicap he had overcome: Banks had only one eye.

On Sunday, 22 October 1972, Banks had been involved in a head-on collision while overtaking on the B5038 between Whitmore and Trentham near his home in Staffordshire. He had just signed a six-year contract with Stoke City.

Gordon Banks, left, and John Marsh of Stoke City hold aloft the League Cup, 1972.

World Cup

Special Commemorative Issue

FIRST DAY COVER

England - 'World Champions'

A Royal Mail first day cover commemorating England's victory in the World Cup, 1966.

Banks was heading home to watch the highlights of Stoke's game against Liverpool the previous day. He had been infuriated by two rulings by the referee Roger Kirkpatrick, whom Banks blamed for Liverpool's two goals. He wanted to watch replays of the incidents to see if he'd been right.

Banks retired from English football in 1973 as a result of his serious facial injury, taking a job as a coach at Stoke City. Then, four years later, came the surprise offer from the United States, where he played for two seasons.

'I was very surprised by the standard I attained at Fort Lauderdale,' he recalled. 'I realised that, with training and practice, I

Gordon Banks poses for pre-season photo, 1969.

▶ talking point

As he threw himself across goal in the 1970 World Cup group game against Brazil, Gordon Banks realised that he would have to do more than just get his hand to the ball; somehow he had to get the thing over the crossbar. A moment later, the England man had pulled off perhaps the most celebrated save of all time.

'If I didn't get the ball up and away,' Banks explained later, 'Pelé would have simply followed up his header and had a simple tap-in. I knew I had to get under the ball somehow and flick it upwards, out of harm's way.

'When the cross came over I had to take up a position at the near post to cover a run by Tostao. That's why I had so far to go across to make the save.'

Pelé was so convinced his header was about to open the scoring, he shouted 'Golo!' 'It was the greatest save I've ever seen,' Pelé said later. 'It was incredible that he managed to push the ball over the bar, I have never had such a surprise in football.' The next day the Mexican newspapers nicknamed Banks 'El Magnifico'.

Banks had to contend with alien conditions in Mexico: the ball flew faster and swerved more in the thinner air, and the sunlight was so harsh that he would often lose sight of the ball.

'Before the corner Bobby Moore made me laugh when he said, "You're getting old, Banksy. You used to hold on to them."'

could readjust to my restricted vision.

'In hindsight I could have taken a year away from the game after the car accident and then given it a go back in the Football League. But after the long gap, and now those two years in the States, it was too late to try again in England.'

JACK CHARLTON

▶▶▶▶▶▶▶▶▶▶▶▶▶▶▶▶

1935–

Jack Charlton cut an unmistakable figure on the football field. A commanding centre-half for Leeds United and England, and future manager at both club and international level – everyone recognised 'Big Jack'.

Tall, with an unusually long neck, receding hairline and gangly limbs, the loud and outspoken Charlton always stood out in company. Even Pope John Paul II knew him by sight: 'Yes, I know who you are: you're the boss,' the Pontiff said on meeting the then Republic of Ireland manager in 1990.

As a player Charlton was a late developer, and the prospect of his England debut in 1965 – at the age of 29 – generated little enthusiasm in the media. As Bobby Moore later reflected: 'Well, Jack didn't seem to look much like an England player, but appearances can be deceptive.' Alf Ramsey certainly agreed.

Jack Charlton shoots at goal during warm-up, 1971.

PLAYER • INDUCTED 2005 • 35 CAPS • 1 WORLD CUP • 2 DIVISION ONE CHAMPIONSHIPS

2 FAIRS CUPS • 1 FA CUP • 1 LEAGUE CUP

> **'Between 1963 and 1972, Jack was the best centre-half in English football.' – Johnny Giles**

In the uncomplicated, competitive and conservative Charlton, the England manager had belatedly found the ideal partner for the stylish, more adventurous Moore. 'You're a good tackler, Jack, and good in the air, and I need those things,' Ramsey told him. 'I know that as soon as Bobby goes upfield with the ball, you will always fill in behind him as cover.'

Their partnership was the defensive foundation for Ramsey's side; Charlton played in

Jack Charlton salutes the crowd before his 600th appearance for Leeds United, 1972.

26 of the next 27 internationals, including all six World Cup matches in 1966. England lost only three of the 35 games in which he played, and in one of those matches, against Scotland in 1967, he was handicapped by a painful broken toe.

Perhaps his most significant contribution came during the World Cup came against Portugal in the semi-final. 'He was embroiled in a titanic struggle for aerial superiority with Torres, the giant Portugal forward,' Gordon Banks recalled. Charlton won that battle. His brother Bobby said: 'Jack played what I consider to be his best game for England.'

Bill Shankly, who twice attempted to sign Charlton for Liverpool, rated him 'the best English centre-half I've ever seen'. Others came to share Shankly's opinion and in 1967 Charlton was voted Footballer of the Year.

Over a 20-year career, Charlton made a club record 773 appearances for Leeds, before retiring in 1973 at the age of 37. Such longevity hardly seemed possible in his youth.

Initially, Don Revie was far from alone in regarding Charlton as surly, disruptive and undisciplined. 'You've got a chip on your shoulder,' the manager told him. Years later Charlton acknowledged: 'I was a bit of a one-man awkward squad in those days.'

Significantly, however, Revie also realised Charlton's potential. Once his attitude improved, so did his form. 'If you keep on like this, you'll play for England,' Revie told him.

'Jack turned it round for himself,' team-mate Johnny Giles said. 'He was outstanding: always competing and getting his foot in when it mattered.'

In addition to his strength at the back, Charlton was a threat at set-pieces. His favourite trick involved standing in front of a goalkeeper on the goal-line. On the ball, his technique and passing ability was often underrated.

As Shankly predicted, Charlton later thrived in management. In 1974 he was voted Manager of the Year when Middlesbrough won promotion. 'He gives a straight answer to a straight question,' Shankly once said, 'and that's always a good sign.'

▶ key match

England 2 Scotland 2, Home International Championships, Wembley Stadium, 10 April 1965

It made for a good newspaper story when Jack Charlton made his debut for England. Not only was he nearing 30 but Jack was also lining up alongside brother Bobby – making them the first siblings to play in the same England side that century. 'The football writers liked the angle even more when I passed to Bobby for him to score,' Jack said later.

The brothers became even closer during the game when Bobby was drafted in as an emergency left-back. Even with only nine fit players, England managed a draw. 'It meant that I had to get my head down and battle, which suited me,' Charlton said. 'I had no time to be distracted by the occasion.'

BILL SHANKLY ▶▶▶▶▶▶▶▶▶▶▶▶▶▶

1913–1981

Bill Shankly was a folk hero whose infectious enthusiasm, energy, charisma and wise-cracking humour transformed Liverpool from a club mired in mediocrity into a major power in European football.

'Shanks arrived at Anfield and changed the whole thing,' recalled Ian Callaghan, the Liverpool and England midfield player. 'When you look at the club now, it was Bill Shankly who put down the foundations.'

For 15 years, between 1959 and his shock resignation in 1974, Shankly preached the same basic message. 'We would pass the ball 20 yards to a team-mate and then support,' Kevin Keegan said. 'It was as simple as that: keeping the ball moving.'

During that time Liverpool won promotion, secured the title three times, the FA Cup twice and the UEFA Cup. Bob Paisley, Shankly's assistant and then successor, won the European Cup three times as manager. 'I just carried on what Billy had started,' Paisley said.

Shankly was eulogised by Liverpool supporters, and the respect and admiration was mutual. One Saturday he stood on the Kop with 'the boys', as he called them. In the dressing room, the Liverpool players heard the chant: 'Shankly! Shankly! Here he is. Here he is.'

In 1965, at the victory parade to celebrate the club's longed-for first FA Cup success, Shankly stepped forward to speak from the Town Hall balcony. 'He simply put up his hand and 250,000 people fell silent,' recalled Ron Yeats, the Liverpool captain. 'He had this connection with people.'

As far as we are concerned, we want Bill to be with us for ever,' John Smith, the Liverpool chairman said in 1974 – a statement that only added to the sense of shock when Shankly retired in the summer.

Bill Shankly travels to Liverpool by train with the FA Cup, 1974.

▶ key match

Liverpool 3 Internazionale 1, European Cup semi-final, first leg, Anfield, 4 May 1965 (Inter won the tie 4–3 on aggregate)

Internazionale were feared and highly disciplined European champions, but they had never been tested by the type of experience Bill Shankly served up on the first of Liverpool's great European nights at Anfield.

Shankly tapped into the energy of a packed Kop to intimidate and unnerve the Italians. 'Inter first lost psychologically and then went to pieces in play,' the *Corriere Della Sera* newspaper reported.

Shankly whipped up the energy levels at Anfield another notch with a calculated gesture before the kick-off; he instructed two injured players – Gerry Byrne, the hero of the FA Cup final victory the previous Saturday, and Gordon Milne – to parade the trophy.

Once the game began, Liverpool tore into the Italians. 'We've been beaten before but tonight we were defeated,' said Helenio Herrera, the Inter manager.

MANAGER • INDUCTED 2002 • 1 UEFA CUP • 3 DIVISION ONE CHAMPIONSHIPS • 2 FA CUPS

**'If ever Liverpool lost twice in a row, it was a full-blown crisis in Bill's eyes, and he would grill us in his office one by one.'
– Ian Callaghan**

When Bill Shankly took up his job as manager of Liverpool in 1959 he was shocked to find that one of the toilets at Anfield had no running water. 'What an eyesore,' he thought to himself, looking round the dilapidated ground.

It was not only the stadium that was in a state of decay. In each of the previous three campaigns, Liverpool had narrowly missed out on promotion to Division One. The club had not won a major honour since 1946–47. Supporters were frustrated and dispirited.

'In the post-war years Liverpool were not a team of winners,' Paisley recalled. 'There was a feeling that we belonged in the middle of the table, but Bill changed that.'

Shankly first sought stability. He assured the training staff that their jobs were safe. There was one condition: 'At this club there will be no stories about another man, no talking behind backs', he told them.

The staff began to meet in a small room under the stand to discuss their work, a habit encouraged by Shankly. It was the start of the 'Boot Room' tradition at Anfield.

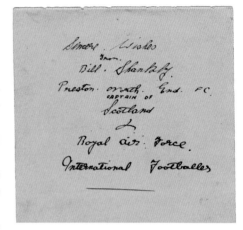

↗
A collectors book featuring an autograph of Bill Shankly, signed during his playing days with Preston North End.

On Shankly's orders the team shed their white shorts and socks in favour of an all-red kit. 'I wanted Liverpool players to look more imposing,' he said. From the outset, in his dealings with the media, he was outspoken and partisan – often embellishing his comments with a pre-rehearsed quip for effect.

Shankly had insisted on selecting the team as a condition of taking the job. The directors had to content themselves now with finding money to buy new players.

Shankly spent those funds wisely, buying Ron Yeats, a centre-half, and a forward, Ian St John, from Scotland. All but a handful of the players he inherited were sold to pay for further reinforcements.

↖
Bill Shankly talks to a group of schoolboys in Liverpool, 1965.

In the season before his arrival Liverpool were beaten in the FA Cup by Worcester City, a non-League side. By 1961–62, promotion had been won. Two seasons later, Liverpool were champions.

Professional footballers loved to work for Bill Shankly. He gave them self-belief, a football to kick about in training – and a taste for success. The Liverpool players spent much of their time in training playing five-a-side. Shankly – a passionate man with an evangelical zeal – always insisted on keeping things simple.

At his previous club, Huddersfield Town, the reserve-team players threatened to go on strike when Shankly was put in charge of the first-team training. 'We wanted a share of Bill as well,' recalled Ray Wilson, the future England defender. 'He made training ever so

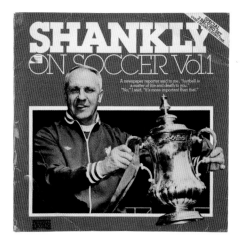

↗
The cover of a Bill Shankly LP record.

enjoyable. All he wanted to do was play.'

Shankly had an eye for leadership quality in others. Ron Yeats was made captain before he had played in a single game. A few weeks later, after his home debut, journalists were invited 'to take a walk around our new centre-half'. Yeats recalled: 'I was a bit embarrassed but it made me feel 10 feet tall.'

He also made players believe in themselves. In his early days at Anfield, as a raw 20-year-old, Kevin Keegan was told that he would go on to play for England within 18 months. Buoyed by this statement, Keegan made it with a couple of months to spare. He, in turn, was devoted to Shankly, dedicating an autobiography to his memory.

Shankly once told Emlyn Hughes, one of

↖
Bill Shankly joins in training watched by coach Joe Fagan, 1965.

his favourite players: 'When I die I only hope that people will be able to say he played the game, he was fair, he never cheated anyone. And if they can say that, I know I will be able to rest in peace.'

Bill Shankly died in 1981. He had touched everyone in the city. When his funeral procession drove past the Everton training ground, the players, still wearing their muddy kit, stood in a line at the side of the road, heads bowed.

NOBBY STILES

▶▶▶▶▶▶▶▶▶▶▶▶▶▶▶▶▶▶

1942–

When Nobby Stiles joyfully placed the Jules Rimet trophy on his head as part of his victory jig at Wembley Stadium late on a summer's afternoon in 1966, he created one of the most abiding images in the history of English football.

A fiercely committed ball-winner for England and Manchester United, Stiles shares with Bobby Charlton the distinction of being the only Englishmen to be on the winning side in a World Cup and European Cup final.

In 1968, Stiles returned to Wembley Stadium to help his beloved United, the team he supported as a boy, defeat Benfica in the Continent's premier club competition.

'As a defender, Nobby had a kind of sixth sense for danger and he would nip it in the bud,' Bobby Charlton said. 'So much of his work went unnoticed by the crowd. But all his team-mates knew his value.'

Nobby Stiles turns on the ball, 1966.

PLAYER • INDUCTED 2007 • 28 CAPS • 1 WORLD CUP • 1 EUROPEAN CUP

2 DIVISION ONE CHAMPIONSHIPS

**'The main factor in our winning the World Cup was the introduction of Nobby.'
– Jack Charlton**

Short of stature, prematurely balding and missing his two front teeth, Stiles hardly cut the figure of a traditional sporting hero. Alan Ball once called the spectacle-wearing Stiles 'the oldest-looking Under-23 international in the history of the game'. The public adored him, though, no matter his appearance.

Tactically, Stiles was 'the central figure of our defensive set-up,' Alf Ramsey wrote later. 'Instead of a sweeper behind the defence, we had a ball-winner in front of it.'

An outstanding schoolboy international, Stiles became frustrated at his lack of progress after joining Manchester United as an inside-forward in the late 1950s. Struggling to make an impact in attack, he eventually took action.

Analysing his strengths and weaknesses, Stiles realised that he might thrive in a defen-

↗
Nobby Stiles ties his laces.

sive role. 'I was very competitive,' he wrote later. 'Over five to ten yards I was whippet-quick, and with those few yards of genuine pace, I could exploit my good defensive antennae.'

Then, in 1964, circumstances intervened: Stiles was given a chance to stake a claim for a position alongside Bill Foulkes, United's veteran centre-half. The challenge was a tough one: to mark Jimmy Greaves, the most prolific goalscorer in English football.

After the game, which Manchester United won, Matt Busby praised Stiles' performance. 'A job well done,' Busby said. It was the turning point in his career; he was now an automatic choice -- an advance that brought him to the attention of Alf Ramsey.

During the World Cup tournament in 1966, Ramsey famously put his job on the line by refusing to drop Stiles despite heavy pressure from the Football Association and FIFA.

↖
Nobby Stiles trains at Old Trafford, 1969.

Severely criticised for a bad tackle, Stiles was asked by Ramsey whether it was deliberate. Stiles replied emphatically: 'No.' Ramsey was satisfied. 'If he goes, I go,' was the gist of his ultimatum to officialdom. Stiles kept his place, and Ramsey stayed on.

It was extremely rare for Ramsey to single out an individual for praise, but he did so for Stiles during the 1966 tournament, prompting a spontaneous round of applause from his team-mates.

After one international at Wembley, Ramsey was giving an interview on television when Stiles walked past. 'There,' he said, pointing at his number four, 'is an Englishman.' For Ramsey, the proudest of patriots, there was no greater compliment.

▶ **talking point**

An immensely popular figure amongst his peers, Nobby Stiles was jokingly nicknamed 'Happy' – because on the pitch he wasn't. All the more so, if he thought his team-mates could work harder, particularly when it came to keeping the opposition from scoring. 'Nobby was the England team's sergeant major,' forward Geoff Hurst said. 'If I wasn't pulling my weight he would scream unrepeatable abuse at me.'

In training during the build-up to the World Cup in 1966, Stiles and Jackie Charlton were embroiled in a fierce, toe-to-toe argument over England's defensive tactics. The equally forceful England centre-half towered over his team-mate. 'Nobby didn't give an inch,' Charlton said. 'I remember thinking that he was a bit scary.'

IAN CALLAGHAN

▶▶▶▶▶▶▶▶▶▶▶▶▶▶▶▶▶▶▶▶▶▶▶▶▶▶▶▶▶▶▶▶▶▶▶▶▶

1942–

When describing Ian Callaghan as 'a manager's dream and model professional', Bill Shankly was paying tribute to the one player who rose with Liverpool from second-tier obscurity in English football to victory in a European Cup final.

'Ian typifies everything that is good in football, and he has never changed. You could stake your life on Ian,' the Liverpool manager wrote.

In a career of extraordinary longevity and remarkable consistency, Callaghan made a club-record 857 appearances – between 1960 and 1978. Operating on the right wing and then in central midfield, the modest and unassuming Callaghan won five League championship medals, two FA Cups, two European Cups – in 1977 and 1978 – and two UEFA Cups.

Ian Callaghan, 1967.

PLAYER • INDUCTED 2010 • 4 CAPS • 1 WORLD CUP • 5 DIVISION ONE CHAMPIONSHIPS

2 FA CUPS • 2 EUROPEAN CUPS • 2 UEFA CUPS

'If there were 11 Ian Callaghans at this club, there would never be any need to put up a team sheet.' – Bill Shankly

At international level, the Liverpool-born stalwart was a World Cup winner in 1966, making one appearance on the right wing for Alf Ramsey in the finals tournament: a group game against France, in which he set up one of the goals in a 2–0 win.

In all competitions, Callaghan played more than 950 first-class games, spread across all four divisions of English football, including stints with Swansea City and Crewe Alexandra as his career finally wound down. His last competitive appearance as a professional came one month before his fortieth birthday.

'How was he capable of his achievements over such a long period?' Shankly once asked rhetorically, before answering his own ques-

Ian Callaghan takes on an Everton defender, 1971.

tion. 'Because he listened to the gospel: the gospel of dedication and enthusiasm. Ian will go down as one of the game's great players.'

As a local lad trying to break into the first team at Anfield, Callaghan had the additional pressure of succeeding Billy Liddell, the great idol of the Kop during the 1950s.

Throughout the 1960s, Callaghan plied his trade near the touchline. Initially he operated along traditional lines, taking on his full-back and then getting his cross in, ideally from near the by-line. However, gradually as the decade wore on he began to tuck in more often, as a deep-lying winger, when the opposition had the ball.

In 1971, following a cartilage operation, and the arrival at the club of Kevin Keegan, Callaghan was switched to a more central role in midfield. 'We discovered that he was a great tackler and passer of the ball,' team-mate John Toshack recalled. 'Ian ran the show.' Three years later he was voted Footballer of the Year by the football writers.

'Ian was a superbly consistent player,' Keegan said. 'Sure, he would have a bad game occasionally – like once every other season. His enthusiasm for the game and his hard work were fantastic.'

Physically, Callaghan was remarkably robust. Only one other injury – an Achilles problem in 1977 – would seriously disrupt his career. 'Whenever Ian goes down on the field, he bounces straight back up again,' Shankly said, likening him to a rubber ball.

Ian Callaghan runs with the ball, 1971.

▶ **talking point**

Eleven years had elapsed since Ian Callaghan last played for England. Then suddenly, in 1977, he made a remarkable comeback – in his testimonial season with Liverpool. 'It really is a fairytale,' he said. 'Unbelievable.'

In his first act as caretaker manager Ron Greenwood selected the 35-year-old stalwart for the friendly against Switzerland at Wembley. Never before had an Englishman waited so long between caps, it was reported.

With little time to prepare following the sudden departure of Don Revie, Greenwood selected a core of Liverpool players, including Callaghan, for England's next World Cup qualifier. Though victory was achieved, England ultimately failed to qualify; the damage had already been done.

'If every player in the game was like Ian Callaghan there would be no managers left, simply because they would not be needed,' Bob Paisley once said.

TEAM INDUCTEE
ENGLAND
▶▶▶▶▶ **1963–1966**

5 February 1963

In his first significant act since his appointment, Alf Ramsey overhauls England's tactics. Abandoning the idea of specialist roles, Ramsey opts for dual-purpose inside-forwards – players both dangerous near goal and active in midfield.

27 February 1963

England are knocked out of the European Nations Cup after a demoralising 5–2 defeat against France in Paris. Ramsey observes afterwards: 'There must be a new pattern of defence against Continental opposition.'

May 1963

England win all three games on tour. 'Previously, players were allowed to express themselves on and off the field, and England lost,' Ramsey says. 'On tour they played under direction, and results were good.'

21 August 1963

Alf Ramsey issues his now famous rallying cry: 'I believe we will win the World Cup in 1966.'

23 October 1963

England defeat a strong Rest of the World side 2–1 at Wembley. Djalma Santos, the veteran Brazil defender, says: 'This is by far the best England side I have played against.' The home side wear a new kit, with round-necked shirt collars. A new-look, more confident England is emerging.

June 1964

England suffer defeat against Brazil and Argentina at a mini-tournament in South America. Doubts are raised about the effectiveness, notably in defence, of England's new 4-2-4 tactics against top-class opposition. Will Ramsey change tack again?

2 October 1964

In response to several instances of indiscipline within the squad, Ramsey relieves Bobby Moore as captain for a brief period. 'I must make sure I have the right man for the job,' Ramsey says. Once Moore re-affirms his commitment he is re-instated. 'I am convinced I have done the right thing,' Ramsey says afterwards.

12 October 1964

Bobby Charlton is dropped from the England team after a disappointing performance as 'a link-man' in midfield against Northern Ireland. 'We need a player to pass accurately and quickly,' Ramsey explains.

10 November 1964

'I am no nearer finding the ideal combination of players,' Ramsey tells the football writers. 'By the end of this season I must know what individual players can or cannot do, and then decide on the combinations of players and decide the tactics.'

10 April 1965

After handing both centre-half Jack Charlton and the combative Nobby Stiles their England debut, Alf Ramsey watches a 2–2 draw against Scotland. With Gordon Banks confirmed as an automatic choice in goal, behind established full-backs Ray Wilson and George Cohen and sweeper Bobby Moore, Ramsey has found the defensive unit upon which he will pin England's World Cup hopes.

↖

Bobby Moore and the England squad, 1966.

10 November 1965

England labour to a 2–1 win over Northern Ireland at Wembley. 'Judging this in relation to our World Cup preparations I was not satisfied,' Ramsey says afterwards.

8 December 1965

Alf Ramsey unveils his 4-3-3 formation against Spain in Madrid. There is no place for a specialist winger. When England have possession, five forwards attack through the middle. England win 2–0. 'It was now that the players really began to believe we could win the World Cup,' George Cohen later reflects.

4 May 1966

After playing inconsistently in several attacking positions, Bobby Charlton finds his feet as a deep-lying centre-forward in a 2–0 win over Yugoslavia.

June 1966

Determined to make England the fittest team at the World Cup, Ramsey takes his squad to Lilleshall for an intensive training camp. 'Honestly, the programme we planned for them was murder,' Harold Shepherdson, the assistant manager, says two weeks later. 'I felt sorry for the lads. For two weeks they were on their knees, but not one man belly-ached.'

5 July 1966

England conclude a brief overseas tour with victory over Poland. That makes it four wins out of four since leaving home.

20 July 1966

England qualify for the quarter-finals by defeating France 2–0 at Wembley. The biggest talking point is the shin injury sustained by Jimmy Greaves.

23 July 1966

Geoff Hurst scores the winning goal against Argentina. As the great selection debate – Greaves or Hurst? – rages in the national newspapers, England revert to a formation without a specialist winger.

26 July 1966

Bobby Charlton inspires a thrilling victory over Portugal in the semi-final. 'Reaching the final is the most important thing in our lives,' Ramsey says. Hurst plays his part by creating the second goal.

30 July 1966

Geoff Hurst scores a hat-trick as England become world champions with a 4–2 defeat of West Germany.

↘

England players walk to training, 1966.

RON GREENWOOD

▶▶▶▶▶▶▶▶▶▶▶▶▶▶▶▶▶▶▶▶▶▶▶▶▶▶▶▶▶▶▶▶▶▶▶▶

1921–2006

A pioneering coach and loyal servant of both club and country, Ron Greenwood played an important role in making England the best team in the world in the 1960s, and then lifted morale as manager at a time of crisis a decade later.

When the former manager of West Ham United took charge of England in 1977, 11 years had elapsed since Bobby Moore, Martin Peters and Geoff Hurst – three graduates of the Upton Park youth system – took their turn in lifting the Jules Rimet trophy at Wembley.

Another five years on, in 1982, his England side went unbeaten at the World Cup for the first time since 1966, a fitting culmination to a distinguished coaching career spanning four decades.

Trevor Brooking, a stalwart for West Ham and England said: 'Ron will be regarded as one of the best coaches England has produced over the past 50 years.'

Ron Greenwood talks to reporters, 1982.

MANAGER • INDUCTED 2006 • 1 FA CUP • 1 EUROPEAN CUP-WINNERS' CUP

'As West Ham manager, Ron Greenwood opened the door to the world of modern football.'
– Geoff Hurst

In the mid 1960s, Greenwood guided the Hammers to back-to-back success in the FA Cup and European Cup-Winners' Cup with a brand of vibrant, counter-attacking football.

His belief in attacking football never faltered. 'At its best, the game is a joy, a battle of wit and muscle and character; it involves and inspires,' he once wrote. The message to his players was always the same: 'Let's go out there to win, and to win in style.'

Recognising his tactical acumen, FIFA appointed him a technical advisor at successive World Cup tournaments, in 1966 and 1970. Bobby Moore once called him 'an encyclopaedia of football'.

A reliable centre-half who collected a championship medal with Chelsea in 1954–55,

↗
Ron Greenwood walks on the pitch at Anfield, 1969.

Greenwood was persuaded out of retirement to take charge of the national side in 1977, following the unexpected defection of Don Revie.

Tactically, the now veteran manager stayed true to his beliefs: Kevin Keegan and Trevor Brooking were at the heart of things in a positive 4-2-4 formation, with Steve Coppell and Peter Barnes on the wings. After a decade in the international wilderness, England qualified for the European Championships in 1980 and the World Cup in Spain two years later.

On Greenwood's suggestion, the FA appointed managers and coaches at all levels of the England set-up, an arrangement that proffered Bobby Robson and Terry Venables valuable international experience.

Of even greater and lasting significance, Greenwood handed caps to Viv Anderson,

↙
Ron Greenwood coaches the England Under-23 side, 1960.

▶talking point

Following his appointment as West Ham United manager in 1961, Ron Greenwood established a reputation for tactical innovation.

Over the next 13 years, Greenwood encouraged his players to solve their own problems, both on and off the pitch.

In addition to taking a coaching course and final exam at Lilleshall, West Ham players were sent on scouting missions in Europe, with a brief to assess future opponents. 'I want them to have both lively minds and lively bodies,' Greenwood said.

'One of the things Ron taught us was to stay *out* of space until we were ready to make use of it,' Geoff Hurst recalled. 'This was new thinking at the time.'

Laurie Cunningham and Cyrille Regis – the first three black players to represent England. 'The only colour that matters should be the colour of a player's shirt,' Greenwood said.

Looking back over his career in club management, Greenwood had one regret: the failure of West Ham United to win a championship title. Though praised for their positive, attacking football, the Hammers lacked the necessary consistency and 'steel' over a gruelling League season, as their manager, in hindsight, readily conceded.

Perhaps, though, his legacy as a man of integrity and positive values goes beyond the winning or losing of titles. 'I cared more about the purity and finer values of football than I did about winning for winning's sake – and if that is a sin, then I am a sinner,' Greenwood said. 'Football should be about taking risks.'

JIMMY GREAVES ▶▶▶▶▶▶▶▶▶▶

1940–

By his own admission, Jimmy Greaves often appeared innocuous in the air, lacked a physical presence to unsettle his marker and did not possess an explosive shot. Yet, for all his supposed shortcomings, he was justly acclaimed as the greatest goalscorer of the post-war era.

Six times in his career Greaves finished as the leading goalscorer in Division One – first with Chelsea and then, in his prime, with Tottenham Hotspur.

The majority of his remarkable tally of 357 goals in 514 League games were scored from close range, and mainly with his left foot. 'I was born with an instinctive, natural gift for sticking the ball in the net, and I wasn't interested in doing much else,' Greaves once said. 'I don't consciously scheme goals, nor take up pre-determined positions,' he explained. 'I don't have a thunderous shot like Bobby Charlton, nor have I spent hours working out shooting angles. I just get in as close as I can and let rip.'

Bill Nicholson, the Spurs manager, famously described the accuracy and efficiency of Greaves' finishing in these terms: 'Jimmy made it simple. All he did was pass the ball to the stanchions.' One national newspaper likened the inside-forward's deft scoring style to 'closing the door on a Rolls-Royce'.

At international level Greaves scored 44 goals, including a record six hat-tricks, in 57 appearances between 1959 and 1967. Johnny Haynes, the England captain in the early part of Greaves' international career, said: 'No player has ever had such cold finishing power.'

A forward of exceptional balance, even at speed, Greaves returned to English football with Spurs after a brief, unhappy spell with AC Milan in November 1961. In each of the next three full seasons, Greaves finished as leading scorer in Division One.

↖
Jimmy Greaves poses for a team photo during pre-season training, 1965.

▶key match

Tottenham Hotspur 3 Burnley 1, FA Cup final, Wembley Stadium, 5 May 1962

The Duke of Edinburgh was surprised to see Jimmy Greaves standing before him during the presentation of the two teams before the game.

After shaking Greaves' hand the Duke said: 'I thought you were in Italy.' Overhearing the remark Danny Blanchflower, the Spurs captain, replied: 'No, sir, we bought him back, and he cost enough, believe me,' referring to the record fee Spurs had recently paid Milan.

On the day, Spurs won quite easily, giving the 22-year-old Greaves his first major honour. 'Our dressing room before the game was very calm,' he said. 'It's nerves that lead to scrappy play, and at Wembley we didn't have any.'

Inside five minutes, Greaves deliberately over-ran a flick-on by centre-forward Bobby Smith, confusing the Burnley defenders and giving himself the small amount of space he needed before delivering a finish of trademark precision.

PLAYER • INDUCTED 2002 • 57 CAPS • 1 WORLD CUP • 2 FA CUPS • 1 EUROPEAN CUP-WINNERS' CUP

**'With that poacher Greaves around you don't need a half-back, you need a gamekeeper with a 12-bore and a mantrap.'
– Jimmy Armfield, 1961**

At the age of 20 years and nine months, Jimmy Greaves became the youngest ever player to score 100 goals in the Football League. Almost exactly three years later he equalled – to the day – Dixie Dean's age record for scoring the quickest 200 League goals.

'A million words will be written about this lad's goalscoring ability,' one *Daily Express* football writer predicted in 1961, and he was right.

After making his debut for Chelsea at the age of 17, Greaves played 169 games for the club, scoring 132 goals. At the end of his final game for the club the tearful youngster was carried from the field on the shoulders of sup-

porters. More and more the emphasis in English football was being switched to youth, and Greaves embodied a growing sense of optimism in the game. He was, quite simply, a sensation. A phenomenon, some said.

Following his transfer to Milan for a fee of £80,000 in 1961, not even the massed defences in Italy could stop him – as his record of nine goals in 12 games in Serie A testified. Greaves, though, hated Italian football, describing it as 'an outrageous, petty, laughable world where everything was done in the name of football and the spirit of the game was battered beyond recognition'. On his return to the familiar surrounds of the Football League in late 1961, Greaves, his enthusiasm restored, registered 21 goals in 22 games for Spurs.

On joining the double-winning side for a British record transfer fee of £99,999, Greaves added a cutting edge to an attack, with Dave Mackay, Johnny White and Danny Blanch-

↗
Jimmy Greaves, (Trevillion).

flower creating the openings from midfield. 'They were talented enough to read my off-the-cuff runs and instinctive play and skilful enough to make the right pass,' Greaves said. 'It was a great experience.'

In hindsight, the career of Jimmy Greaves can be divided into two halves: before and after 1965. He was never quite the same following a debilitating bout of hepatitis in November of that year. He was lighting a bonfire for his

↖
Jimmy Greaves evades three Mexico defenders, 1966.

children when he suddenly felt 'as if someone had chopped my legs off'.

The illness weakened Greaves, sidelining him for three months. The long-term consequences, however, were even more serious. 'When I came back I realised I had lost a vital half-yard of pace, and speed was vital to my game,' he said. Though he still regarded himself, with some justification, and despite the illness, as the country's best marksman, his scoring rate did slow noticeably in the second half of the decade.

Disillusionment may also have played a part. As the game gradually became more defensive, Greaves found himself increasingly at odds with the negative tactics being adopted by many managers.

As the pace and ferocity of the game also quickened, some observers questioned his work-rate. Not Joe Mercer, though. He expressed admiration for the way in which Greaves was prepared at times to do 'absolutely nothing' during a game.

'Jimmy is the greatest finisher I've ever seen,' the Manchester City manager said. 'You can't mark him. The reason: he is prepared to

'I have never seen a greater positional player, and I'm not just talking British football.' – Stan Cullis

stand still. It takes great courage as a footballer to appear lazy, to look as if you're doing nothing. But then, all of a sudden, when the chance arises, Jimmy is gone. He had left his shadow standing.'

Stan Cullis of Wolves celebrated Greaves' technique in front of goal: 'He has the rare gift of sizing up a goalkeeper and leaving him helpless with a shot that barely moves off the ground.'

Nearer to home, Bill Nicholson described Greaves as 'a natural', adding: 'Jimmy's muscular reaction is fantastic, and this is why he is able to get his foot to a ball a split-second before a defender. He also has a great coolness in finishing, another gift which can scarcely be taught.'

Often, it all seemed to be ridiculously easy. Terry Venables once joined his team-mate for a pre-match meal in a favourite pub. Venables ate a grilled chicken breast; Greaves ordered roast beef, Yorkshire pudding, carrots, peas, cauliflower and potatoes, roasted and boiled, followed by steamed pudding and custard. 'I gazed at him in disbelief,' Venables recalled. 'Was this any way for a professional sportsman to carry on? Evidently it was. We won 6–1 that

Jimmy Greaves reads a newspaper over the shoulder of Roger Hunt, 1966.

afternoon and Jim scored five of the goals.'

Johnny Haynes was equally amazed as he watched Greaves score a hat-trick in England's 9–3 win against Scotland in 1961. 'When Jimmy plays as he did that day I find myself wondering if there has ever been a player like him in the entire history of the game,' the England captain said.

GEOFF HURST

▶▶▶▶▶▶▶▶▶▶▶▶▶▶▶▶▶▶

1941–

Geoff Hurst, the prototype 'target man' of English football, emerged as a household name overnight in 1966 when he became the first, and so far only, player to score a hat-trick in a World Cup final.

Those three goals at Wembley – a superbly timed header, a shot on the turn with his right foot and a thunderous drive with his left at the end of a 40-yard run on the ball – illustrated the all-round ability of the West Ham United forward.

His third goal was the last kick of the final. 'I knew I would never hit a better shot so long as I lived,' he recalled. 'The sound, the feel of the leather on leather was exactly right.'

'Brave as they come,' Ron Greenwood said. 'The strength of his running and his ability to drag defenders out of position are phenomenal.'

Geoff Hurst in West Ham kit, 1968.

PLAYER • INDUCTED 2004 • 49 CAPS • 1 WORLD CUP • 1 FA CUP • 1 EUROPEAN CUP-WINNERS' CUP

> 'I have watched how Geoff has added refinements to his basic qualities of courage and strength – timing, positional sense and a willingness to create space.'
> **– Ron Greenwood**

The hat-trick did wonders for his confidence. 'I came back from the World Cup feeling 10 feet tall,' he wrote in 1967. 'I have scored goals this season in a way that would have been quite beyond me a year ago.'

In the autumn of 1966, Hurst scored 22 goals during a run of 14 games, justifying West Ham manager Ron Greenwood's decision to make him one of English football's highest earners, on a new six-year contract.

The Hammers' resolve to keep him was tested in 1967 when Matt Busby put in a bid of £200,000 – double the existing record – by telephone from Poland, where United were playing a European tie. Greenwood sent a now famous telegram in reply. It read: 'Busby, Manchester United. Gornik. No. Greenwood.'

Geoff Hurst beats a defender, 1964.

Alf Ramsey selected Hurst as his first-choice in the England attack for six years between 1966 and 1972, the longest run of any forward during his time as manager. At club level, West Ham lifted the FA Cup in 1964 and the European Cup-Winners' Cup the following season. In 1972 Hurst left West Ham for Stoke City, having scored 248 goals in 499 games.

At one point Greenwood advised the football authorities to compile a film of Hurst's running off the ball for distribution to clubs as a coaching guide. 'His movement off the ball was fantastic,' Greenwood noted. 'Sometimes he was a decoy; other times he would just knock the ball off, one touch, and then away; or alternatively he would go wide to give the attack width and create space for others.'

Rival managers were equally impressed. 'I took it as a professional compliment when the Spurs manager Bill Nicholson sent his new

Geoff Hurst scores the fourth goal of the World Cup final, 1966.

signing Martin Chivers to watch me and study the way I played,' Hurst wrote.

England had gone into the World Cup final without an orthodox winger. As a result the ball tended to be played forward from deeper positions. Hence the need for a 'target man', though that term had yet to enter football's vocabulary.

Alf Ramsey had a long list of requirements for the role: mobility, hard work, unselfishness, physical strength, robustness and the ability to finish. Ultimately, Hurst fitted the bill perfectly.

'I was always more confident that we would keep possession when I hit long passes if Geoff was in our side,' said Ray Wilson, the England left-back.

THROUGH THE AGES
FOOTBALL
IN THE 1960s

▶▶▶▶▶▶▶▶▶▶▶▶▶▶▶▶▶▶▶▶▶▶▶▶▶▶▶▶▶▶

THIS PAGE: **Above** Sheffield Wednesday players in the snow at Highbury, 1967. **Right** Jimmy Greaves goes for a header, 1968.

OPPOSITE: **Above left** Tommy Smith receives treatment from Bob Paisley, 1969. **Above right** Jack and Bobby Charlton head home to Ashington for a civic reception in their honour, 1966. **Below left** England players enjoy a game of cards at Hendon Hall, 1966. **Below right** Denis Law and Jack Charlton square up, 1965.

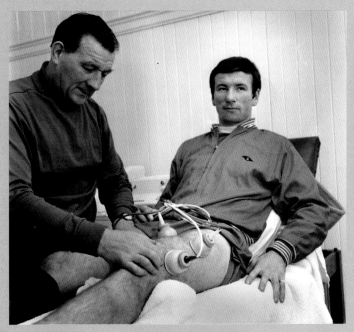

DON REVIE

▶▶▶▶▶▶▶▶▶▶▶▶▶▶▶▶▶▶

1927–1989

Don Revie was ridiculed in the national newspapers as something of a pretentious upstart when he declared: 'We are going to become a Real Madrid. One day, this club will rule in Europe.'

Behind his back, even some of his own Leeds players were mocking him over the statement of intent, and they did so all the more after Revie announced a change of club colours from blue and yellow to the all-white strip made famous by Real.

The sniggering was hardly surprising given the circumstances: Revie had no experience as yet in management, and Leeds United, a club of little pedigree, were languishing at the time in the Second Division, where they had been stuck for a generation.

Yet, remarkably, for a brief period at least, Revie did fulfil his seemingly ludicrous promise. In the years between promotion in 1963–64 and 1974, Leeds won more trophies in European football than the Madrid aristocrats.

Don Revie walks out of the tunnel at Elland Road, 1970.

MANAGER • INDUCTED 2004 • 2 DIVISION ONE CHAMPIONSHIPS

1 FA CUP • 2 FAIRS CUPS • 1 LEAGUE CUP

The younger players on the staff back then had reacted differently to his prophecy than the more cynical older pros. Norman Hunter, a future England defender, said: 'I took it as read. I totally and utterly believed in Don Revie.'

Under Revie, Leeds were the most consistently successful team in England; for a decade they finished no lower than fourth in the top flight. They were champions twice, and runners-up five times.

His record at club level made Revie the obvious choice as successor to Sir Alf Ramsey for the England job in 1974, and the Leeds side that he had built reached the European Cup final the following season. Unfortunately, his reputation would not survive the appointment by the Football Association intact.

Faced with failure to qualify for a second successive major tournament, Revie caused a sensation, generating enormous public and media hostility when he broke his contract in order to accept a lucrative and secret offer

↗
Don Revie holds aloft the League championship trophy, 1969.

from the United Arab Emirates. It proved to be the end of his career in English football.

Years earlier, before taking the job at Elland Road, Revie sought the advice of Matt Busby, the man he most admired in football. 'Be loyal and honest to your players, never lie, and they will do anything for you in return,' the Manchester United manager told him.

In the transfer market Revie paid Everton £25,000 for Bobby Collins, persuading the former Scotland international to drop down a division. The diminutive Collins eventually led the team to promotion as captain by his own fiercely competitive example.

Most significantly, Revie gathered together an outstanding crop of youngsters. Billy Bremner, Peter Lorimer and Eddie Gray all chose Leeds ahead of bigger, more established clubs. Defenders Paul Reaney, Norman

↖
Don Revie gives instructions to Kevin Keegan, 1976.

▶ key match

Liverpool 0 Leeds United 0, First Division, Anfield, 28 April 1969

Billy Bremner could not believe it when his manager told him to parade the championship trophy Leeds had just won in front of the Kop.

Though fearful that the gesture might backfire, the players complied when Don Revie insisted. Respectful of Liverpool as a club, he wanted Leeds' achievement to be properly acknowledged. The Kop responded with chants of 'Champions! Champions!'

It had been a typically disciplined defensive display, with Billy Bremner outstanding in a makeshift role as sweeper. They came for a point, and got it. Afterwards, Bill Shankly offered Leeds this praise: 'You didn't fluke or pinch the title, you deserved it,' he said. 'You're a wonderful team.'

Hunter, Paul Madeley and goalkeeper Gary Sprake also emerged.

After several near-misses, Leeds finally won the First Division title in 1969. It was a turning point for the club. Previously, Leeds were a disciplined, aggressive side specialising in 1–0 away wins. 'We went a wee bit over the top at times,' Bremner said. 'We weren't going to be intimidated.' Their detractors, though, accused them of cynicism and gamesmanship.

From 1969 onwards, Revie gave his players more freedom. 'We've changed our style,' he said, 'because now I believe we've got the players to win matches by scoring goals, rather than winning by keeping the opposition out.' Their reward was another title in 1973–74.

ROGER HUNT

▶▶▶▶▶▶▶▶▶▶▶▶▶▶▶▶▶

1938–

From his position alongside Alf Ramsey on the bench, Harold Shepherdson was struck by the reaction of the England players when Roger Hunt scored his second goal of the game against France at Wembley in 1966.

'Instead of the usual dignified congratulations when a man scores,' the England trainer recalled later, 'the players ran over and mobbed Roger in celebration.'

Inside the stadium the sense of relief, Shepherdson noted, was palpable. In scoring his third goal in as many group games, Hunt guaranteed England's progress to the knock-out stage of the World Cup.

Such exuberant behaviour, then a rare sight in football, provided proof of Hunt's popularity, and the professional respect that he commanded in the England dressing room. 'Roger has tremendous moral fibre,' Nobby Stiles once said.

Roger Hunt poses for a pre-season photograph, 1968.

PLAYER • INDUCTED 2006 • 34 CAPS • 1 WORLD CUP • 2 DIVISION ONE CHAMPIONSHIPS • 1 FA CUP

Disappointed with England's attitude and performance in beating France 2–0, Ramsey accused the team of complacency at a hastily-convened meeting that evening. In making his criticism, however, he made one exception. 'Roger always has the right attitude,' was the gist of Ramsey's message to the squad. 'He always plays well.'

Up to that point, Hunt had scored a remarkable rate of almost a goal a game for England. 'And even if he didn't score,' Martin Peters observed later, 'we all knew that Roger would run his socks off for the good of the team.'

The modest Liverpool goalscorer had found form at exactly the right time. From squad regular, he'd made himself an automatic choice in a matter of weeks during the build-up.

'Most of the football writers back then didn't grasp his importance to the side, but, believe me, the England players didn't underestimate his contribution,' Nobby Stiles recalled.

Ramsey wanted someone up front who was prepared to work tirelessly off the ball. By

↗
Roger Hunt chases a through-ball, 1969.

proving his willingness to follow orders, Hunt made himself indispensable. Initially handed the number 21 shirt, he was the only attacker to start every game during the World Cup.

At club level, Hunt had a different role. 'It was his job to get on the end of things in the penalty area,' Ian Callaghan explained. 'Bill Shankly didn't want him chasing about all over the place, wasting energy.' Liverpool won the title in 1963–64 and 1965–66; Hunt was leading goalscorer on both occasions.

'We wanted him to concentrate on goalscoring in the same way Jimmy Greaves did at Tottenham,' Shankly explained later. 'Mind you, Roger didn't just slide them in quietly, like Jimmy. He blasted them in.'

Though subsequently nicknamed 'Sir Roger' by team-mates and the Kop, the demands of the World Cup seemed to drain Hunt both physically and psychologically. The following season he struggled for form; and

↖
Roger Hunt signs autographs for a group of boys, 1963.

Ramsey dropped him, albeit briefly, in 1967.

Even though his scoring rate for both club and country slowed markedly in the second half of the decade, he remained an England regular until January 1969, when he finally decided that he'd had enough of the public and media criticism, much to Ramsey's disappointment.

Hunt scored 18 goals in 24 appearances for England; although perhaps more significantly, in the seven years since his debut, England had lost only two games in which he played.

'Through sheer effort, he would make what was, in fact, a bad ball, look like a good one.' – Alan Ball

DENIS LAW ▶▶▶▶▶▶▶▶▶▶▶▶▶▶▶▶▶▶▶▶

1940-

Matt Busby paid a British record transfer fee of £115,000 to bring Denis Law to Old Trafford in July 1962. 'Denis would have been good value at twice the price,' Busby wrote later.

'Denis was the sharpest striker I had ever seen, and he was also the most unselfish,' the Manchester United manager said. 'He was seconds quicker than anyone else in thought and deed.

'Goals that looked simple as Denis tapped them in were simple only because he got himself into position so quickly,' added Busby. 'He leapt Olympian heights. He headed the ball with almost unbelievable accuracy. And he had the courage to take on the biggest and most ferocious opponents.'

After heading south from his native Scotland, Law made his debut for Huddersfield Town in 1956 at the age of 16 years and 303 days. Within a matter of weeks Busby had submitted a bid for his transfer.

The offer of £10,000 – an unheard of sum for a player of that age at the time – was turned down flat by Bill Shankly, the then Huddersfield manager. A year later, Busby, in his role as part-time manager of Scotland, gave Law his debut at full international level. He was the youngest player ever to represent the country.

After a brief spell at Manchester City, Law was sold to Torino in 1961 for a fee of £100,000. Within months, he was describing Italian football as 'sick, ruined by money'. Turin, he said, was like a 'prison for a footballer'.

His escape followed a chance meeting. Law was playing for the Italian League against the Football League at Old Trafford. 'I don't like playing in Italy,' Law told Busby. 'Why don't you come and buy me?' Busby needed no encouragement. 'It was one of my best ever bits of business, in terms of value for money,' he said.

Denis Law holds aloft the League championship trophy, 1965.

PLAYER • INDUCTED 2002 • 55 CAPS • 2 DIVISION ONE CHAMPIONSHIPS • 1 FA CUP

'**Denis was rarely even aware of his opponent in the penalty area because he only ever saw the ball and the goal in front of him.'**
– Bobby Robson

'Without my temperament I would be nothing as a footballer,' Denis Law said. 'It's the source of my success as well as my mistakes.'

Throughout his career Law possessed an intense will to win. 'I'm a bad loser,' he said. 'I play it hard. I have to dominate my opponent. Some people criticise such sentiments. I see them as a source of pride.'

Occasionally, if he thought himself unfairly provoked, he would retaliate. He once famously chased Ian Ure, the Arsenal centre-half,

around the pitch in a fury seeking retribution for a tackle. Both players were sent off.

Three times, between 1963 and 1967, Law received lengthy suspensions from the football authorities for his behaviour on the field. 'Learning to live with my temperament is my private battle,' he once said.

But there was also no doubting his bravery. 'I have seen his legs virtually cut to ribbons, with blood and cuts, and covered in bruises from kicks in a game,' Busby said.

One knock to his knee during the 1965–66 season would have unforeseen consequences. The injury was misdiagnosed and the condition of the joint steadily deteriorated. By May 1968, the pain was unbearable, forcing Law to undergo corrective surgery. He watched his team-mates win the European Cup final on television in hospital.

↗
A Charity Shield plaque, 1967.

'Trying to kick Denis is a waste of time,' Bobby Charlton said at the time. 'It never stops him, and he is fiery enough to hit them harder than they hit him.' Dave Mackay once described Law as 'well built and hard as teak'.

It is hard to imagine a more unlikely looking aspiring professional footballer than Denis Law at the age of 15. 'I was weak, puny and bespectacled with a dreadful squint,' Law recalled.

Andy Beattie, the Huddersfield Town manager, took one look at the boy standing in front of him, barely five feet tall, a boil on his cheek, and wearing round, standard-issue National Health glasses to correct his vision. 'The boy's a freak,' he told his colleague.

But his unlikely appearance hid a raw, natural talent. An abnormally slow heart beat, instant acceleration from a standing start and

↖
Denis Law picks himself up, 1968.

'Denis is a real will-o'-the-wisp player. He perfected the art of getting in behind the defender, the hallmark of any great striker.' – Bobby Charlton

razor-sharp reflexes made young Law stand out. A diet heavy in steak and milk soon built up his strength and stamina.

Speed was the essence of Law's game. 'I had to get in front of the defender,' he said. 'It was all about getting that half-yard on my

Denis Law shoots at goal, 1959.

Denis Law, (Trevillion).

marker.' He also worked tirelessly during games. 'Training and practice bores me,' he said. 'I like to save everything for Saturday. If I don't finish a game feeling half dead I have a sense of failure.'

The 1963–64 season was perhaps his peak. 'I was flying,' he said. 'I finished with 30 goals

▶ talking point

On 27 April 1974, Denis Law scored his last goal at Old Trafford. His back-heel flick in the 82nd minute won a crucial derby game.

Law had a distinctive way of celebrating a goal; raising one arm and pointing his index finger to the sky. Law set the trend according to Matt Busby. 'Before Denis, such salutes to the crowd were rare,' Busby said.

But there was no trademark celebration on this occasion. Law was playing for Manchester City, and everyone inside Old Trafford knew that his goal had condemned Manchester United to relegation.

Law had left Old Trafford against his will in 1973. At the age of 33 he returned for one season to Maine Road, where he had played in 1960–61, before his £100,000 transfer to Torino in Italy.

He had not wanted to play at Old Trafford for fear of exactly this eventuality. 'United meant too much to me,' he wrote later, 'but as a professional, once I had been selected I had to play. When the goal went in, I was feeling sick. I was totally depressed and I wished that the ball had gone wide.'

Law was substituted immediately. That summer he played for Scotland in the World Cup in West Germany. He won the last of his 55 caps against Zaire in his final game as a professional. On his return home, Law retired.

'My last ever touch in League football was the goal that sent United down,' he said. 'So I left the stage, without really taking a bow.'

in as many League matches, with 15 more in Cup ties.'

Bobby Charlton described Law as 'easily the best inside-forward in Britain'. 'Denis was a bargain,' Charlton wrote. 'When he is really in form, he is virtually unstoppable.'

JOE MERCER

▶▶▶▶▶▶▶▶▶▶▶▶▶▶▶

1914–1990

After resurrecting the fortunes of two famous clubs and taking another to a peak of European football, Joe Mercer answered the call of England at a time of upheaval and uncertainty for the national side.

In the wake of the sudden departure of Sir Alf Ramsey in 1974, the Football Association turned to the genial and trusted Mercer, whose wise counsel and cheery disposition restored morale within the England team.

His brief and successful stint as England caretaker manager was a fitting reward for an outstanding career at club level, the pinnacle of which was achieved with Manchester City during the latter half of the 1960s.

Asked to identity the single attribute in a manager that is a pre-requisite for a side to be successful, Mercer replied: 'Above all else, he must be an eternal optimist.'

Joe Mercer, 1960.

MANAGER • INDUCTED 2009 • 1 DIVISION ONE CHAMPIONSHIP • 1 FA CUP

2 LEAGUE CUPS • 1 EUROPEAN CUP-WINNERS' CUP

'I could always answer players if they asked me why they were left out.' – Joe Mercer

After winning promotion in 1965–66, Manchester City made the breakthrough two years later when they captured the championship title for the first time since 1937.

When City then lifted the FA Cup the following season with victory over Leicester City at Wembley, the former Arsenal captain and Everton wing-half became the first man in history to win League and Cup honours as both a player and manager.

Then, in 1970, there came another first: as winners of the League Cup and European Cup-Winners' Cup, City became the first English club to achieve the 'double' of European trophy and major domestic prize in the same season.

Mercer made his name as a manager by winning promotion to the top flight with Sheffield United and Aston Villa, where he also won the League Cup. Gerry Hitchins noted

Mercer's integrity and honesty during their days working together at Villa Park. The England forward recalled Mercer assembling the players. 'Let's get it straight,' he said. 'I'm always looking for new players. But I can promise you this: nobody will come here and get special treatment or privileges from me that you don't enjoy.'

In later years Mercer detailed his methods as a manager: 'I gave marks to every boy who played for me. I would assess how he played in each match and write a report on the game. I could always answer players if they asked me why they were left out.'

At Maine Road, Mercer was responsible for overall strategy and team selection. A figurehead and spokesman for the club, he outlined his tactical approach: 'We have a number of basic plans dealing with simple things, such as throw-ins, but we don't wrap it up in analysis, diagrams and over-elaboration. A team must be able to play "off the cuff", adapting your tactics to suit conditions and opponents.'

His first major decision as manager turned out to be the most significant: the appointment of Malcolm Allison as coach. Under Mercer and Allison, Manchester City concentrated on attack. As *The Times* reported in 1968: 'City took the First Division crown on their own skilful merit. They have emerged as a breath of fresh air in English football.'

When the Mercer-Allison partnership broke down, Mercer moved on to Highfield Road where he helped Coventry City consoli-

↗
Joe Mercer lights a cigar for Malcolm Allison.

date their position in the top flight. Then came that call from the FA for 'Good old Uncle Joe,' as Kevin Keegan, the England star of the day affectionately called him.

↖
Joe Mercer waves to supporters, 1970.

▶talking point

Joe Mercer had no time for detailed, lengthy team talks. He preferred to keep it simple, and, whenever possible, amusing.

In his time at Aston Villa he prompted laughter in the dressing room by quoting from Shakespeare's *Henry V* before a vital promotion game in 1960: 'We few, we happy few, we band of brothers.'

Or he would remind them: 'The grass is green, the sky is blue, go out and rejoice in the fact that you are professional footballers.'

Mike Doyle, the Manchester City midfielder, said: 'He would scribble some thoughts down on his newspaper. Sometimes it was hilarious, because his remarks would be spiced with real humour.'

BILLY BREMNER

▶▶▶▶▶▶▶▶▶▶▶▶▶▶▶▶▶▶

1942–1997

Nailed to the wall in the Leeds United dressing room at Elland Road during the 1960s was a sign. It read: Keep Fighting. 'It hangs above my peg, appropriately; for I am the captain,' Billy Bremner said. 'I'm the one supposed to set an example to the other lads.'

Over a period of 16 years, this '10 stone of barbed wire', as the *Sunday Times* newspaper described Bremner, did just that, inspiring the most consistently successful team in England over a period of 16 years of first-team action.

The diminutive Bremner was a vital cog in the Leeds machine – an indispensable and irrepressible force in midfield. When Don Revie heard that the Scotsman might be sold, the Leeds manager gave his board of directors an ultimatum: 'If he goes, I go.' Both Bremner and Revie stayed put.

↖
Billy Bremner stares into the camera, 1970.

PLAYER • INDUCTED 2004 • 54 CAPS • 2 FAIRS CUPS • 2 DIVISION ONE CHAMPIONSHIPS

1 FA CUP • 1 LEAGUE CUP

'Billy was ... exactly the type of player you want in your team.'
- Denis Law

'Above all, Leeds have Bremner, the best footballer in the four countries,' John Arlott wrote in the *Guardian* in 1970. 'If every manager in Britain were given his choice of any one player to add to his team, some, no doubt, would toy with the idea of George Best; but the realists, to a man, would have Bremner.'

By his own admission, Leeds United followed their 'Keep Fighting' motto a little too enthusiastically on occasions, particularly in the mid 60s, when the club was attempting to establish itself as a major power following promotion. 'We were so determined that none of the elite clubs were going to get in our way,' Bremner wrote. 'We weren't star-gazers.'

Billy Bremner in action, 1974.

Mentally, too, they fought on, undaunted, despite the disappointment of missing out narrowly on major honours three seasons in succession. Their remarkable resilience was finally rewarded with a breakthrough victory in the League Cup final in 1968. 'Now that we've won some silver at last, we'll go on to collect other trophies,' Bremner said at the time, and he was right.

Defeat irritated Bremner, even when it came to the hobbies Revie famously introduced as a way of avoiding boredom at the team hotel. 'I never won at bloody carpet bowls,' Bremner once complained. His competitive nature inspired others. 'Billy simply couldn't bear losing, and we picked up on that,' team-mate Norman Hunter recalled.

'Billy played more with his heart than his head,' Eddie Gray, the Leeds winger, wrote later. 'He had a heart the size of Elland Road. He was a free spirit who worked on instinct.'

Billy Bremner leads the salute to Leeds United fans, 1973.

►talking point

Leeds United 1 Manchester United 0, FA Cup semi-final, City Ground, 31 March 1965

Billy Bremner had a happy knack of scoring vital goals, but none stirred as much feeling as this one: the late header that put Leeds United through to their first FA Cup final.

In the final seconds, Bremner, his back to goal at the far post, twisted his body to direct the ball into the top corner. 'Billy's record for scoring vital goals speaks for itself,' team-mate Eddie Gray recalled.

Neither side had yielded an inch in a game one newspaper described as 'a sordid battle'.

'His speciality was the reverse pass,' Gray added. 'Billy could deliver the pass without giving any indication of his intent by his body shape when playing the ball.'

Bremner was versatile, too. When the situation demanded, he would drop back to play sweeper, particularly away from home. 'He was brilliant at the job,' Hunter said, 'and those performances at the back just highlighted his all-round ability.' At the other end, Bremner also scored goals; often important ones.

Over the years Revie increasingly insisted that his players turn out even when they were unfit. With Bremner, however, the practice often went to extremes. 'Billy once played with a hairline fracture in his leg,' one Leeds player said.

Bremner recalled one conversation: 'The boss once said to me: "I'd rather have you with one leg than anybody else with two, to gee the other lads up." I thought that was rubbish, but that's what he said.'

GEORGE BEST ▶▶▶▶▶▶▶▶▶▶▶▶▶▶

1946–2005

George Best, the mercurial genius of Old Trafford and the best footballer in Europe at his peak, was the game's first celebrity icon, a young lad from Belfast who counted the Beatles and the Rolling Stones as friends.

Best arrived in Manchester as a shy, nervous, skinny 15-year-old in 1961. Seven years later the once homesick teenager scored the most crucial goal of a European Cup final at Wembley.

Denis Law described Best as 'a complete footballer'. Matt Busby said: 'George had more ways of beating a player than anyone I've ever seen. Every aspect of ball-control was natural to him. He would use an opponent's shins to play a one-two.'

By the age of 17, Best was a first-team regular; in 1968 he was the youngest-ever Footballer of the Year. The following year he won the same accolade in Europe and by the mid-1960s he was famous across the Continent as 'El Beatle', the brilliant footballer with the pop-star good looks.

'I stepped over the line from being an athlete and became a personality or pop thing,' Best said. At the height of his popularity he received 10,000 fan-mail letters a week.

Best played 466 League and cup games for Manchester United, scoring 178 goals, including the precious strike that gave his team the lead in extra time at Wembley in 1968. United went on to beat Benfica 4–1. Best finished that season as the leading goalscorer in Division One with 28 goals, a remarkable return for a winger.

'I always used to say to George: "You could score 30 goals a season, if you look for Denis Law, give him the ball and go for the return,"' Jimmy Murphy, the Manchester United assistant manager said. 'But then, how can you tell a genius how to play?'

George Best runs at the Everton defence, 1972.

▶ key match

Benfica 1 Manchester United 5, European Cup quarter-final, Lisbon, 9 March 1966

Both Bobby Charlton and Denis Law rate this match as George Best's greatest in a Manchester United shirt.

The Portuguese newspapers dubbed Best 'the fifth Beatle', a theme taken up by the *The Times* in its match report: 'With his long, dark mop of hair, he ... set a new, almost unexplored beat.'

Best scored his side's first goal with a soaring header, then stunned the 90,000 crowd by 'gliding past three defenders like a dark ghost to break clear and slide the ball home', as *The Times* football writer Geoffrey Green memorably put it. 'George just went out and destroyed them,' Matt Busby said.

Before flying home Best deliberately bought the biggest sombrero he could find. When the waiting pressmen greeted him in Manchester, they had their picture. For the first time the image of Best featured on the front as well as the back pages. Overnight, he became the first celebrity footballer.

PLAYER • INDUCTED 2002 • 37 CAPS • 1 EUROPEAN CUP • 2 DIVISION ONE CHAMPIONSHIPS

'There are times when I think George Best has ice in his veins.' – Jimmy Murphy

George Best was first spotted by Bob Bishop, a Manchester United scout who ran a youth club in Belfast. Bishop sent a message to Busby, saying his new find, although small and skinny, had 'an enormous ration of football gifts'.

Best practised those skills endlessly. 'Even when it was dark I'd still be there, smashing a ball against the garage doors,' Best said. 'I tried to hit the same spot. Accuracy was the key, I always thought.'

Arriving in Manchester for a trial, Best was intimidated by the city. So much so that he went straight back home the next day. Only then did he find the nerve to give professional football another go. At 15 he was small and frail for his age. On first meeting him the landlady at his club digs thought he was an apprentice jockey.

Right from the start he showed an appetite for work. Described by Murphy as 'a fantastically hard trainer', Best often practised alone, determined to make himself genuinely two-footed. A favourite drill was to try to score direct from a corner kick with his left foot. Other times he would try to hit the cross bar from the edge of the penalty area. 'By the time

George Best, (Trevillion).

I was 19 or 20 most people couldn't tell which was my stronger foot,' he said.

Best's leaping ability and heading were helped by the fact that he played rugby at school. He also enjoyed the physical side of football. 'The manager always said that I was the best tackler at the club, which I took as a great compliment.'

'There are times when I think George Best has ice in his veins,' said Jimmy Murphy, who had seen nothing like him before. 'He was only

George Best takes on a Wolves defender in April 1971.

17 when he made his debut, and there he was before the game, sitting on his own, quietly reading the club programme.' Denis Law said, 'Really, I often think that George is completely nerveless.'

His rise was rapid. As a first-team player Best was still eligible for the youth team in 1963–64 and he helped Manchester United win the FA Youth Cup for the first time since the heyday of the 'Busby Babes' in the mid 1950s. Best made his international debut for Northern Ireland the same season.

George Best could see possibilities on a football field that simply did not occur to other players. 'Some young players just have it so naturally that it shines out, like a beacon,'

↗
The Manchester United shirt worn by George Best for the FA Cup tie against Northampton Town in 1970. Best scored six goals.

Bobby Charlton said. 'George all but missed the reserves, going straight from the youth team to the first team.'

The only criticism levelled at Best in those days concerned his tendency to over-elaborate. 'When he has eradicated this small failing I'm sure he will be numbered among the greats,' Charlton wrote in 1967.

Everyone at the club admired his courage.

↖
George Best, 1972.

▶ talking point

George Best had a knack for the unexpected, as Gordon Banks the England goalkeeper was about to find out.

Playing for Northern Ireland against England in 1971, Best combined original thinking, skill and athleticism to manufacture an audacious scoring opportunity for himself.

He had already noticed that Banks threw the ball up in the air when kicking the ball downfield. Best spotted an opportunity. Timing his move perfectly, he waited until the ball was in the air before flicking it with his outstretched leg over the goalkeeper's head.

As the ball bounced towards goal, Banks turned and frantically raced back, only to be beaten to it by Best, who had a simple tap-in into an empty net.

'No one else in the game would have even thought of trying it,' Matt Busby said. 'It was a marvellous, inspired bit of improvisation that deserved reward.'

The referee, however, did not agree. He disallowed the goal, even though Best had not touched the goalkeeper when he knocked the ball away. 'Foot up' was the only possible explanation the newspapers speculated the next day.

'I have never stopped believing that it was a perfectly good goal,' Best said later.

'Even in the face of the most cruelly desperate tackle, George never shirks,' Denis Law said.

Eventually, however, the strain of celebrity, and the frustration he felt at playing for a team in decline while at his peak as a footballer in the early 1970s, proved too much. He began drinking heavily. In May 1977, at the age of 30, after a stint playing at Fulham and overseas, Best quit top-level football.

JOHNNY GILES

▶▶▶▶▶▶▶▶▶▶▶▶▶▶▶

1940–

Johnny Giles shaped the football played by Leeds United from 1965–75, during which period the Yorkshire club challenged for honours on a more regular basis than any other club in the English game.

From his position in central midfield, the mercurial and elusive Irishman orchestrated the transformation of Leeds from second-tier nonentities into a giant of the game, both here and in Europe.

In that 10-year spell from the mid 1960s, Leeds secured all three domestic honours – the League championship and FA Cup twice, and the League Cup once; whilst in Europe, they added two Inter-City Fairs Cups, and reached the European Cup final.

'Johnny was able to get hold of a game by the scruff of the neck and direct it,' Norman Hunter, a Leeds team-mate, said. 'Nobody was better at that than him.'

Johnny Giles, 1973.

PLAYER • INDUCTED 2010 • 59 CAPS • 2 DIVISION ONE CHAMPIONSHIPS • 2 FA CUPS

2 FAIRS CUPS • 1 LEAGUE CUP

'As I look at all the talent and character at my disposal today, my one regret is that John Giles wasn't born an Englishman.'
– Sir Alf Ramsey

For all his value to the team, Giles had little interest in becoming a crowd favourite. 'I was never involved with the fans during a game,' he said. 'The one thing I wanted was the respect of the players, they know you better than anybody else.'

That respect spread far beyond the confines of Elland Road, as Steve Perryman, the Tottenham Hotspur captain confirmed: 'Bill Nicholson keeps telling me to watch Johnny Giles,' Perryman said at the time. 'I'm

doing just that. There is so much to learn from his play.'

As a young boy, Giles already held lofty ambitions, and he looked to two of the outstanding inside-forwards of the post-war era for inspiration. 'I wanted to be a great player, to emulate the likes of Raich Carter and Peter Doherty,' he recalled.

'I had a gift to play football which was no personal reflection on me. That's no false modesty; anybody can be gifted. As a kid I knew it was there. I could kick a ball in the classical way. Nobody can teach you that.'

His career in England began at Manchester United where he broke into the first team at outside-right. But, ultimately, he failed to settle at Old Trafford, despite featuring in a losing FA Cup final in 1963.

In August that year, Giles was transferred for a club record fee of £32,000, after Matt Busby agreed to his transfer request. Five years later, former team-mate Nobby Stiles described the transfer as 'the worst day's work United have ever done'.

Initially, Giles made his mark at Elland Road on the wing, a position that allowed him to study the play of diminutive schemer Bobby Collins. Eventually, after the combative Scot suffered a badly broken leg, Giles took over in the middle – a position he then cemented as his own.

For some observers, Giles personified Revie's Leeds United: hard, professional and ambitious; ruthless, even, if confronted. Some

Johnny Giles in possession, 1974.

opponents later accused him of 'leaving his foot in'. In reply Giles has always maintained that his first thought was self-protection. If they wanted to mix it, 'our attitude was an eye for an eyelash', he said. 'But it would be wrong to think that it was Leeds against a gang of angels.'

In 1975, Giles left Leeds for West Bromwich Albion, where he was appointed the club's first player-manager. Promotion to the top flight was secured with victory at Oldham on the last day of the 1975–76 season. Giles left Albion the following year.

Joe Jordan, the Leeds United centre-forward, has since pinpointed what, in his view, made Giles great: 'With Johnny it was never an issue of the long ball or the short ball, it was only ever a question about the right ball.'

MALCOLM ALLISON

▶▶▶▶▶▶▶▶▶▶▶▶▶▶▶▶

1927–2010

As a coach and manager Malcolm Allison created a succession of teams that reflected his personality: flamboyant, adventurous, unpredictable and, above all, positive.

Often outspoken, always quotable, Allison revelled in his chosen role as one of the game's great showmen and self-publicists. Over the years, this larger-than-life Londoner honed his public image – the trademark fedora hat, sheepskin coat and occasional cigar.

Summoned to the Manchester City cause by Joe Mercer in 1965, Allison transformed the mood at Maine Road, winning over the players with his confident manner and coaching ideas, paving the way to a period of unprecedented success for the club. 'Malcolm Allison was a great tactician. Brilliant.' Francis Lee, the City and England forward, said. 'Analytically brilliant. He saw things no one else did.'

Above Malcolm Allison answers questions from the media, 1969.
Below Malcolm Allison shouts instructions from the bench, 1965.

MANAGER • INDUCTED 2009 • 1 DIVISION ONE CHAMPIONSHIP • 1 FA CUP

1 LEAGUE CUP • 1 EUROPEAN CUP-WINNERS' CUP

'In my opinion, Malcolm is the best coach that has ever been. So much of what he did was years ahead of its time. Without question, he was the driving force behind the success we had at City.' – Colin Bell

From his earliest days in management at Plymouth Argyle, Allison took risks: notably, the deployment of a sweeper – a novel tactic in English football at the time. He then found an ally in Mercer at Maine Road. 'I had all these new training methods and fancy ideas,' Allison recalled, 'and I used to say: "Look, Joe, I fancy doing this," and he always gave me encouragement. Joe was like a father figure to me.'

At their peak between 1967 and 1970, City captured, in order, the League championship, FA Cup, League Cup and European Cup-Winners' Cup – a trophy they secured 'in the grand manner of true champions', the *Daily Mirror* reported. In 1972, with Allison in sole charge, City came within a point of winning the title.

His boastful nature energised the City faithful, and football writers thrived on an almost continuous supply of newsworthy quotes. Allison revelled in his 'champagne lifestyle' and attracted attention. It kept him – and the clubs he managed – in the headlines.

'Allison is a man who by physique, nature and temperament cannot help stealing the spotlight,' the *Daily Mirror* commented. These traits, coupled with an outspokenness and deep knowledge of the game, made him an obvious candidate for inclusion on ITV's groundbreaking panel of experts for the 1970 World Cup.

Another of his innovations involved the adoption of a new away kit – the red and black stripes associated with European giants AC Milan – in order to make City appear more imposing to the opposition.

Later, in 1973, following the disintegration of the partnership with Mercer, Allison departed Maine Road for Crystal Palace. There he instigated more change: on his instruction, out went the club's rather homely nickname 'The Glaziers' and the old kit. 'The Eagles' were soon playing in a distinctive all-white strip with red and blue sash.

And it was at Selhurst Park, during a thrilling ride to an FA Cup semi-final, that Allison skilfully manufactured a newspaper story surrounding his 'lucky' fedora hat that he donned for Cup ties – to the delight of the press photographers.

Though Allison would go on to achieve significant success overseas – offsetting the disappointment of a second unsuccessful stint as City manager, starting in 1979 – his professional heyday came a decade earlier. 'In my opinion, Malcolm is the best coach that has ever been,' Colin Bell once wrote. 'So much of what he did was years ahead of its time. Without question, he was the driving force behind the success we had at City.'

Malcolm Allison smokes a cigar, 1975.

MARTIN PETERS

▶▶▶▶▶▶▶▶▶▶▶▶▶▶▶▶▶

1943–

One of only two Englishmen to score a goal in a World Cup final, Martin Peters was once described by Ron Greenwood as 'the answer to a manager's prayers'.

A subtle, elusive midfield player of drifting menace who combined poise, stealth and intelligence, Peters was an automatic choice in the England team for seven years. 'Not just a good player, but a great one', Sir Alf Ramsey said in 1968.

Often bracketed with fellow Hammers and World Cup winners Bobby Moore and Geoff Hurst, Peters was 'the most gifted of them all, a natural talent', according to Greenwood, their manager at Upton Park.

Asked to identify his strength as a player, the modest Peters said: 'I am always prepared to take a chance with a run.'

↗
Martin Peters runs with the ball, 1973.

PLAYER • INDUCTED 2006 • 67 CAPS • 1 WORLD CUP • 1 EUROPEAN CUP-WINNERS' CUP

1 UEFA CUP • 2 LEAGUE CUPS

Nicknamed 'The Ghost', Peters was a 'masterly technician with a sure and flexible finish who developed an impeccable timing and understanding of space', the official history of the Football Association stated. 'Time and again, he arrived, unnoticed, at the point of greatest threat at the critical moment.'

The most notable and memorable of those interventions occurred on the afternoon of 30 July 1966. At Wembley that day, with only 13 minutes left to play in the final, Peters displayed outstanding technique in keeping his close-range volley under control. England were ahead. 'I know I had my mouth open, but nothing came out,' Peters recalled, describing his goal celebration. 'I was literally speechless with joy.'

Sometimes underrated by the football writers and fans on the terraces, Peters' reputation for excellence within the game was acknowledged in 1970 when Tottenham Hotspur signed him from West Ham in a record transfer deal worth £200,000.

A member of West Ham's successful European Cup-Winners' Cup side in 1964–65,

Martin Peters and Bobby Moore, 1965.

Peters went on to win League Cup and UEFA Cup honours with Tottenham. As his career wound down he helped Norwich City win promotion to the top flight.

'In some ways, his ability goes over supporters' heads,' Ron Greenwood once said. 'They're following the ball, so they don't necessarily notice what he's doing for the team in both attack and defence.'

During his career, Peters played in every outfield position for West Ham. This versatility prompted Ramsey to describe him, in 1968, as being '10 years ahead of his time' – an English footballer ideally suited to the fluent, role-switching 'Total Football' tactics championed by Ajax and Holland during the 1970s.

Peters was a diligent marker, good in the air and he tackled strongly, according to international team-mate Ray Wilson. 'Defensively,

Martin Peters, 1975.

Martin was very good, and he gave the team balance as a result,' the England left-back said.

Two years before the 1970 World Cup in Mexico, Ramsey publicly identified Peters as one of the four players who were certainties for selection in his squad. In 1973, when England faced a decisive qualifier against Poland at Wembley, Ramsey made Peters captain. 'It was my 63rd cap and I was easily the most experienced player in the team,' Peters recalled. England's cruel elimination that night, however, effectively ended his international career.

In assessing his team-mate, Bobby Moore valued, above all, Peters' passing ability. 'People didn't notice him because he played so many perfect first-time balls – the kind of passes that others would deliver after taking a touch. A great, great player.'

▶ talking point

In the searing heat of Leon, Martin Peters convinced every Englishman in the ground that Alf Ramsey's side would march into the last four of the 1970 World Cup in Mexico.

Latching on to a cross from full-back Keith Newton, Peters added a trademark finish that put England two-up against West Germany. Then, with time ticking away, and England still ahead, Alf Ramsey substituted Peters for the first time in his international career. 'I'm saving you for the semi-final,' Ramsey said.

Of course, Germany fought back to win 3–2. 'Years later, Alf told me, in private, that it had been a mistake to take me off,' Peters said.

FRANCIS LEE

▶▶▶▶▶▶▶▶▶▶▶▶▶▶▶▶▶

1944–

Francis Lee runs with the ball, 1969.

'When Francis Lee embarks on a run with the ball at his feet toward the opposition penalty area, he is probably the most dynamic and exciting player in the world.'

These were the words of Joe Mercer, in reply to a question about the attributes of a striker who achieved the notable feat of winning championship medals with two different clubs – Manchester City and Derby County.

'Francis starts to play where other people finish off,' Mercer, the then City manager said. 'He shows his strength in the penalty area. He is squat and strong and so very, very brave.'

In 1971–72, those qualities enabled the barrel-chested Lee to finish top scorer in the First Division, with 33 goals in the League, as City narrowly missed out on another title.

PLAYER • INDUCTED 2010 • 27 CAPS • 2 DIVISION ONE CHAMPIONSHIPS • 1 FA CUP

1 LEAGUE CUP • 1 EUROPEAN CUP-WINNERS' CUP

Francis Lee in action, 1968.

At international level, Lee made his debut for England in 1968, and he went on to win 27 caps over a four-year period, scoring 10 goals. At the 1970 World Cup in Mexico, Lee was an automatic choice for Sir Alf Ramsey up front, typically in a free, support role, either side of Geoff Hurst, the target man. 'I started out as a winger, so I could play there, but support striker was really my best position,' Lee said.

Those early performances for England prompted the *Daily Express* to describe Lee as the 'new wing wonder who, on his day, is a wrecker of the best opposition defences'.

Joe Mercer signed Lee from Bolton Wanderers for a club-record fee of £60,000 in the autumn of 1967. At Burnden Park, Lee had been a consistent goalscorer for several seasons, a run that began when he was 17 years of age. In 1964–65, Lee scored 16 goals in a run of 14 games. By now, however, Wanderers had been relegated, and when they failed to return – and then refused him a pay rise – Lee requested a transfer.

On meeting Lee for the first time, Mercer said: 'I hope you sign for us. We feel that we are one player short at the moment. You are that final piece in the jigsaw. The odd goal or two will turn City into a great team.' And it did.

Many of those goals scored by Lee were crucial, including the fourth goal in the title-deciding victory at Newcastle in 1968, and the second, ultimately decisive goal in the European Cup-Winners' Cup final two years later.

Later in his career Lee earned a reputation as a winner and taker of penalties. His method was always the same: a long run-up, so that the keeper had less chance of 'reading' his intentions, and turn down the power about 25 per cent. 'I never blasted them,' Lee said, 'and I never changed my mind about which side to put it.'

Another contract dispute led to Lee's transfer to Derby County in the summer of 1974 for a fee of £110,000. Dave Mackay, the Derby manager, was adding an experienced, wily operator to the side that he inherited from Brian Clough. 'He has made more of an impact than anyone dared hope,' reported the *Guardian* the following year.

Francis Lee takes a penalty, 1970.

**Manchester City 1 Derby County 2,
Maine Road, 29 December 1974**

Derby County took an important step on their way to winning the title when Francis Lee returned to his former club for a game that produced a memorable television image.

Deep into the second half, with the scores level, the *Match of the Day* cameras filmed Lee when he took a pass on the left wing.

'Interesting,' Barry Davies, the BBC commentator said, as Lee cut inside, beating two defenders, '*very* interesting'. He then thumped the ball into the opposite top corner of the net for a winning goal that prompted an understandable celebration. 'Look at his face!' Davies exclaimed, his voice rising as sharply as the shot. 'Just look at his face!'

BERTIE MEE

▶▶▶▶▶▶▶▶▶▶▶▶▶▶▶▶

1918–2001

Few managerial appointments have been greeted with such surprise as the elevation of Bertie Mee from the backroom staff at Arsenal. Yet the former physiotherapist proved the doubters wrong by guiding the Gunners to a famous double as manager in 1970–71.

The former Army officer and disciplinarian – a man barely known outside the confines of the Highbury treatment room – transformed the fortunes of the club following his appointment in the summer of 1966.

It was a time of crisis and plummeting attendances for a club that had last tasted success in the early 1950s. With morale and confidence restored, Arsenal lifted their first European trophy – the Fairs Cup – in 1970.

His basic aim never altered. 'I want to prevent mediocrity being perpetuated,' Mee told his players.

Bertie Mee leads out the Arsenal team at Wembley, 1971.

MANAGER • INDUCTED 2008 • 1 DIVISION ONE CHAMPIONSHIP • 1 FA CUP • 1 FAIRS CUP

At the time of his appointment, even Mee expressed surprise at the board's decision. His lack of experience in management and moderate playing career was not lost on Arsenal's rivals, notably Liverpool, the then champions.

On hearing the news, Bill Shankly, that great player of mind-games, scoffed: 'They have appointed the medicine man.' Yet Mee was the one who tasted success over the ensuing five years, culminating with victory over Shankly's side in the 1971 FA Cup final.

Above all, perhaps, Mee instilled discipline. Drawing heavily upon his Army experience, he imposed stringent codes relating to dress and conduct – 'Managing with enlightened discipline,' as he put it. Values and tradition were important, Mee insisted. 'Remember who you are and what you represent,' he told the Arsenal players time and again.

'Bertie was a very good psychologist and man-manager,' Bob Wilson recalled. 'Fear-

↗
Bertie Mee celebrates the clinching of the League championship, 1971.

somely hard, but always fair,' the Arsenal goalkeeper added, citing the attributes that would keep Mee in his job for a decade.

Dignified and unassuming, proud and aloof, Mee recognised his own limitations, and then delegated accordingly. Certain duties, most notably tactics, were left largely to first-team coach Dave Sexton and his successor Don Howe, both of whom went on to manage at the highest level. In appointing them, Mee revealed another attribute: an ability to identify talent.

In the late 1960s, Howe was instrumental in changing the way Arsenal defended. With Mee's approval, the future England coach scrapped man-for-man marking in favour of a zonal system – a tactical switch that paved the way for Arsenal's return to the top.

The buying and selling of players, however, remained the preserve of the manager, and Mee made two important early signings:

↖
Bertie Mee supervises training in his role as Arsenal physiotherapist, 1960.

► **talking point**

Arsenal put together an outstanding late run to pip Leeds United for the title – and so complete the double – in the 1970–71 season.

Soon afterwards, Bertie Mee offered this explanation for their achievement. 'Success,' he said, 'results from a combination of hard work and a determination to figure in Arsenal's return to greatness. Confidence and character are our greatest qualities. To win the League you need a squad of footballers who will give you 45 top-class performances out of 50. Occasional brilliance is no good over a long season. We kept and recruited those who had that attitude. The others could go.'

forward George Graham from Chelsea and Bob McNab, the promising Huddersfield Town defender. Fortunately for Mee, Frank McLintock, the inspirational captain of the double side, was already on the books.

Mee also inherited an outstanding crop of youngsters in forwards Charlie George, John Radford and Ray Kennedy, and full-back Pat Rice. Later, when they emerged through the ranks, he had found his winning formula.

Famously, the double was secured with victory on the ground of rivals Tottenham Hotspur. During the run-in, Mee delivered a timely rallying cry following victory over Stoke City in the FA Cup semi-final. Imploring them, this one time, to put the club first and family second, he said: 'You have the chance to put your names in the record books for all time.' And with his help, that is exactly what the Arsenal players did.

TEAM INDUCTEE
MANCHESTER CITY
▶▶▶▶▶▶▶▶▶▶▶▶▶▶▶▶▶▶ 1965–1970

July 1965

In one of his first tasks since taking over as Manchester City manager, and as a condition of taking the job at Maine Road, Joe Mercer appoints former Plymouth Argyle boss Malcolm Allison as assistant manager and coach. The *Daily Express* devotes two paragraphs at the bottom of its main sports page to the news.

4 May 1966

City clinch promotion to the top flight with four games left to play, with a 1–0 victory at Rotherham. Recent signing Colin Bell scores the vital goal.

October 1966

After a lacklustre return to the top flight following promotion, City management bring in Derek Ibbotson, a British international athlete, to oversee training. Ibbotson introduces a new, gruelling programme of running drills. Initially, his pupils are not too happy. 'We're footballers, not track and field athletes,' they complain.

9 December 1967

Tottenham Hotspur are overwhelmed 4–1 in the snow at Maine Road, prompting Spurs manager Bill Nicholson to say: 'City produced some great stuff. They were easily the best team we have played this season. If they keep this up, they are going to take some stopping.' As always, results change the way footballers think: few of the City players are complaining about Ibbotson's training regime now.

27 March 1968

In the last seconds of a pulsating match, an injured Colin Bell, lying on a stretcher on the sidelines, lifts

↖

Manchester City players celebrate a goal against Manchester United, 1969.

his head to see Francis Lee seal a 3–1 victory over champions Manchester United from the penalty spot. Seeing the determination etched on Bell's face, Joe Mercer later told friends: 'The boys have grown up.'

20 April 1968

After a run of inconsistent results, the respected football writer Geoffrey Green reports in The Times 'a general feeling that Manchester City and Liverpool are just about out of the title race, leaving the Uniteds of Leeds and Manchester to fight it out'.

6 May 1968

After watching City complete the double over his Tottenham side, Bill Nicholson is reminded of Spurs' famous 'push and run' side of the early 1950s. 'There is the same quick, accurate passing and tremendous, energetic running.'

11 May 1968

Knowing beforehand that only victory would guarantee the title, City defeat Newcastle United 4–3 in a thrilling match. 'It was worth every yard for a southerner to make this long haul to the north-east, to see the title won in this style and in the grand manner,' writes Geoffrey Green, in *The Times*.

13 May 1968

An ebullient Allison declares: 'We will score Europe to death next season. You have not seen the best of Manchester City because we can be twice as good.' In September, City are knocked out by Fenerbahce, the Turkish champions, in the first round of the European Cup. Lessons, though, have been learned.

11 April 1969

Newspapers report the joint award of the Footballer of the Year trophy to Dave Mackay of Spurs, and Tony Book, whose absence during the first half of the season because of injury stalls City's title defence. 'The other players respect, admire and believe in Tony, and they follow him as captain,' Mercer said. 'That's the secret of his leadership.'

26 April 1969

In the FA Cup final, a Neil Young goal secures victory over Leicester City. As Tony Book lifts the trophy, Malcolm Allison turns to Joe Mercer and declares: 'We have built the foundation for greatness.' The next step? 'We have got to win something in Europe.'

17 December 1969

A late goal from Mike Summerbee sends City to Wembley for the League Cup final, at the expense of Manchester United, prompting one national news-

 The Manchester City squad, 1967.

paper to state in its match report: 'The change of soccer power in Manchester must surely be complete now.'

15 September 1970

Although the new season would bring no additional honours, there is still something left in the City tank. Asked to name the best side he has seen so far this campaign, Sir Alf Ramsey says: 'Manchester City – by some distance.'

29 April 1970

Manchester City win the European Cup-Winners' Cup in the pouring rain of Vienna with a 2–1 win over Gornik, the highly-rated Polish side. 'We went out at the start of the season and demanded that this

competition would be ours,' Allison tells reporters. 'It came to us because we were stronger, braver and, at the tensest moments, the cooler team.'

7 March 1970

Francis Lee endures severe pain to play his part in the victory over West Bromwich Albion in the League Cup final on a muddy pitch at Wembley. 'My knee was on fire during extra-time,' Lee tells reporters after-wards, 'but when I saw our winning goal go in, I felt no pain at all.' Meanwhile Joe Mercer likens the out-standing Colin Bell to Peter Doherty, the great, all-action City inside-forward of the 1930s.

SUE LOPEZ

▶▶▶▶▶▶▶▶▶▶▶▶▶▶▶▶▶

1945–

Sue Lopez has made an outstanding contribution to women's football in England as a pioneer footballer, coach and manager during a career in the game spanning five decades.

Lopez was the first Englishwoman to play semi-professional football as an overseas player in Italy in 1971, returning home to help establish the first ever officially sanctioned England women's team. An automatic choice for seven years, she won 22 caps.

In 1978, she played a major role in organising the first England women's international to be played on a Football League ground following the rescinding of a ban on the use of such venues that dated back to 1921.

As a club player, she was the lynchpin on the left side of midfield for Southampton, the team that was almost unassailable during the 1970s. As a coach she nurtured 12 England youth internationals over a period of seven years.

Sue Lopez in training, 1974.

PLAYER • INDUCTED 2004 • 22 CAPS • 8 FA CUPS

'I am immensely proud of the work I have done to help develop the administrative side of the game and to promote the national side.' – Sue Lopez

Lopez played for Southampton in the first 10 Women's FA Cup finals, starting in 1971, amassing eight winners' medals. About the only thing she hasn't done in football is head the ball very often. 'I rarely do that because I get concussed easily,' she explained. Stan Cullis, the great Wolves centre-half, had the same trouble.

Following her retirement as a player in 1985, she became the second woman to gain the FA Advanced Licence coaching qualification. In 1999 she was named *Sunday Times*

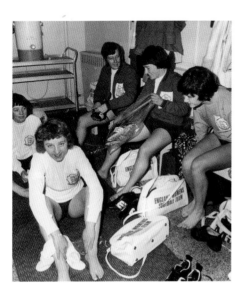

England players prepare for training, 1972.

Female Coach of the Year. The following year she was awarded an MBE.

Lopez made a dramatic impact on Roma during 1971–72, her only season in Italy, after impressing scouts at an international tournament in Turin in 1969. 'Roma Revival with Lopez' was the headline in *Corriere dello Sport*, the daily Italian sports newspaper, in May 1971. 'The newspapers in Italy took us seriously, devoting a whole page to women's football,' Lopez recalled.

Brought in to revitalise the former champions, Lopez scored 13 goals in 11 League matches. 'It was a fantastic experience,' she added.

The highlight of her stay came in a quarter-final of the National Cup. Napoli were winning 2–0 in front of a partisan home crowd of 1,000. Playing at centre-forward, she scored a hat-trick. 'Lopez lets fly at Napoli with three splendid goals,' the newspaper reported. Roma defeated Fiorentina 1–0 in the final. In the League, Roma finished runners-up, two points behind champions Piacenza in the 14-team division.

Lopez then sacrificed her career as a player in Italy to help consolidate the progress of the Women's FA following its inception in 1969, and to ensure her availability and eligibility to play for the England team.

An inaugural member of the Women's FA, Lopez assisted with administration, acting as voluntary assistant secretary for a year. In the 1980s she took on the role of vice-chair of the

► key match

England 3 Belgium 0, The Dell, Southampton, International Friendly, 31 October 1978

Sue Lopez did more than play on the left side of midfield: without her work off the field this historic fixture would not have happened. Lopez helped organise what was the first women's match to be played on a Football League ground since the rescinding of a ban first introduced in 1921.

For it to happen, she found a sponsor to cover the £2,000 expenses and performed press duties, alongside Southampton manager Lawrie McMenemy.

A crowd of 5,500 saw Lopez create the first goal with a telling pass to striker Elaine Badrock.

It was an unofficial international; the Women's FA would not come under the umbrella of the Football Association until 1993.

ruling body, before a spell as International Officer in 1992.

A highlight of her international career came in 1982 when England reached the final of the European Championships, only to lose out in a penalty shoot-out against Sweden at the end of the second leg at Kenilworth Road
.

'Roma revival with Lopez.' – headline in the *Corriere dello Sport* newspaper

ALAN BALL

▶▶▶▶▶▶▶▶▶▶▶▶▶▶▶▶▶

1945–2007

It was rare for Alf Ramsey to single out an individual for praise, but after the most important match in England's history, he made a point of speaking to Alan Ball. 'Young man,' Ramsey said, only minutes after the final whistle of the World Cup final in 1966, 'you will never play a better game in your life.'

Ramsey was not alone in his thinking. Bobby Charlton and Geoff Hurst were two of the England players most vocal in nominating Ball, then still only 21, as their man-of-the-match. Helmut Schoen, the West Germany manager, also praised his performance.

'If we had to pick a star,' Charlton said later, 'it had to be Alan. His skill, hard work, control, footwork and devastating use of the ball in the final were a revelation, and he did it all against a world-class full-back in Karl-Heinz Schnellinger.'

Alan Ball, 1968.

PLAYER • INDUCTED 2003 • 72 CAPS • 1 WORLD CUP • 1 DIVISION ONE CHAMPIONSHIP

'Stanley [Matthews] was a wonderful man, but I didn't care for reputations. I was going to walk through everybody to get where I wanted to be.' - Alan Ball

Having concluded that his team could not accommodate specialist wingers against the most powerful opposition, Ramsey needed Ball in order to make his radical tactical blue-print work. In possession the England number seven was instructed to break wide whenever possible. When Germany had the ball, it was his job to drop back, in support of full-back George Cohen and ball-winner Nobby Stiles.

The winner of 72 caps, Ball was twice sold for record transfer fees. In 1966, Everton paid Blackpool £110,000, a record sum between British clubs. Six years later, Everton realised

their profit, selling him on against his wishes to Arsenal for £220,000.

Ball was the epitome of the type of foot-baller Ramsey admired. Way back in 1952, Ramsey had written about the need for versa-tility. High in energy, Ball was prominent in a new generation of players who were capable of the multiple roles in attack and defence that Ramsey had in mind. He was determined, too.

'When I was a boy, just 17, and starting out in the professional game, people asked me what my ambition was. I told them: "To play for England in the 1966 World Cup."' In the mid 1970s, Ball was briefly made England captain. 'It was such a proud moment,' he said.

Fiercely patriotic, Ball shared Ramsey's frustration when England failed to win the European Nations Cup in 1968. He felt this was not England's proper place. He told reporters that he threw his medal for third place out of the window afterwards.

Ball won a championship medal with Everton in 1969–70, his only major club honour. 'We played purely off-the-cuff foot-ball,' he recalled. 'The improvisations were inspired.'

Either side of this triumph, Ball appeared in two FA Cup finals – for Everton in 1968 and with Arsenal in 1972 – only to finish on the losing side on both occasions. In December 1976 he joined Southampton, helping the club win promotion to the First Division in 1977–78.

Alan's six seasons at Goodison Park marked his peak as a player. 'Alan was quite

↖

Alan Ball practises one of his tricks, 1965.

↗

Alan Ball shouts instructions, 1970.

possibly the finest midfield player Everton has ever had – or is likely to have,' said team-mate Howard Kendall. Before leaving for Arsenal, Ball received a phone call from Liverpool manager Bill Shankly, who told him: 'You were great on Merseyside, son, really great.'

▶talking point

At the age of 17 Alan Ball vowed to play for England within three years, and he was not going to allow anyone, regardless of reputa-tion, to slow his progress.

As an apprentice at Blackpool it was Alan's job to clean the boots of the great Stanley Matthews. In training one day, Ball put a ball through for the winger to chase but Matthews just stood there pointing to his feet in an obvious message to his brash team-mate.

Ball had yet to play a first-team game for Blackpool, but his callowness did not stop him telling the most revered footballer in the country: 'If the pass is on, you chase it and get there.'

TEAM INDUCTEE
MANCHESTER UNITED
▶▶▶▶▶▶▶▶▶▶▶▶▶▶▶▶▶▶▶▶▶▶ **1966–1968**

20 April 1966

Matt Busby experiences defeat at the semi-final stage of Europe's top club competition for a third time. Unlike before, however, this loss – against Partizan Belgrade – creates doubt in the manager's mind. Perhaps now, at the veteran stage of his career, the last chance has gone. At this point Pat Crerand has a quiet word: 'Never mind, boss,' the midfielder says, 'we will still win this European Cup.' First, though, United have to qualify, and that means regaining the title.

George Best congratulates Bobby Charlton, 1968.

5 September 1966

The newspapers report Busby's intention to strengthen his team with the signing of a new goal-keeper. Alex Stepney duly arrives from Chelsea for a fee of £50,000.

5 November 1966

Busby describes the away match against Chelsea, the League leaders, as 'the key match of the season'. Defender Bill Foulkes is recalled after a stint in the reserves. 'The team that wins this one will win the League,' Busby tells reporters privately. The result: Chelsea 1 Manchester United 3.

10 December 1966

On the strength of a run of six successive victories, United go top. There then follows a surprise defeat at Aston Villa. Now they face third-placed Liverpool at Old Trafford in a match that sold out a fortnight ago. The match ends in a draw. The 62,500 attendance strengthens United's position as the best-supported club in England.

28 December 1966

Having surrendered top spot to Liverpool for a day, Manchester United go back to the summit with a 2–0 victory over Sheffield United.

18 February 1967

Norwich City cause the FA Cup upset of the season, inflicting United's first home defeat since the previous April. 'The Norwich goals were heart-breaking,' Busby tells reporters. In the dressing room afterwards the players are furious with themselves. 'They were now more determined than ever to win the title,' Busby said later.

25 March 1967

'We got some knocks today, but the goalless draw was worth two points for us,' Busby says, reflecting on the goalless draw at Anfield. Liverpool, Nottingham Forest and Spurs are all challenging United in this 'enthralling title race'.

6 May 1967

In its match report of the 6–1 victory at Upton Park

that secures Manchester United the title, the *Daily Express* states: 'West Ham were broken by a team who played it as it came – centre-forward David Sadler as centre-half, and every man in defence, apart from goalkeeper Alex Stepney, storming forward until West Ham were completely overrun.'

18 July 1967

Looking ahead to the following season, Matt Busby says: 'Above all else we want to win the European Cup.' Newspapers report that success in Europe will yield the club 'as much as £30,000'.

28 October 1967

Newspapers report that Denis Law will miss seven games after being suspended for fighting with Ian Ure, the Arsenal defender. In a double blow, Nobby Stiles is then ruled out for seven weeks with a cartilage injury.

Matt Busby walks towards the League championship trophy, 1967.

15 November 1967

After eliminating part-timers Hibernians, of Malta, Manchester United survive the brutal tactics of Sarejevo in the European Cup. 'That was the most disgraceful exhibition I have seen,' Busby says. 'We were lucky to get away with just a few bruises.'

27 November 1967

Newspapers report that Busby has promised his players a £10,000-a-man bonus if they win the treble of League championship, FA Cup and European Cup. Defeat against Spurs in the third round of the FA Cup puts paid to that.

13 March 1968

Manchester United overcome Gornik Zabrze in the quarter-final of the European Cup. Busby describes the second leg in Poland as 'one of our greatest nights'. Stanislay Oslizlo, the Gornik captain, says afterwards: 'We hope Manchester United win the European Cup.'

20 April 1968

The importance of the European Cup is confirmed when Busby ponders resting George Best and Bobby Charlton ahead of the semi-final against Real Madrid. In the event, both play in the League fixture against Sheffield United. Despite this victory, United go on to lose out in the title race to Manchester City.

15 May 1968

Matt Busby weeps unashamedly, and an emotional Bobby Charlton collapses on the turf after United go through to their first European Cup final after drawing 3–3 with Real Madrid in the second leg in Spain. Velazquez, the Real inside-forward says: 'I would rather United won the Cup than any other team – except, of course, Real.'

29 May 1968

Manchester United 4 Benfica 1. On hearing the result, MPs cheer in the House of Commons. Meanwhile, Otto Gloria, the Benfica manager says: 'The title of European champions is in very good hands. Manchester United are a very good club, and congratulations to them.'

EMLYN HUGHES

▶▶▶▶▶▶▶▶▶▶▶▶▶▶▶

1947–2004

After being earmarked for greatness by Bill Shankly, Emlyn Hughes twice lifted the European Cup as Liverpool captain, having established himself as a cornerstone of a side that dominated English football in the late 1970s.

Soon after signing Hughes from Blackpool for a club-record fee of £65,000 in 1967, Shankly famously – and prophetically – described his latest recruit, then a raw 19-year-old with barely two dozen first-team appearances behind him, as 'a future captain of England'.

Boundless in his energy and enthusiasm, Hughes was indefatigable, much like Shankly had been during his own days as a wing-half with Preston North End. However, of the two, Hughes was the more adaptable, excelling at both full-back and in midfield before finding a niche with both club and country as a left-sided central defender.

↖
Emlyn Hughes celebrates victory, 1977.

PLAYER • INDUCTED 2008 • 62 CAPS • 4 DIVISION ONE CHAMPIONSHIPS • 1 FA CUP

1 LEAGUE CUP • 2 EUROPEAN CUPS • 2 UEFA CUPS

> **'To the Kop, [Emlyn] was one of them – and they loved him for it.'**
> **– Graeme Souness**

The ebullient Liverpool manager had tried to buy Hughes on the spot after witnessing by chance his debut for Blackpool the previous season. Now, within a month of his arrival, Hughes was playing in front of the Kop. This was, Shankly declared emphatically, 'one of the most important signings of all time'.

In making 665 appearances and scoring 48 goals for Liverpool over the next 12 years, Hughes did all he could to justify such a bold judgement on the part of his manager.

An important turning point in Hughes' career occurred during the 1973–74 season when Shankly switched him to central defence alongside Phil Thompson. Tactically, the switch paved the way for Liverpool's emer-

Emlyn Hughes volleys the ball, 1976.

gence as the supreme power in European football under Bob Paisley.

'Liverpool had played with a big centre-half for years, but then suddenly that changed,' Hughes wrote later. 'Neither of us were particularly tall but we could play on the ground.'

By now, Hughes was an established international, having made his debut in 1969 during the Alf Ramsey era. In all, Hughes won 62 caps, 59 of them with Liverpool, establishing him as the most-capped Englishman in the club's history up to that point.

Handed the England captaincy by caretaker manager Joe Mercer in 1974, Hughes kept the job when Don Revie took over on a permanent basis. Their relationship turned sour, however, when Hughes was dropped, seemingly for good, during the 1976 European Championship qualifying campaign.

Two years and 15 internationals later, Hughes was back. In his autobiography

Emlyn Hughes raises a bottle of champagne in celebration, 1976.

published in 1980, Hughes wrote: 'Don later apologised for dropping me. He told me: "Emlyn, you proved me wrong."' His outstanding form had forced Revie's hand, and impressed the football writers who voted him their Player of the Year in 1977.

Hughes completed his haul of domestic honours in 1980 when he lifted the League Cup as captain of Wolves following a £90,000 transfer to Molineux. As he neared retirement, Hughes said: 'I would like to think I never cheated anyone on the field.'

> **'Emlyn Hughes can play in four or five different positions and still look a star.'**
> **– Bill Shankly, 1973**

▶talking point

Emlyn Hughes did more than enough to justify the nickname given to him by Liverpool fans: Crazy Horse.

It stuck with him following an incident early in his career at Anfield when he rugby-tackled an opposing forward. 'Fans saw that Emlyn was ready to die for the club,' said team-mate Graeme Souness.

His good humour was infectious but Hughes could also be distraught in defeat on the big occasion. 'Emlyn wore his emotion like a badge,' Souness added.

His lively, jocular character made Hughes an ideal team captain on the BBC's long-running quiz show *A Question of Sport*.

PAT JENNINGS

▶▶▶▶▶▶▶▶▶▶▶▶▶▶▶

1945–

Pat Jennings, the unflappable Irishman with giant hands and trademark one-handed catch, played at the highest level for 23 years, changing the way goalkeepers went about their job in the process.

The affable Jennings played for Tottenham Hotspur and Arsenal, without ever generating the animosity of either set of rival supporters; and when he staged a testimonial at Highbury in May 1985, Spurs happily accepted his invitation to be the opposition.

Jennings introduced a new style of shot-stopping, according to Bob Wilson, the goalkeeper in Arsenal's double-winning side in 1971. 'Pat's style of goalkeeping was unique in the 1970s,' Wilson said. 'No one had used their feet in the natural way Pat had. These days, saving with the feet is commonplace, is essential, and its origin lies with him.'

Pat Jennings stands in goal at Highbury, 1982.

PLAYER • INDUCTED 2003 • 119 CAPS • 1 UEFA CUP • 2 FA CUPS • 2 LEAGUE CUPS

'Pat Jennings was as calm, cool and collected as anyone could possibly be. For a goalkeeper he was like Buddha. In fact, at Arsenal, we called him "God".' – Viv Anderson

Jennings, the oldest British player to appear in a World Cup finals tournament, was voted Footballer of the Year in 1972–73 during his time at White Hart Lane.

'Pat was a brilliant shot-stopper, his positional sense was outstanding and he commanded his area,' Jimmy Greaves said. 'His remarkable consistency and dependability spread confidence through, not just the defence, but the entire team.'

Sir Alf Ramsey recognised Jennings' ability by selecting him in a British XI in a match to celebrate entry into the Common Market in 1973. 'I was thrilled to get the nod ahead of Peter Shilton and Ray Clemence, both of

Pat Jennings holds the ball, 1964.

whom I rate as exceptional goalkeepers,' Jennings said.

Terry Neill, the Arsenal manager, described the outlay of £40,000 to bring Jennings, then aged 32, to Highbury in August 1977 as 'one of the best transfer deals I made during my career'.

In contrast, his counterpart at Spurs, Keith Burkinshaw, later admitted that the deal was the worst decision he ever made. There was plenty of time for the Tottenham manager to rue his mistake: Jennings made another 300 plus first-team appearances.

As a teenager growing up in Northern Ireland, Jennings played Gaelic football, a sport that demands physical strength, courage, good handling skills and kicking – all vital attributes for a goalkeeper.

'You have to withstand knocks, and all the time you are leaping to catch the ball against opponents,' he said. 'Catching the ball one-handed was another skill I developed, and

Pat Jennings and Joe KInnear walk out of the tunnel at Wembley, 1971.

that's been useful for crosses that might otherwise be just out of reach with two hands, even if it might appear a trifle showy.'

In 1963 Jennings represented Northern Ireland at an international youth tournament at Wembley, attracting the interest of Bill McGarry, the Watford manager. After one season at Vicarage Road he joined Spurs for a fee of £27,500, a sizeable sum for a goalkeeper at the time. At the age of 19 he was thrown straight into action.

Jennings also made his international debut as a teenager. Almost two decades later he finally achieved his ambition of playing in a World Cup. Remarkably, Northern Ireland qualified again four years later. In his record 119th and final appearance for his country, Jennings made an emotional farewell – against mighty Brazil in Mexico – on his 41st birthday.

▶talking point

No one inside Old Trafford knew quite how to react when Pat Jennings scored the equalising goal in the Charity Shield game in August 1967.

The crowed went strangely quiet, almost in disbelief. His stunned team-mates did not even congratulate him. 'It was a freak goal,' Jennings said.

Jennings' prodigious kick down field had sailed, first bounce, over the head of the advancing Alex Stepney, his opposite number in the Manchester United goal.

'I wasn't even sure if it counted in the laws of the game, so I didn't celebrate,' Jennings recalled. 'Even the referee seemed to hesitate before deciding it must be a goal.'

FRANK McLINTOCK

▶▶▶▶▶▶▶▶▶▶▶▶▶▶▶▶

1939–

Frank McLintock made things happen. From his position in either midfield or defence he transformed the fortunes of every club he played for. His influence worked the other way, too. Each time he left a club the team went into relative decline. The pattern was repeated at Leicester City, Arsenal and Queens Park Rangers.

As a young, dynamic wing-half, McLintock made his name at Leicester – winners of the League Cup, two-time FA Cup finalists and challengers for the title in the early 1960s. Then, in later years, he utilised his experience as 'the spare man at the back' when QPR came within one point of the championship title in 1975–76. In doing so, Rangers qualified for Europe for the first time.

Of course, the competitive Scot made his greatest impact as the captain of Arsenal, winners of the League and FA Cup double in 1970–71. His influence over the side was recognised and celebrated by football writers, who voted him their Footballer of the Year.

Frank McLintock, 1972.

PLAYER • INDUCTED 2009 • 63 CAPS • 1 DIVISION ONE CHAMPIONSHIP

1 FA CUP • 1 LEAGUE CUP • 1 FAIRS CUP

'The greatest captain in English football.'
– Don Howe

The previous season, following his switch from midfield to central defence, McLintock led the Gunners to their first European triumph – victory over Anderlecht in the Fairs Cup final.

The then Arsenal coach Don Howe rated McLintock the best captain in the game. 'I am beginning to feel obsolete in the dressing room,' Howe said. 'Frank is doing as much talking as I am – and he's working wonders with his words. He lifts players up. His influence runs right through the team.'

McLintock had made his debut for Leicester in 1959. Two years later, Leicester finished sixth in the First Division, the club's best posi-

Frank McLintock intercepts a pass, 1972.

tion since the late 1920s, and reached the FA Cup final. His disappointment in defeat against Spurs was so great that he threw away his losers' medal in the dressing room but fortunately one of his team-mates picked the medal up and gave it back to him later.

Rival clubs were now circling. Both Bill Shankly and Don Revie wanted to sign him. McLintock ended up, however, at Arsenal. There would be more Cup final disappointments at Wembley before McLintock finally led a team to victory under the Twin Towers. Reporting the defeat of Liverpool in the 1971 FA Cup final, *The Times* stated: 'McLintock has proved himself Arsenal's big man by example and resilient leadership.'

All of which made his subsequent departure from Arsenal, in 1973, incomprehensible

Frank McLintock celebrates victory in the Fairs Cup final, 1970.

for many of his team-mates. Years later, Bertie Mee, the Arsenal manager, was reported as describing his decision to allow the transfer to QPR as 'the biggest mistake of my career'.

At Loftus Road, McLintock played a crucial role, as Rangers manager Dave Sexton introduced a variation of 'Total Football', the tactics honed by Ajax and the Holland national side. QPR relied heavily on the veteran McLintock's passing ability and vision, as the west London club enjoyed its heyday.

In 1979, the Liverpool manager Bob Paisley selected McLintock as his 'player of the decade'; meanwhile, former team-mate Alan Ball described him as 'the best, most forceful captain I have ever played under'.

BOB PAISLEY ▶▶▶▶▶▶▶▶▶▶▶▶▶▶▶

1919–1996

Bob Paisley was reluctant to take charge at Liverpool because of the doubts he had about his ability to do the job. It was a rare example of poor judgement by a shrewd man who went on to become the most successful club manager in history.

Paisley had been a loyal assistant manager at Anfield for three years before the sudden, shock retirement of Bill Shankly in 1974 thrust him into the limelight at the age of 55. It was the beginning of the most illustrious chapter in the history of the club.

'I never wanted this job in the first place, and I'm not even sure that I can do it,' Paisley told the players at his first team meeting as manager. 'I need all the help I can get from you lads. There will be no disruption to the team. Let's just keep playing the Liverpool way.'

Although impressed by his 'refreshing honesty and modesty that typified his personality', Kevin Keegan worried that Paisley might be overwhelmed by the challenge of succeeding Shankly. 'Bob surprised us all, even himself,' Keegan recalled. 'He grew into the job, sensibly sticking with the team and the tactics he had inherited from Shanks while gradually implanting his own ideas.'

Over the next nine years Liverpool established themselves as the most powerful club in Europe, winning the European Cup three times, a feat beyond any other British manager in history, and a host of domestic honours. 'The sort of lad I am looking for as a Liverpool player will try to nutmeg Kevin Keegan in training, but will then step aside for him in the corridor,' Paisley said.

A modest, unassuming man with 'no airs or graces about him', Paisley was very decisive when it came to tactics and substitutions, according to Kenny Dalglish, who added: 'his knack of making the right decisions under pressure made him a great manager.'

Bob Paisley travels by train to Liverpool with the European Cup, 1978.

▶ key match

Liverpool 1 Real Madrid 0, European Cup final, Paris, 27 May 1981

Bob Paisley took particular professional satisfaction in this defeat of the Spanish aristocrats who dominated European football with such panache during the 1950s.

'Real Madrid set standards of excellence in the European Cup,' Paisley said later, 'so it means all the more that English teams are now providing the benchmark for quality.'

With the minutes ticking away in a tight game, Alan Kennedy the Liverpool left-back, scored the winner with a rising shot from a narrow angle.

'I'm so proud to be the manager of the first British club to win the European Cup three times,' Paisley said. 'We controlled most of the second half, and I am sure that Real don't begrudge us our victory.'

As ever, Paisley fought against complacency. Considering this side past its peak, he dismantled it. The following season, Liverpool won the title and League Cup double.

MANAGER • INDUCTED 2002 • 3 EUROPEAN CUPS • 1 UEFA CUP • 6 DIVISION ONE CHAMPIONSHIPS

3 LEAGUE CUPS

'**A master tactician. I cannot recall him ever shouting at me. If he had something to say he would have a quiet word with the player on one side.**'
– Ian Callaghan

Bob Paisley devoted his working life to Liverpool Football Club. Forty-four years almost to the day after signing for the club in 1939, he walked down the tunnel at the end of his last game in charge as manager. He was 64 years of age. The only interruption came during the war. For years the players knew him affectionately as 'The Rat', the nickname he was given after fighting in the Army as a Desert Rat in North Africa.

Born in County Durham, Paisley arrived at Anfield just before the war after winning an FA Amateur Cup medal with Bishop Auckland. He served the club as player, trainer, physiotherapist, coach and assistant manager before succeeding Shankly.

On taking over, Paisley refused to be awed by the intense, passionate bond between Shankly and the Kop. Indeed, he was prepared to challenge the status quo. Liverpool, he argued, had a habit of playing flat-out all the time.

'At Anfield the crowd makes demands on us as to how we should play,' Paisley said. 'There is all this energy coming down from the terraces. This is not always the best thing. We are looking to balance our play a bit more. To have a bit more variety.'

Paisley emerged from the shadow of his extrovert predecessor in 1975–76, when Liverpool won the League championship and the UEFA Cup double. Even then he deflected attention. 'The club has been geared for this for 15 years,' he said. 'I just helped things along. This success is down to our players doing the simple things well,' he added. 'That's the way we intend to continue, the Liverpool way.'

Bob Paisley carries Emlyn Hughes off the pitch, 1968.

A decade earlier Paisley had identified the recipe for success in Europe. 'We must learn from teams on the Continent that we can't go and win the ball individually, we're to win the ball collectively,' he told the players. In 1977, Liverpool became only the second English club to lift the European Cup.

Paisley described the performance against Borussia Mönchengladbach as 'one of the best ever seen' in a final. 'I hope I am not being boastful when I say I think that this is only the start. There is no team in the world that we need fear,' he said. Liverpool defended the trophy the following season.

In 1978–79, Liverpool amassed a record total of 68 points and a goal difference of plus 69 in the League. There were 28 clean sheets, and only four goals were conceded at Anfield. 'We have won the championship with a style

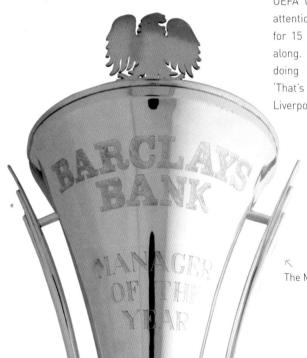

The Manager of the Year trophy.

The Canon League Division One trophy, 1983.

Bob Paisley holds aloft the League championship trophy, 1983.

that shows British football at its best,' Paisley said. 'It is a triumph for teamwork.'

Through it all, Paisley wore his flat caps and cardigans, a homely image that belied his single-minded determination to succeed. Matt Busby spoke of his friend's 'inner steel and his tough, stubborn streak'.

Alan Hansen noted 'an absolute lack of sentiment' in Paisley when it came to selecting a team. The best 11 fit players took the field – regardless of past results. Meanwhile, no one stayed at Anfield beyond his 'sell-by-date' in football terms, irrespective of reputation or past service. 'Once they have come down from that level it is not fair to them or the club to keep them,' Paisley said.

'This game can kick you in the teeth,' the manager repeatedly told his players. 'If we give in to complacency, there is only one way to go, and that is down.'

RAY CLEMENCE

▶▶▶▶▶▶▶▶▶▶▶▶▶▶▶▶▶▶

1948–

'We had a great team in the 1960s,' Bill Shankly once wrote, 'but if we'd had Ray Clemence in goal, Liverpool would have won the European Cup and all the cups under the sun.'

Of course, once Clemence had established himself as Liverpool's number one, Liverpool *did* go on to win European Cups and a host of other honours during the 1970s. Of all the factors behind that success, Shankly pinpointed his keeper's excellence and consistency as the most important.

His signing by Shankly from Scunthorpe United in 1967 for a fee of £18,000 proved to be one of the best bits of business ever conducted by Liverpool. Fourteen years and 665 appearances later, when Clemence joined Tottenham Hotspur, Liverpool received 20 times their original outlay.

'Before a big game Ray had this look about him,' Graeme Souness recalled. 'We knew then that there'd be little in it for the opposition.'

Ray Clemence watches the action, 1983.

PLAYER • INDUCTED 2010 • 61 CAPS • 5 DIVISION ONE CHAMPIONSHIPS • 2 FA CUPS

1 LEAGUE CUP • 3 EUROPEAN CUPS • 3 UEFA CUPS

His last competitive act as a Liverpool player was to keep a clean sheet in the 1981 European Cup final against Real Madrid. When his departure was confirmed, Bob Paisley the then Liverpool manager, said: 'This is the biggest blow to me since I had to let Kevin Keegan move to the Continent in 1977.'

Physically, the right-handed Clemence – who unusually kicked with his left foot – considered himself a natural for the job. 'I had the perfect balance for a goalkeeper,' he once wrote. 'There was no secret behind it. I was lucky. It was the way my body was made to work. Diving one way or the other felt just the same for me.'

Only six times during the previous 11 years had Liverpool taken the field for a League

↖

Ray Clemence holds aloft the FA Cup, 1974.

game without him – testimony to his remarkable consistency and durability. 'Ray can play with his eyes shut,' Bob Paisley said.

Having waited patiently for his chance to succeed Tommy Lawrence, Clemence initially operated behind a defence marshalled by centre-half Ron Yeats, a dominating figure in the air near goal. Yeats was followed by Larry Lloyd, a number five in the same mould.

As his confidence grew, Clemence won over the Kop with his sharp reflexes, safe handling, keen positional sense and exceptional anticipation. His one obvious weakness – goal-kicking – was put right with hard work on the training ground.

When Liverpool revised their tactics with the introduction of more mobile, skilful centre-backs in Phil Thompson and Alan Hansen, more responsibility fell on Clemence – both in the air, when crosses came in, and on the ground.

'Ray was a great communicator, repeatedly shouting about my positioning,' Hansen recalled. 'Our back four pushed up, defending a line further up the field. Ray was like a third back, even a sweeper, with the speed and understanding to go straight to the source of any threat.'

Following his transfer to White Hart Lane, Clemence added another FA Cup and UEFA Cup medal to his collection. In total, he made more than 300 appearances for Spurs.

Forced to retire in 1988 because of injury, Clemence stayed on as a goalkeeping coach, a

↗

Ray Clemence patrols his goal area, 1971.

role he would later perform for England. 'You don't lose a player of Ray's quality without it having an effect,' said Terry Venables, the then Spurs manager.

▶ talking point

Ray Clemence was engaged in a lengthy and ongoing battle with Peter Shilton for ownership of the green England number one jersey.

A winner of 61 caps over a period of 11 years, Clemence enjoyed his best run at international level during Don Revie's time in charge in the mid 1970s. His consistency so frustrated his rival that at one point Shilton seriously contemplated retirement from international football.

The next England manager, Ron Greenwood, could not separate them, opting at first to alternate his keepers. 'Both Ray and Peter were magnificent,' he said.

A highlight of his career occurred when Clemence became the first goalkeeper to captain England since Frank Swift in 1948.

LIAM BRADY

▶▶▶▶▶▶▶▶▶▶▶▶▶▶▶▶▶▶

1956–

Three decades after Liam Brady last wore the red and white of Arsenal in a competitive fixture, he remains a cult figure in the eyes of Gunners fans.

The club's official history referred to the Irishman reverentially as 'a midfield general of sublime vision and skill who could drift past opponents as though they were not there'. In another passage, particular and fulsome praise was reserved for Brady's passing ability with a left foot described, rather poetically, as 'an instrument of almost celestial precision'.

The history, published in 2004, dwells understandably on one match: the extraordinary 'Five-minute final' at Wembley in 1979, when Brady's talent and courage lifted Arsenal off the floor in the dying seconds, propelling them to a stunning victory.

As had happened so often during his seven-year career at Highbury, when the Gunners needed inspiration, it was their curly-haired linchpin who supplied it.

↖
Liam Brady brings the ball under control, 1979.

PLAYER • INDUCTED 2006 • 72 CAPS • 1 FA CUP

'In football parlance, if you cut him he [Brady] would bleed Arsenal. He was revered by every single Arsenal supporter.'
– Nick Hornby, *Fever Pitch*

That defeat of Manchester United gave Brady his only honour as an Arsenal player. There would be three other finals with the Gunners – in the FA Cup, twice, and the European Cup-Winners' Cup; although each ended in disappointment.

His contribution was recognised both inside and outside the club. According to the official history, Brady – voted Footballer of the Year by his fellow professionals in 1979 – was 'the choice of many fans as the finest

↗
Liam Brady salutes the Arsenal fans, 1978.

player in Arsenal's history'.

For fans, 'Chippy' Brady was one of them: a Gooner who loved his chips – hence the nickname. His background as a product of the youth system only added to his popularity.

Brady joined the Gunners at the age of 15, in 1971. Two years later he made his debut for a side then in decline. By the end of the decade, under manager Terry Neill, Brady had established himself as a playmaker.

As Brady improved, so did Arsenal – proof of which came with three successive FA Cup final appearances between 1978 and 1980, with victory over Manchester United sandwiched between defeats against Ipswich Town and West Ham United.

Victory in the 1979 final was all the more important to him because Brady had by now decided to leave the club – once his contract expired in 1980. In response, Arsenal offered to make him the best-paid player in England,

↖
Liam Brady celebrates a goal, 1980.

but Brady was determined to pursue a career in Italy where he went on to enjoy championship success with Juventus.

So, at the age of 24, Brady walked away from Highbury after scoring 59 goals in 306 appearances. Terry Neill described the departure as 'a tragedy of monumental proportions for the club'. It would be another seven years before Arsenal won another major honour.

At international level, Brady amassed 72 caps for the Republic of Ireland between 1974 and 1990. 'Liam is the most accomplished player ever to represent this country,' said Eoin Hand, the Irish manager.

After leaving Juventus, Brady enjoyed spells at Sampdoria, Internazionale and Ascoli, before returning to Britain to play out his career at West Ham United.

BRIAN CLOUGH ▶▶▶▶▶▶▶▶▶▶▶

1935–2004

A mercurial master of man-management, Brian Clough astonished the football world when he took a modest, previously unheralded provincial club and moulded them into European champions.

When Nottingham Forest rose from second-tier mediocrity to the summit of the European game, Clough achieved an unprecedented feat – no manager before or since has caused such an upheaval in the established order. No respecter of hierarchy, Clough challenged the elite – and beat them.

Having defeated Malmo of Sweden in the 1979 European Cup final, the charismatic, idiosyncratic and unpredictable Clough proved his point by defending the trophy – this time against even greater odds, by defeating Hamburg.

A champion of English football, like Alf Ramsey before him, Clough said afterwards: 'We gave Hamburg a lesson in application, determination, dedication and pride; all the things that are taken for granted in our domestic football.'

Such achievements were no fluke. Clough had followed a similar path before with another provincial club – Derby County. In the late 1960s, they too rose from a lower division. As champions, their challenge for the European Cup ended in failure – a defeat Clough always attributed to Continental bribery and corruption.

Domestically, Clough was the first manager to win the championship with two different clubs since the inter-war years when Herbert Chapman achieved the feat with Huddersfield Town and Arsenal. More recently, Kenny Dalglish did the same, with Liverpool and Blackburn Rovers. Of the three managers, however, Clough had by far the most meagre financial resources at his command compared to his rival clubs of the day.

Brian Clough looks on from the dug-out, 1988.

▶ key match

Nottingham Forest 1 Malmo 0, European Cup final, Munich, 30 May 1979

Brian Clough proved the value of his unconventional methods by inviting the Forest players to drink a beer with him on the coach journey to the ground.

Clough wanted his players relaxed and their minds distracted. 'Better for them to have a drink than sit there bored to a stupor watching a bloody video of opponents who weren't as good as us,' Clough said later.

The Swedes were a dour, defensive side who relied on rare breaks against Forest. Clough would not be drawn into their trap. 'He told us not to be reckless when going forward,' Peter Shilton recalled.

To counter Malmo's offside trap, Trevor Francis was deployed in midfield, with orders to join the attack late. When John Robertson began a weaving run down the flank, Francis sensed his chance. A diving header at the end of a 50-yard run gave Forest their winner.

MANAGER • INDUCTED 2002 • 2 EUROPEAN CUPS • 2 DIVISION ONE CHAMPIONSHIPS • 4 LEAGUE CUPS

He compensated for this relative lack of financial clout with a mastery of psychology and a genius for publicity. Sometimes, he kept his players mentally alert by doing the unexpected – such as preparing for a European Cup final by taking the players on a week's holiday to Majorca. Other times, it was all about keeping his players relaxed. 'No one can achieve anything worthwhile in life unless they are relaxed,' he always said.

'A player can never feel too sure of himself,' said Archie Gemmill. 'That is the manager's secret,' Peter Shilton said. 'He had a unique style, but it certainly worked.'

Brian Clough enjoyed almost all his success working in partnership with Peter Taylor. They complemented each other perfectly. Clough was brash, opinionated and unpredictable; Taylor was calm, methodical and calculated. The pair met as players at Middlesbrough and worked together in man-

The Simod Cup, a trophy won by Nottingham Forest in 1989 versus Everton at Wembley.

agement at Hartlepool United, Derby County and Nottingham Forest.

'Nobody could touch Peter as a judge of talent,' Clough said. 'His sense of humour was also a key component of our success together.' Clough recognised the contribution made by Taylor by inviting him to lead out the Forest side before the League Cup final in 1979.

Taylor was also a masterful operator in the transfer market. While the duo were at Nottingham Forest, Archie Gemmill was bought from Derby County for a fee of £20,000 plus goalkeeper Jim Middleton. Then, in 1979, Gemmill was sold on to Birmingham City for £150,000. 'What an amazing deal!' Clough said later. But Clough was also prepared to spend money and he became the first manager to pay £1 million for a player when he signed Trevor Francis from Birmingham City in February 1979, doubling the previous record.

Under Clough, Forest looked for experienced players who had yet to achieve success but who still burned with ambition. In July 1977 he signed Kenny Burns, 'an overweight striker at Birmingham City', and promptly converted him into a sweeper. Even Burns was

Brian Clough works in his office, 1969.

taken aback. The following season he was Footballer of the Year.

Gary Birtles was another find. A carpet-fitter by trade, he was bought from non-League football for £2,000 and went on to play for England.

Clough did not lack self-belief. Before the start of the 1968–69 season, he predicted during a television interview that Derby would win promotion. The previous season the club had finished fifth from bottom. At the risk of looking foolish, Clough agreed that the interview should be screened at the end of the season. In May, Derby were crowned champions.

Some observers accused him of arrogance, and when he was awarded the OBE in 1991, Clough played up to his reputation by joking that the letters stood for 'Old Big 'Ead'.

His self-belief lay at the root of his unorthodox behaviour. As Derby manager, he wanted to sign David Nish, the Leicester City

Brian Clough poses for promotional photos for ITV programme *The Big Match*, 1973.

full-back. 'I actually gate-crashed a board meeting at Leicester,' Clough recalled. 'I breezed straight in, large as life, and told them I'd come to sign Nish.' And he did, for a British record fee of £225,000.

At the other end of the scale, Clough was prepared to wait several hours in the reception rooms at White Hart Lane in order to sign Dave Mackay from Spurs.

His motivational team-talks could be equally unconventional. At half-time at one home game, with Forest losing, he locked the players out of the dressing room. Taken aback, the players were handed a football. 'You were rubbish,' he told them. 'Now go out there and do something to entertain the crowd for ten minutes.' Forest won the game.

He did not hesitate to confront authority

brian clough

Centre-forward   MIDDLESBROUGH & ENGLAND

> ## ▶ talking point

During his time as a prolific goalscorer with Sunderland, Brian Clough spent a lot of time studying the approach of Alan Brown, the disciplinarian manager at Roker Park. What he saw shaped his own managerial style.

'The manager detested shabby appearance and unkempt hair,' Clough recalled. 'I always maintained those same standards with my players when I became a manager.'

Clough, like Brown, forbade dissent to referees. Indeed, he encouraged officials to book anyone who challenged authority. Arguing, he told his players, disrupted concentration, led to unnecessary bookings, which in turn disrupted the team because of suspensions.

To maintain a silence in the face of provocation or perceived injustice required discipline, and Clough believed this mental strength was essential if his teams were to succeed in Europe, especially when playing in front of hostile crowds away from home.

There was one other lesson Clough learned from the dictatorial, uncompromising Brown. 'Most of all he taught me that a football manager is boss,' Clough said. When injury forced him to retire as a player at the age of 29, Clough soon had the chance to put his theories to the test.

when he thought the cause right. At the end of the League Cup final in 1979 he broke with custom by walking up the steps to the Royal Box. No manager had ever done that, not even Alf Ramsey after England won the World Cup in 1966. Forest had won, and Clough decided the manager deserved some recognition.

An ABC picture card dating from the 1950s.

COLIN BELL

▶▶▶▶▶▶▶▶▶▶▶▶▶▶▶

1946–

Colin Bell, the footballer nicknamed after a famous racehorse because of his extraordinary stamina, supplied the energy and skill that propelled Manchester City's rise to prominence in the late 1960s.

Bell played 48 times for England, establishing him as Manchester City's most-capped player. For several seasons he was an automatic choice at international level but his ambition to reach a century of caps was ruined by serious injury. 'I felt I could have played for England for another six years,' Bell said.

'A world-class player,' said Malcolm Allison, the Manchester City manager. 'The City team had a beautiful balance of strength and skill, and Colin was the key piece in the jigsaw. He was so versatile in central midfield: he defended well, could break from deep positions, and he scored goals. He ran all day and had a real footballer's brain,' wrote Allison, the originator of Bell's nickname, Nijinsky, the thoroughbred Derby winner.

Colin Bell, 1972.

PLAYER • INDUCTED 2005 • 48 CAPS • 1 DIVISION ONE CHAMPIONSHIP • 1 FA CUP

1 EUROPEAN CUP-WINNERS' CUP • 1 LEAGUE CUP

Over a period of three seasons starting in 1967–68, Manchester City collected four major club honours. By the end of the decade, as Bell departed with England for the World Cup in Mexico, his club laid claim to having the best team in the League.

Harold Shepherdson, assistant to Alf Ramsey, was asked soon afterwards to name the fittest footballer in Britain. 'I have no hesitation in giving the title to Colin Bell,' he replied.

In their preparations for the tournament, the England players competed against each other in various disciplines one day as a way of adding interest in training. 'It was like a small athletics meeting,' Shepherdson recalled, 'and the whole squad took it very seriously. We had sprints, races over 220 yards and one mile, jumping, bench hurdles, javelin-throwing, shot-putting, long jump, pull-ups, and throwing a cricket ball.' Bell dominated his team-mates throughout, winning a total of seven 'gold medals'.

'I was at my best once we got beyond 220 yards or so,' Bell recalled. 'I was very good at running at three-quarters maximum pace. I could go at that pace all day.'

For City and Bell, a serious title challenge and losing League Cup appearance followed in the 1970s; then, suddenly, it was effectively all over. 'Basically, one tackle ... ended my career,' Bell said, referring to the injury he sustained in a League Cup tie against Manchester United in the 1975–76 season.

He fought doggedly to regain full fitness, making several comebacks, but each time he broke down. Finally conceding defeat, he retired in 1979.

After emerging as a prospect at Bury, Bell was signed for a fee of £45,000 in March 1966. 'What an unbelievable bargain,' Malcolm Allison said a decade later.

After securing promotion, City won the championship in 1967–68. City's captain Mike Doyle highlighted Bell's performance in the penultimate fixture, a 3–1 win at Tottenham Hotspur, as critical. 'Colin was everywhere that day. It was one of the finest displays I've ever seen.'

Doyle was the first person to run over when Bell sustained his appalling knee injury. 'I heard Colin say through clenched teeth, "It's gone, good and proper." It was a terrible blow for the club and a personal tragedy for Colin,' Doyle wrote. 'For me, he was the perfect inside-forward.'

Colin Bell gets the better of Germany's Franz Beckenbauer, 1970.

GRAEME SOUNESS

▶▶▶▶▶▶▶▶▶▶▶▶▶▶▶▶

1953–

A commanding midfielder of deft touch and crunching intent, Graeme Souness was the most successful Liverpool captain in history – and an inspirational figure whose departure challenged the Anfield doctrine that no player is irreplaceable.

Soon after arriving at Liverpool for a record fee, the combative Scot delivered the incisive pass that set up Kenny Dalglish for the winning goal in the 1978 European Cup final against Bruges at Wembley Stadium.

With his last kick for Liverpool, six years later, the owner of the famous moustache in football converted a vital penalty as the Reds won Europe's most prestigious club competition for a fourth time.

Graeme Souness was not one to fluff his lines, on or off the field – not even when it came to his cameo role as himself in the 1982 television drama *Boys From The Blackstuff*.

↖
Graeme Souness holds up the League championship trophy, 1982.

PLAYER • INDUCTED 2007 • 54 CAPS • 3 EUROPEAN CUPS • 4 LEAGUE CUPS

5 DIVISION ONE CHAMPIONSHIPS

'Graeme was so important to Liverpool as a tremendous driving force. He kept the whole midfield and front line going. A world-class player.' – Ian Rush

Dictatorial and all-pervading, Souness combined skill and aggression in equal measure. He was abrasive and calculating, clever and precise. Possession was sought with a relentless ferocity; then, once won, Souness turned creator, spearing passes in all directions. 'Graeme has got vision and he's got strength,' Bob Paisley noted.

Never one to lack belief in his own ability, Souness began his career at Tottenham Hotspur, whose manager at the time, Bill Nicholson, compared him to Dave Mackay the great Spurs leader of the 1960s.

Convinced that he merited a first-team place, despite his youth and inexperience,

Souness became impatient with his lack of progress at White Hart Lane. A transfer to Middlesbrough secured first-team football, under the tutelage of Jack Charlton, the then Boro manager. Charlton put him in the middle of the park and told him to keep things simple. Boro duly won promotion to the top flight in 1973–74; and Souness now had the stage he wanted.

His performances over the next four years alerted Liverpool, and as soon as Middlesbrough decided to cash in, Paisley moved swiftly, finalising the deal within a matter of minutes. The fee of £352,000 was a record cash deal between English clubs.

The 24-year-old made an immediate impact at Anfield. His first goal – a stunning left-foot volley into the top corner against Manchester United in 1978 – endeared him to the Kop.

At his peak, Souness embodied the Liverpool side that dominated English football during the Paisley era. Nicknamed 'Champagne Charlie' on account of his extravagant lifestyle off the pitch, Souness combined toughness and relentless ambition with power and panache – just like Liverpool at their best. Paisley saw in him a touch of arrogance, a quality the Reds manager thought essential in a captain.

As captain, Souness refused to be intimidated, no matter the provocation or threats. He demanded the highest standards, other-

Graeme Souness shields the ball from Everton defender Kevin Ratcliffe, 1984.

▶ key match

Liverpool 1 Roma 1 (aet, Liverpool won 4–2 on penalties), European Cup final, Rome, 30 May 1984

The final was to be played at the Olympic Stadium – the home ground of their Italian opponents. 'We've no worries about going there,' Graeme Souness said beforehand. 'When you're under pressure, it puts you on your toes.'

Full-back Phil Neal put Liverpool ahead from close range, only for Roma to equalise late in the half.

There were no more goals, so it all came down to penalties. Steve Nicol missed his spot kick, but the other Liverpool players held their nerve, including Souness and match-winner Alan Kennedy. 'When Alan scored I went berserk,' Souness said. 'For the first time in my career I wept tears of joy.'

wise 'tea cups would fly in the dressing room', recalled team-mate Ian Rush.

Before his departure to Italy in 1984, the Scot scored the winning goal in the League Cup final replay, the first part of an unprecedented treble. In seven seasons at Anfield, Souness helped Liverpool win 12 major trophies, including five titles and three European Cups.

In their heyday, Liverpool always seemed to replace their best players seamlessly, most notably when Dalglish took over from Kevin Keegan in 1977. But when Souness left for Sampdoria, he left a void that could not be filled immediately. 'Graeme was the top man,' Ian Rush said. 'Simply irreplaceable.'

PETER SHILTON ▶▶▶▶▶▶▶▶▶▶▶

1949-

After overcoming the most daunting challenge imaginable for a teenage goalkeeper, Peter Shilton ended a career of exceptional longevity as the most-capped Englishman in history.

At the age of 17 Shilton was already deemed ready and able to supplant Gordon Banks – a World Cup winner with England the previous summer – as first-choice goalkeeper at Leicester City.

With two such outstanding keepers on their books, Leicester opted to cash in on Banks, such was the strength of their conviction that Shilton had a glittering future in the game. It was a faith Shilton vindicated to the full over the ensuing three decades.

After making his debut for England in 1970, Shilton went on to collect a record 125 caps spread over a 20-year period – a length of service surpassed only by the great Stanley Matthews during the modern era.

At club level, following a stint at Stoke City, Shilton moved on to Nottingham Forest where he collected two European Cup winners' medals. 'Even as a teenager at Filbert Street, his maturity and technique were outstanding,' Peter Taylor, the then Forest assistant manager wrote later. 'He instinctively knew the tricks of the trade at that age. Signing Peter in 1977 was a highlight of my career.'

Brian Clough paid a fee of £275,000 – a record sum for a keeper – to bring Shilton to the City Ground. 'He was worth twice the price,' the Forest manager said, citing as evidence the 24 goals Forest conceded in 42 games on their way to the title in 1977–78.

During that outstanding campaign, Shilton kept 25 clean-sheets. 'We had a firm belief that if we scored, there was no way we'd lose because the opposition would not be able to score against our defence and goalkeeper,' Clough said.

Peter Shilton makes a diving save in training, 1973.

PLAYER • INDUCTED 2002 • 125 CAPS • 2 EUROPEAN CUPS • 1 LEAGUE CUP

1 DIVISION ONE CHAMPIONSHIP

'A phenomenal goalkeeper. Simple as that.' – Bobby Robson

As a boy, Peter Shilton was prepared to stretch himself – literally! – in pursuit of his ambition to become a top-class goalkeeper.

He began training at Leicester City, his hometown club, at the age of 11. At home, he stood under a streetlamp for up to two hours at a time in the evening, catching a ball as it rebounded off a wall. 'It was great practice for my handling and footwork,' he said.

Fearing that he might not grow tall enough to make the grade as a goalkeeper, the young Shilton took to hanging from the banister at home. 'My mum would hang on to my legs and try to stretch me! Whether this had any effect I don't know, but I shot up from the time I was 13.'

Shilton studied the great goalkeepers of the time in order to learn his trade. He tried to copy the positional sense of Gordon Banks,

the presence in goal of Lev Yashin, the Russian goalkeeper, and the agility and distribution of Peter Bonetti of Chelsea.

'I noticed that Gordon was never caught out as the ball was struck; that Yashin projected an aura of invincibility; and that Peter was willing to take responsibility for crosses, and I wanted to bring these qualities to my game.'

Established as an England Youth regular at the age of 17, Shilton was the subject of a transfer bid by Arsenal in 1967. It was now that Leicester City decided to sell Gordon Banks for a world record fee of £60,000 for a goalkeeper.

However, the search for improvement went on, and Shilton found inspiration in some unusual places. In 1974 he sought the advice of a ballroom dancer whose ideas on balance, foot movement and running found a receptive audience. 'I changed my posture, how I turned from the hips,' Shilton said. 'I threw my weight slightly forward and learned how to keep my feet light and close to the ground, moving them as if skating on ice.'

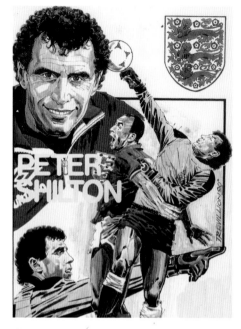

Peter Shilton, (Trevillion).

Peter Shilton was the first-choice goalkeeper for England at three successive World Cup tournaments – 1982 in Spain, 1986 in Mexico and 1990 in Italy. In 125 international appearances he conceded 80 goals.

His career with England covered the eras of four national team managers: Alf Ramsey, who gave him his debut in 1970, Don Revie, Ron Greenwood and Bobby Robson. Had it not been for the challenge of Ray Clemence during the mid to late 1970s, Shilton would almost certainly have amassed a world record 175 or more caps.

Peter Shilton playing for Nottingham Forest, 1980.

↗
Peter Shilton catches the ball, 1973.

By the early 1980s Bobby Robson had identified Shilton as the best goalkeeper of the post-war era. 'I think the likes of Lev Yashin, Dino Zoff of Italy and the Brazilian Gilmar could consider themselves lucky to be classed in his company,' he said.

A decade later, during which time Shilton enjoyed stints with Southampton and Derby County, Robson wrote: 'Peter was always the first name I wrote on the England team-sheet. He was so consistent – big in goal, long arms and a good leap.'

↖
The PFA Footballer of the Year trophy.

Leyton Orient laid out the red carpet for Peter Shilton when he became the first player in the history of English football to play 1,000 League matches – 31 years after he signed professional forms with Leicester City.

Fittingly, he kept a clean sheet in a 2–0 win over Brighton, the third time he had stopped the opposition scoring in his four appearances for the club. After playing five more League games, Shilton finally hung up his goalkeeping gloves in 1997. In total, he had played in 1,391 official games.

'I never lost my appetite for the game,' Shilton said. 'Even late in my career I enjoyed testing myself in games and in training. It was always a challenge to be the best goalkeeper possible.'

No one has bettered his total of 88 appearances in the FA Cup, and his total of 17 appearances in the World Cup, stretching over three tournaments, is also a record.

Shilton kept a clean-sheet 66 times for England, a ratio of more than one every two games. On 14 occasions he captained his country.

In order to prolong his career he cut out alcohol from his diet in 1988, ensuring his selection by Bobby Robson for Italia '90. 'He never lost his agility or his handling in his latter years because of the work he put in,' Robson said. 'He was magnificent.'

Shilton remained fit and agile enough to play first-class football until the age of 47. In a career spanning 31 years he played a record 1,005 Football League games.

'Perfection as a goalkeeper is unachievable,' Shilton once said. 'But it is what motivated me. By aiming for it, I reasoned I would achieve a higher standard than anyone else.'

THROUGH THE AGES
FOOTBALL IN THE 1970s

▶▶▶▶▶▶▶▶▶▶▶▶▶▶▶▶▶▶▶▶▶▶▶▶▶▶▶▶▶▶▶▶▶▶▶▶

THIS PAGE: **Above** Bobby Moore, second from left, competes against a host of leading sportsmen on the BBC programme *Superstars*, 1973. **Right** George Best arrives at Euston Station, 1970.

OPPOSITE: **Above left** The referee speaks to Billy Bremner and Kevin Keegan, 1974. **Above right** Brian Clough speaks to the crowd in Ashbourne, 1975. **Below left** Jack Charlton leads the Leeds United players, 1972. **Below right** Jimmy Greaves in training for the 1970 London-Mexico rally.

KEVIN KEEGAN ▶▶▶▶▶▶▶▶▶▶▶▶

1951–

Kevin Keegan perfected a knack for the grand finale – after lifting himself from the depths of the Football League to the England captaincy by dint of sheer force of will and hard work.

Twice Keegan made his exit from a club in a European Cup final, winning one, losing the other. Then, after his final appearance as a player before retirement, he waved goodbye to an adoring Newcastle United crowd from a helicopter.

Keegan made an equally dramatic impression on his debut for Liverpool as a raw 20-year-old in 1971: within 12 minutes he had scored in front of the Kop at Anfield and the *Match of the Day* cameras. 'A fairytale start,' he recalled.

The first Englishman to be twice voted European Footballer of the Year, Keegan was never dropped during his six-year Liverpool career. 'I didn't play one reserve game. Whenever I was injured or suspended I went straight back into the team.'

Off the field, Keegan has been described as England's first 'post-modern footballer'. With sponsors and advertisers seeking his endorsement, Keegan realised the commercial value of his 'image rights'. Footballer-businessman Stanley Matthews had led the way two decades earlier; now Keegan, the perm-haired, pop-singing, TV celebrity, further blurred the lines between sport, popular culture and show business.

Bill Shankly paid Scunthorpe United £33,000 for Keegan, whose refusal to admit defeat and willingness to run until he dropped mirrored his manager's own qualities as a player during the 1930s. 'All bustle and explosive energy,' Keegan said.

'When Kevin was on the books at Anfield he was, without argument, the best player in Britain,' Emlyn Hughes, the Liverpool captain, said. 'He was magnificent, a superb, all-round professional whose consistency was incredible.'

Kevin Keegan emerges from the tunnel at Anfield, 1975.

PLAYER • INDUCTED 2002 • 63 CAPS • 1 EUROPEAN CUP • 2 UEFA CUPS

3 DIVISION ONE CHAMPIONSHIPS • 1 FA CUP

'We had to simmer him down in training. Kevin was first in everything because he was so fit.' – Bill Shankly

The arrival of Kevin Keegan at Anfield acted as a catalyst for the resurgence of Liverpool as a pre-eminent force in English football.

His impact was immediate. 'Shanks told me after I had played three games for Liverpool that I'd go on to play for England within a year and a half,' Keegan recalled. The raw recruit from Scunthorpe could hardly believe it. 'I remember thinking to myself, "Eighteen months! He can't be serious, surely."'

The official poster for the 1982 World Cup finals.

As it transpired, Keegan didn't need as much time as he'd been given. In November 1972, several months earlier than predicted, he made his England debut against Wales in Cardiff.

By now, Liverpool had gone six years without winning a trophy, yet by the end of that season, with Keegan an indefatigable menace up front, they were champions of England again and had claimed their first European trophy – the UEFA Cup.

At Anfield Keegan formed a partnership up front with John Toshack, a tall Welshman whose ability in the air provided a consistent and accurate supply of headed flick-ons.

Put simply, Keegan revelled in taking defenders where they least wanted to be. 'If he was big and tall, I dragged them into the open spaces out wide where I could exploit my pace,' he explained. 'Alternatively, if he was small, I put myself in the penalty area, so that I could get my head on crosses. I wasn't all that tall, but I had a good leap in me.'

In 1976 Keegan captained England for the first time. Within weeks he was voted Footballer of the Year. In his acceptance speech Keegan said: 'I am not the best player in the country by a mile, but I'm working on it.'

In his last game for Liverpool, Keegan tormented his marker, Berti Vogts, throughout the duration of the 1977 European Cup final. Frustrated, the experienced West Germany defender tripped the marauding Keegan for the penalty that sealed victory over Borussia Möenchengladbach in Rome.

Kevin Keegan scores for Newcastle United, 1984.

That summer Keegan signed for Hamburg. At the end of his second season in Germany Keegan was voted European Footballer of the Year a second year in succession.

As champions, Hamburg reached the European Cup final the following season, only to endure the disappointment of defeat against Nottingham Forest. Time to move on again – this time, back to England.

After a successful stint with Southampton, whose sixth-place finish in the top flight in 1980–81 recorded a high-point in the club's history, Keegan signed for Newcastle United the following year. Invigorated by his presence, Newcastle duly won promotion in 1984. 'Two thousand fans were turning up to watch our training sessions,' recalled team-mate Chris Waddle.

Finally, at the age of 33, Keegan retired, departing St James' Park by helicopter. 'To

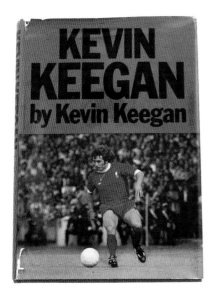

An autobiography published in 1977.

add to my dramatic exit, I dropped my number seven shirt as we took off,' he wrote later.

At international level Keegan endured the disappointment of successive failures to qualify for the World Cup. Then, in 1982, when England finally made it, he was sidelined by injury for all but 18 minutes of the tournament in Spain. 'It disappoints me greatly that the least successful part of my career should have been played out on the international stage,' Keegan wrote.

Ron Greenwood, the England manager between 1977–82, was more generous: 'Kevin

was a great international player, and the man around whom I built my team.'

Years later Keegan said: 'I was never the prettiest player to watch but it was the end product that I was interested in.'

Kevin Keegan runs with the ball,
with Colin Todd in support, 1976.

TREVOR BROOKING

▶▶▶▶▶▶▶▶▶▶▶▶▶▶▶▶▶

1948–

Respected throughout the game for his skill and sportsmanship, Trevor Brooking was the creative lynchpin in midfield for West Ham United and England – a loyal and celebrated one-club man of fluid style, inspired vision and calm demeanour.

Born within a few miles of Upton Park, where he stood on the terraces behind the goal as a boy, he emerged alongside Bobby Moore, Martin Peters and Geoff Hurst in the late 1960s.

For almost two decades he wore the famous claret and blue with pride, notably in 1980, when a rare header of his secured victory over Arsenal in the FA Cup final.

Fellow Hammer Frank Lampard once said of his tall, graceful, two-footed team-mate: 'Our tactics were always the same: get the ball and give it to Trevor.'

Commenting on his longevity with West Ham, Brooking said: 'In an unstable industry like football, I've been lucky enough to find stability and order.'

Trevor Brooking, 1981.

PLAYER • INDUCTED 2009 • 47 CAPS • 2 FA CUPS

'Our tactics were always the same: get the ball and give it to Trevor.' – Frank Lampard

With England, Brooking formed an outstanding partnership with Kevin Keegan. 'They are my trump cards,' said Ron Greenwood. Ray Clemence described the pair as 'two great football brains working together'.

To Greenwood's great regret, injury ruled out both Brooking and Keegan for all but 20 minutes of the 1982 World Cup, as England narrowly failed to reach the last four. 'We

Trevor Brooking runs with the ball, 1976.

would have won the tournament if they had been fit,' Greenwood said.

An outstanding youth international, Brooking established himself in the West Ham first team in 1969–70. Under the tutelage of Greenwood, the then Hammers manager, Brooking developed gradually. 'I accepted Ron's advice that I should be more aggressive and more involved in matches,' he recalled.

Receiving the ball, Brooking had outstanding spatial awareness. Rather than always controlling the ball he was adept at letting the ball run – a rare attribute in English football said Greenwood, who also described Brooking as 'expert' in shielding the ball.

Enzo Bearzot, a World Cup-winning manager with Italy in 1982, once said of Brooking: 'Like Johan Cruyff, he is deceptive, yet so perceptive. It is not his pace, as much as his change of pace that makes him so difficult to mark.'

In 1972–73 Brian Clough, the then Derby County manager, offered West Ham £400,000 for Brooking and Bobby Moore. Then in 1974, rumours circulated in the game that Tottenham Hotspur were offering £425,000 for Brooking's signature. The deal did not eventuate, and the following season Brooking collected a winners' medal after victory over Fulham in the FA Cup final.

As a one-club man, Brooking offered a throwback to the earlier days of Tom Finney and Nat Lofthouse. On his last appearance at Upton Park in 1984, Brooking was carried off

the field on the shoulders of supporters at the end of the game – a scene reminiscent of the celebrations surrounding Stanley Matthews' testimonial two decades earlier.

In 2009, the club renamed the Centenary Stand at Upton Park after Brooking as a permanent tribute.

Having witnessed Brooking's emergence in the mid 1960s, Bobby Moore spoke of him in the same breath as three of the then greats of world football: the German Gunter Netzer; the Brazil playmaker Gerson; and Italy's Gianni Rivera. 'A fabulous player,' Moore said. However, the final word goes to Ron Greenwood: 'The hardest thing to do in football is to make the game look simple, and Trevor was able to do that.'

KENNY DALGLISH ▶▶▶▶▶▶▶▶

1951–

A cult hero of the Kop, Kenny Dalglish repaid Liverpool fans their rapturous welcome by inspiring a period of unprecedented success at Anfield during the 1970s and 1980s. Having previously idolised Bill Shankly, the Liverpool crowd focused their adulation on their new number seven following his arrival from Celtic. Then, in later years, Dalglish became the most celebrated and high-profile player-manager of the modern era.

Arriving on Merseyside, Dalglish faced the daunting challenge of succeeding another Anfield hero, Kevin Keegan, following his transfer overseas in 1977. Any doubts there might have been as to whether he was up to the challenge were soon answered. The following season Dalglish scored the winning goal in the European Cup final. Twelve months on, and Liverpool were League champions again, and Dalglish was Footballer of the Year.

Bob Paisley, the Liverpool manager, paid Celtic £440,000 for the 26-year-old Dalglish. Like Keegan, the Scot could operate either in midfield or up front.

In 1985 Dalglish initiated a gradual transition into management when he succeeded Joe Fagan. In his first season in charge as player-manager, he guided Liverpool to a League and FA Cup double. 'Kenny made a successful switch because he behaved like an orchestra conductor,' Paisley said. 'He brought others into play. He understood that not everyone was blessed with great skill. He had patience, both as a player and as a manager.'

Sir John Smith, the Liverpool chairman, described Dalglish as 'the best player this club has signed this century'. Dalglish made a huge impression, even on the blue half of the city. Late in life, Dixie Dean, the great Everton centre-forward, described him as 'a wonderful player, such skill, so brave. Probably the best combination of goalscorer and goal maker I've ever seen.'

Kenny Dalglish turns on the ball against Manchester United, 1984.

▶ key match

Liverpool 1 Club Bruges 0, European Cup final, Wembley Stadium, 10 May 1978

Kenny Dalglish produced an exceptional piece of skill to achieve his great ambition in club football at the first attempt with Liverpool. Watching from the other end of the pitch, Ray Clemence celebrated 'the bit of magic that won us the Cup'.

The finish – a deft chip over the goalkeeper at the moment he tries to smother the shot by spreading himself at the forward's feet – was a Dalglish invention, according to teammate David Fairclough.

'It was something that Kenny designed,' Fairclough said. 'It's become a common-used shot now, but he was probably the innovator. Kenny weighed up the situation and came up with the answer.'

As Kevin Keegan watched the game on television, he initially thought Dalglish had taken the ball too deep. 'But he then conjured up a goal of pure class,' Keegan wrote later.

PLAYER • INDUCTED 2002 • 102 CAPS • 3 EUROPEAN CUPS • 1 FA CUP • 4 LEAGUE CUPS

6 DIVISION ONE CHAMPIONSHIPS

'Of all the players I have played alongside, managed and coached in more than 40 years at Anfield, Kenny is the most talented.'
– Bob Paisley

'Let's get out of here, before they realise what they've done.' These were the words Bob Paisley uttered to John Smith as they left a meeting with Celtic officials. For, although a record fee between British clubs had been agreed only moments earlier, the two Liverpool men knew that the deal represented more than value for money. They had found a bargain.

Soon after, Dalglish played in the Charity Shield fixture at Wembley. It was Liverpool's

first game in the post-Kevin Keegan era, as David Lacey noted in his match report in the *Guardian*. 'Dalglish moved on the ball confidently near goal and struck up a good rapport with those around him,' Lacey wrote. 'A more deliberate player than Keegan, he may give the side better balance in the long run.'

Asked for his comment after the game, Paisley was typically reticent and understated. 'He'll do for me,' the wily manager told reporters.

Emlyn Hughes played alongside Dalglish for Liverpool and against him as a defender with England. It was obvious which situation he preferred. 'Kenny is almost impossible to mark,' Hughes said.

Hughes, the Liverpool captain, praised the intelligence of Dalglish as a footballer. 'His

↗
Kenny Dalglish shoots for goal against Wolves, 1979.

thinking during a game is both incisive and decisive,' he said. In 1981, Paisley said: 'Kevin Keegan was quicker, but Kenny runs the five yards in his head.' Ray Clemence said Dalglish was 'three or four moves ahead of everyone else'.

'What made him unique was his vision,' Paisley added. 'He had this rare quality of being able to know where the other players were without even looking, and to find them with a perfect pass.'

During his time as Scotland manager, Alex Ferguson stressed another aspect of his game. 'It is because Kenny is so skilful that

↖
Kenny Dalglish celebrates victory in the 1986 FA Cup final.

A tracksuit top worn by Liverpool players for the European Cup final, 1985.

his courage as a player is seldom stressed, but he has the heart of a lion,' Ferguson said. 'No defender has ever frightened him, that's for sure.'

A fierce rival at club level, Ferguson also described Dalglish as 'the best bum player in the game', referring to the lower-body strength that enabled him to shield the ball from a defender – a theme also taken up by David O'Leary, the Arsenal defender. 'Trying to take the ball off Kenny once he's got it, is almost impossible,' O'Leary said. 'He crouches over the ball, elbows poking out. Commit too soon, and he will spin and go past you.'

Once passed the age of 30, Dalglish gradually switched to a deeper role in midfield. Ian Rush, the Liverpool striker who was the leading scorer in Division One in 1983–84 with 32 goals, said: 'I just made the runs knowing the ball would come to me from Kenny.'

Inevitably, with the passing years his appearances on the field became less frequent, and finally in May 1990 at the age of 38 Dalglish allowed himself one last run out. With another title secured, the player-manager introduced himself as a substitute against Derby County. 'I just wanted to show my appreciation to the fans at Anfield,' he wrote later.

One abiding memory remained for the Kop faithful: the image of Dalglish, the man they called 'King Kenny', celebrating a goal – arms held aloft and a beaming, infectious smile across his face.

Barclays League Division One trophy, 1988.

GLENN HODDLE

▶▶▶▶▶▶▶▶▶▶▶▶▶▶▶▶▶▶

1957–

Glenn Hoddle earned the admiration of Johan Cruyff, Diego Maradona and Michel Platini for his skill and passing ability during a memorable career dotted with extraordinary moments of sublime improvisation and spectacular goals.

An attacking midfield player of rare balance, vision and relentless, unbreakable ambition, Hoddle was the creative mainstay around whom Tottenham Hotspur built successive teams during the late 1970s and 1980s.

During his heyday in English football, Hoddle orchestrated back-to-back FA Cup triumphs for Spurs – in 1981 and 1982 – and a successful UEFA Cup campaign in 1984.

At international level, after a cameo appearance in the World Cup in Spain in 1982, Hoddle emerged as a pivotal figure for England during the tournament in Mexico four years later – the highlight of an international career spanning nine years, during which time he amassed 53 caps.

Glenn Hoddle celebrates, 1981.

PLAYER • INDUCTED 2007 • 53 CAPS • 2 FA CUPS • 1 UEFA CUP

'Glenn was capable of winning a game in an instant with his exquisite skill.'
– Sir Bobby Robson

A Spurs fan as a lad, Hoddle practised hour after hour with a small rubber ball, developing his technique. On seeing him in action as a schoolboy for the first time, Bill Nicholson, the then Spurs manager, signed him almost on the spot.

Similarly impressed, team-mate Steve Perryman was astonished by Hoddle's 'extraordinary' mastery of the ball, likening him to an expert golfer. 'Glenn swerves the ball, fades it, flips it, spins it, drives it, chips it and uses backspin to make it stop,' the Spurs captain wrote.

During his 12 years at Tottenham, Hoddle made 378 appearances and scored 88 goals –

many of them unforgettable: a breathtaking volley into the top corner against Manchester United; the celebrated, opportunist, inch-perfect chip on the turn at Watford; and a brilliant solo run at White Hart Lane, outwitting several defenders before dummying the keeper and rolling the ball into an empty net against Oxford United.

The so-called 'Great Enigma' of the English game, Hoddle was idolised on the White Hart Lane terraces, admired by neutrals and eulogised by many football writers. Never one to shirk responsibility in striving to identify the 'killer' pass, Hoddle was praised by Brian Clough for his 'moral bravery'.

Within the game, however, there were those who questioned his defensive discipline and stamina. Ultimately, for all his ability going forward, and much to his frustration, none of the managers he worked for in England gave him full rein to express

himself fully for an extended period.

In Europe, however, Hoddle was feted. Growing up in Amsterdam, a young Dennis Bergkamp idolised him. And France playmaker Michel Platini once famously stated: 'Had he been French, he would have won 150 caps.'

Eventually, and perhaps inevitably, Hoddle moved overseas, joining Monaco, whose then manager Arsène Wenger, gave him total freedom in attack. 'Glenn was the most skilful player I have ever worked with,' Wenger said later. After helping Monaco win the French championship, Hoddle returned home as player-manager of Swindon Town and later Chelsea, guiding the latter to a losing FA Cup final appearance in 1994.

Glenn Hoddle shoots, watched by Bobby Robson, 1983.

TEAM INDUCTEE
LIVERPOOL
▶▶▶▶▶▶▶ **1977-1979**

10 August 1977

European Cup holders Liverpool smash the record transfer fee between British clubs when they sign Kenny Dalglish from Celtic for £440,000 – money generated by the £500,000 sale of Kevin Keegan to Hamburg. 'Kenny may prove to be a better player for Liverpool than I did,' Keegan says.

31 August 1977

Newly-appointed England manager Ron Greenwood selects six Liverpool players – Ray Clemence, Phil Neal, Emlyn Hughes, Terry McDermott, Ray Kennedy and Ian Callaghan – in his squad for the friendly against Switzerland.

24 September 1977

At the age of 22, Alan Hansen, a £150,000 signing from Partick Thistle, makes his debut for Liverpool. 'It's up to me to make the most of the chance,' the Scottish defender says.

▶▶▶▶▶▶▶▶▶▶▶▶▶▶▶▶▶▶▶

1 October 1977

Defeat against Manchester United highlights Liverpool's inconsistent start to the season in the League. Asked for an answer, Bob Paisley says: 'It's not a question of more running.' Then, pointing to his temple he adds: 'To be properly fit, it's here that you must be tuned in.'

Kenny Dalglish runs with the ball, with Phil Neal in support, 1978.

19 October 1977

After a bye in the first round of the European Cup, Liverpool overwhelm Dynamo Dresden, the East German champions, 5–1 at Anfield.

11 November 1977

Liverpool remain out-of-sorts in the League. 'A good team does not become a bad team overnight,' Paisley tells reporters. 'I do not believe that chopping and changing does any good.' In their next match Liverpool lose 2–0 at QPR – a fourth consecutive reverse.

▶▶▶▶▶▶▶▶▶▶▶▶▶▶▶▶▶▶▶

10 January 1978

Graeme Souness signs for Liverpool for a fee of £352,000 from Middlesbrough. Paisley describes the abrasive 24-year-old Scot as 'one of the few players out there who come up to our standard'. Souness, the manager adds, 'will play in central midfield, which is his position, and we'll sort out the rest from there.'

▶▶▶▶▶▶▶▶▶▶▶▶▶▶▶▶▶▶▶

1 March 1978

After defeating Benfica in the first leg tie in Portugal,

Emlyn Hughes, the Liverpool captain says: 'Psychologically, our winning the away tie like this must make all the other teams frightened of drawing us next.'

12 April 1978

An imperious performance by Liverpool against Borussia Möenchengladbach in the second leg at Anfield secures a second successive European Cup final appearance. 'Considering the standard of the opposition, that was definitely our best performance of the season,' Bob Paisley says.

13 April 1978

After watching the game from the stands, Matt Busby, the former Manchester United manager is quoted the next day as saying: 'Souness made a vital contribution with his penetrating forward passing. He is a really exciting addition to Liverpool's armoury, because he has the strength to follow up the attack he has begun.'

10 May 1978

An exquisite chip by Kenny Dalglish gives Liverpool victory against Bruges in the European Cup final at Wembley. The following day one national newspaper begins lobbying for Bob Paisley to be knighted. The man himself tells reporters: 'Our next objective is to win our first League match of the season next August.'

2 September 1978

Terry McDermott rounds off a 7–0 humiliation of Tottenham Hotspur with a rousing header at Anfield.

After watching highlights on television, rival managers unite in praise. Ipswich Town's Bobby Robson describes them as 'the perfect football side'; and Steve Burtenshaw of QPR likens Liverpool, in terms of quality, to a Rolls-Royce motor car.

27 September 1978

A highly disciplined defensive display by champions Nottingham Forest at Anfield ends Liverpool's hopes of a third successive European Cup success. In the League, however, they march on relentlessly.

▶ ▶ ▶ ▶ ▶ ▶ ▶ ▶ ▶ ▶ ▶ ▶ ▶ ▶ ▶ ▶ ▶ ▶ ▶

7 April 1979

After watching Liverpool 'steamroller' his Arsenal side 3–0 at Anfield, rival manager Terry Neill says: 'Liverpool are 10 years ahead of us and just about every other club in the country.'

↗
Liverpool players celebrate.

8 May 1979

On the 40th anniversary of his arrival at Liverpool as a player, Bob Paisley watches his side clinch a record 11th championship title with a 3–0 home win over Aston Villa. 'For sheer quality and consistency, this has been our best season,' he says.

▶ ▶ ▶ ▶ ▶ ▶ ▶ ▶ ▶ ▶ ▶ ▶ ▶ ▶ ▶ ▶ ▶ ▶ ▶

17 May 1979

The Liverpool defence, at the heart of which Alan Hansen has been outstanding, keep a clean sheet at Leeds United. It gives them a goals-against total for the season of 16 – a record low. Victory also lifts Liverpool to a record haul of 68 points. 'That sort of record could stand for all time,' a delighted Bob Paisley says afterwards.

VIV ANDERSON

▶▶▶▶▶▶▶▶▶▶▶▶▶▶▶▶▶▶

1956–

Viv Anderson won two European Cup winners' medals after making a vital breakthrough when he became the first black footballer to represent England at senior level.

During a distinguished career with Nottingham Forest, Arsenal, Manchester United and Sheffield Wednesday, Anderson – the winner of 30 England caps – was voted the best right-back of the 1970s in a poll of top-flight managers. 'I like the physical side of football,' he said. 'I enjoy tackling.'

Above all, Anderson regards his international debut against Czechoslovakia at Wembley in November 1978 as a cause for professional satisfaction. 'At the time all I thought about was doing my job and trying to impress the manager enough to get selected again,' Anderson recalls. 'It is only looking back that I realise the importance of it all, and the responsibility I was carrying.' It is not every player who receives a 'Good Luck' telegram from the Queen beforehand.

Viv Anderson moves forward, 1978.

PLAYER • INDUCTED 2004 • 30 CAPS • 2 EUROPEAN CUPS • 3 LEAGUE CUPS

1 DIVISION ONE CHAMPIONSHIP

Ever since his days as an apprentice, Anderson had endured racist abuse from the terraces on a depressingly regular basis. 'Winning that first cap may have been a small step for him in his career but it was a huge leap forward for black footballers in this country,' Ian Wright wrote in 1997.

Nicknamed 'Spider' on account of his long legs, Anderson made his mark when Forest emerged as a major force after scraping promotion from the Second Division in 1976–77. The First Division championship title was won at the first attempt on the back of an undefeated run of 26 games and a defence that let in only 24 goals in the League.

Anderson played in successive European Cup finals, in 1979 and 1980. First Malmo, then Hamburg were beaten 1–0: a total of 180 minutes without Forest conceding a goal. 'Against Hamburg, we were under siege,' Anderson recalled, 'but our concentration and discipline never lapsed.'

Forest gained a reputation for resilience, particularly away from the home, during a record unbeaten run of 42 League games between November 1977 and December 1978.

The Forest fans recognised his contribution. In a poll conducted in 1997, 96 per cent of supporters voted Anderson the best right-back in the club's history.

George Graham brought Anderson to Arsenal in 1984. In each of his three seasons at Highbury, the team's defensive record improved, a run that ended with League Cup success.

Such consistency alerted Alex Ferguson, who made Anderson his first signing as Manchester United manager in 1987. Ferguson wanted to add experience and physical presence to a side that he considered too 'lightweight' to compete for honours. 'His res-

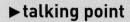
olute professionalism and bubbly, contagious enthusiasm in the dressing room were worth a lot more than the £250,000 we paid for Viv,' Ferguson recalled.

Throughout this time Anderson had been collecting more caps, without ever being an automatic choice. 'I was unable to win an extended run in the side of nine or 10 games unfortunately,' he said, 'but I am delighted with my total of 30 appearances.'

'[Anderson is] exceptional going forward. He's one of England's finest post-war full-backs.' – George Graham

Viv Anderson walks out for his England debut, 1978.

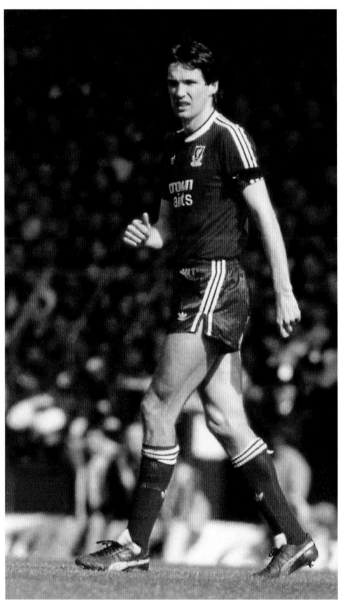

ALAN HANSEN

▶▶▶▶▶▶▶▶▶▶▶▶▶▶▶▶

1955-

An exceptionally skilful and unflappable central defender, Alan Hansen was the one constant presence as Liverpool exercised an unprecedented dominance in English football during the late 1970s and 1980s.

The Scot arrived on Merseyside one month before the club's first European Cup triumph, in 1977. When he retired, 14 years and more than 600 appearances later, the League championship trophy was again on display at Anfield.

In between times, Hansen amassed a then record eight championship medals. For all but one of those seasons Liverpool finished in the top two, and only twice did they end a campaign without a trophy.

As late as 1990 Johnny Giles still rated the veteran Hansen the best player in England. 'He can still zoom clear of trouble in the manner of the great Franz Beckenbauer,' he wrote.

Alan Hansen follows the action, 1988.

PLAYER • INDUCTED 2006 • 26 CAPS • 3 EUROPEAN CUPS • 8 DIVISION ONE CHAMPIONSHIPS

2 FA CUPS • 3 LEAGUE CUPS

> **'The loss of Alan Hansen through retirement is potentially more damaging to Liverpool than the loss of Kevin Keegan and Kenny Dalglish.' - Howard Kendall**

Tall and lean, with a long and distinctive looping stride, the distinguished Hansen was the antithesis of the traditional, no-nonsense, rugged British centre-half. Timing, anticipation and technique shaped his game, rather than strength, aggression and intimidation. Instead of diving into the tackle, Hansen jockeyed forwards, before nicking the ball away.

Once in possession, Hansen came into his own. Not since the heyday of John Charles in the 1950s had there been a centre-half with this much confidence and ability going forward; time and time again, defence was turned into attack, with a surging run on the ball or a clever pass.

As captain, Hansen led Liverpool to the double in 1985–86 at the expense of Everton. 'More than anyone else, it was Alan who underpinned Liverpool's continued success,' Howard Kendall said. 'In many respects, he was their best attacker. My team-talk was always the same: "Stop Hansen".'

Bob Paisley signed Hansen from Partick Thistle without having seen him play, on the recommendation of his coaching staff. The transfer fee of £150,000 – a modest sum even then – represents perhaps the shrewdest deal ever struck by the wily Liverpool manager.

'Alan is the most skilful centre-half I have ever seen in British football,' Paisley said. 'He has such beautiful balance. He never loses control and always looks so graceful. What a joy to watch.'

Defensively, Liverpool adopted a 'flat-back four' pushing up as far as possible in order to compress play. In 1978–79, the tactic restricted opponents to a mere 16 goals in 42 games – a top-flight record. An efficient offside trap offered yet more security.

'Our defence took up a more advanced position than any other team in the history of British football,' Hansen recalled. 'Our aim was to make it difficult for opponents to give

Alan Hansen holds the Charity Shield, with Kenny Dalglish and Graeme Souness, 1982.

their strikers the service they wanted, and to keep the ball a safe distance from our goal.'

It certainly worked on a consistent basis: eight times during his career Liverpool had the best defensive record in the division.

At the age of 35 Hansen announced his retirement. 'I was not only "gone" physically – because of the wear and tear on my knees – but mentally, I knew I'd had enough,' he recalled. Liverpool had lost a unique talent.

'I remember that whenever a new player arrived – especially a defender,' Hansen recalled, 'Ronnie Moran, our coach, would point to me and say, "Don't watch big Al play – don't try to do what he does, because he's a one-off".'

OSSIE ARDILES

▶▶▶▶▶▶▶▶▶▶▶▶▶▶▶▶

1952–

The unforeseen signing of Osvaldo Ardiles by Tottenham Hotspur in the summer of 1978 stunned English football, and his success in North London heralded a more cosmopolitan era for the game.

His transfer was made possible by the lifting of a ban on the import of foreign players, and the move revitalised Spurs, setting them on the path to eventual Cup success.

Only a few weeks after winning a World Cup medal, Ardiles walked out to a familiar sight when he made his first appearance at White Hart Lane: in a tribute to his triumph with Argentina on home soil, Spurs fans replicated the ticker-tape welcome that formed such a memorable feature of the tournament.

Soon afterwards, Cliff Lloyd, the secretary of the players' union, said: 'Seeing Ardiles play may well whet the appetite of fans across the country. We could be about to witness an influx of foreign players into English football.'

Ossie Ardiles celebrates a goal, 1981.

PLAYER • INDUCTED 2009 • 63 CAPS • 1 WORLD CUP • 2 FA CUPS • 1 UEFA CUP

Ron Greenwood, the England manager, was an interested observer in South America, and after the final he selected Ardiles in his imaginary World XI. 'He comes forward and supports others well,' Greenwood wrote. 'He's a fighter who battles hard and plays great passes wide. Ardiles is one of those players who seems to be all over the place.'

Back in the BBC studio, guest pundit Lawrie McMenemy was also full of praise. After watching a clip of film highlighting Ardiles' play, a wistful Southampton manager said: 'I would certainly like him in my team, that's for sure' – a comment that was taken at the time as nothing more than wishful thinking.

Such things simply did not happen, because back then South American players moved to Spain or Italy, not England. Or so it was thought. Meanwhile, Keith Burkinshaw, the Spurs manager, was moving quickly and

Ossie Ardiles introduces himself to Spurs fans, 1978.

quietly to arrange arguably the most unexpected transfer in history.

An avid reader of *The Times* and chess fanatic, Ardiles assessed football with the clinical eye of a grandmaster moving pieces around a board. 'I always wanted to control the game,' he once said. 'I wanted to know what everyone on the pitch was doing at any one time. And to look for weaknesses in the other side.'

In his debut season in English football, Ardiles helped Tottenham consolidate their position in the top flight, following promotion; then in 1981 their resurgence gathered pace with victory over Manchester City in a memorable FA Cup final replay.

On the ball, his darting runs and endlessly probing passes made him a cult hero. Spurs fans also loved his harrying and tackling in midfield. Ardiles did the hard work, always putting his team first. He took the

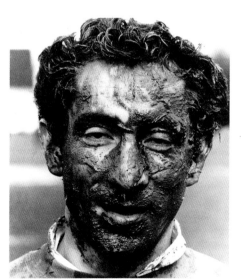

Ossie Ardiles covered in mud, 1993.

knocks and stayed on his feet.

His stature – all five-feet-six-inches of him – and slight frame had prompted many observers and fellow professionals to question his ability to perform – or even cope – in England once the tackles started flying in and the pitches turned to mud. Instead, Ardiles thrived.

From day one the presence of Ardiles was beneficial for English football. Away from home, starting in August at Nottingham Forest, where the attendance was 10,000 above the season-average, the sight of Ardiles – and his Argentina team-mate Ricky Villa – generated huge interest. Once settled, his performances for Spurs proved conclusively that players from South America and Latin countries could thrive here, paving the way for others to follow. Our game had changed for good.

TEAM INDUCTEE
ASTON VILLA
►►►►►►►►►►► 1980-82

10 August 1980

Aston Villa parade Peter Withe, the centre-forward signed from Newcastle United by manager Ron Saunders for a club-record fee of £500,000, in a pre-season friendly. A win at Leeds United kicks off their season in style.

6 September 1980

Villa surrender the only remaining unbeaten record for a top-flight team in all competitions with this

Tony Morley salutes Aston Villa supporters, 1981.

1-0 defeat at Portman Road. 'We scrambled our victory,' observes Ipswich Town manager Bobby Robson. One player in particular stood out for Robson. 'That Gary Shaw will be some player,' he says, referring to Villa's 19-year-old striker. 'He's quick, brave and sees things early.'

10 October 1980

Newspapers report the selection of Gordon Cowan in the England squad for an upcoming international. 'Suddenly my game has come together,' the midfielder says. 'It has helped a lot having as good a target man as Peter Withe up front. He's always easy to find.'

14 November 1980

With Villa five points clear at the top, one newspaper quotes Dennis Mortimer as saying: 'Those people who are waiting for the bubble to burst are in for a big surprise.'

27 December 1980

Peter Taylor, the Nottingham Forest assistant manager, watches his side hold Villa at the City

Ground. 'Villa were superb.' Taylor says. 'They played like we did when we won the title two years ago.'

10 January 1981

Peter Withe and Dennis Mortimer score the goals in a 2-0 victory over champions Liverpool at Villa Park. 'This performance could set us up for the rest of the season,' Saunders says afterwards. 'People talk a lot of nonsense about skill and flair; what's important is the team.'

7 February 1981

On the morning of the League fixture at Everton, Bob Paisley cites Ipswich Town – not Villa – as Liverpool's main rivals for the title. Villa respond with a rousing 3-1 win at Goodison, where television cameramen capture Tony Morley's stunning strike.

14 April 1981

Villa remain a point clear, albeit having played one more game, following a 2-1 home defeat against title rivals Ipswich Town. 'It was like walking into a right hook,' says Saunders. 'We threw it away, but I still fancy us for the title.' The question is: can Villa hold their nerve?

2 May 1981

Aston Villa are champions. Despite defeat at Arsenal, they cannot be denied their first title in 71 years. 'Our potential is enormous,' Saunders says. 'I see no reason why we should not be able to emulate Liverpool and Forest by winning the European Cup.'

Aston Villa players pose with the European Cup, 1982.

4 November 1981

After breezing past FC Valur of Iceland, Villa endure a nervous 90 minutes at Villa Park in the second leg of their European Cup tie against Dinamo Berlin. A 1–0 home defeat means that Villa rely on the away goals rule. 'We don't have the men or mentality to defend a lead – so we went out and attacked throughout,' Saunders comments. 'We gave away a bad goal but that tested our character, and we were not found wanting.'

9 February 1982

After almost eight years in charge, Ron Saunders re-signs as manager of Aston Villa, citing a contractual dispute and a reduction in his authority at Villa Park. 'If I'm going to manage, I want to be allowed to man-age, not be an office boy,' he tells reporters. Villa put

Tony Barton, the chief scout, in temporary charge.

17 March 1982

A rare goal by reliable central defender Ken McNaught completes a 2–0 aggregate victory over Dynamo Kiev in this quarter-final.

7 April 1982

In his first game in full control of the team, Tony Barton looks on as Tony Morley scores the only game of the semi-final first leg against Anderlecht at Villa Park. A goalless draw in Belgium a fortnight later eases Villa through to the final.

25 May 1982

On the eve of the final, Bayern Munich defender Wolfgang Dremmler dismisses the threat of Aston Villa saying he knows little about any of their players. 'The cup is ours,' he says. 'Anything else is too fantastic to believe.'

26 May 1982

On hearing the final whistle in Rotterdam, Tony Barton walks over to the Villa players and thanks each one of them in turn. A special embrace is reserved for Peter Withe, whose close-range conversion of a Tony Morley cross ensured victory. Villa have another hero on the night: inexperienced reserve goalkeeper Nigel Spink. Called upon to replace Jimmy Rimmer after 10 minutes, Spink is reported to have said: 'My mum will be pleased.' Eighty minutes later, tens of thousands of Villa fans shared Mrs Spinks' emotion.

DEBBIE BAMPTON

▶▶▶▶▶▶▶▶▶▶▶▶▶▶▶▶▶▶▶

1961–

Debbie Bampton was still a schoolgirl when she made her England debut against Holland at the age of 16; and she played her last game for her country two decades later on a tour to the United States in 1997.

Despite being sidelined for 12 months after sustaining a serious knee injury in 1982, Bampton won 95 caps for England, scoring seven goals, and she was awarded an MBE in 1998 in recognition of her services to women's football as a player and a manager.

She played in central midfield throughout her career, with the exception of a spell as sweeper for the national team in the mid 1980s.

Debbie Bampton, 1986.

PLAYER • INDUCTED 2005 • 95 CAPS • 5 NATIONAL LEAGUE TITLES • 4 FA CUPS • 1 LEAGUE CUP

**'As a lifelong Arsenal fan I did not hesitate when I had the chance to play for the club.'
– Debbie Bampton**

In 1992–93 she was a member of the Arsenal side that became the first team to win the domestic treble of League championship, FA Cup and League Cup. In 1994–95 Arsenal came close to repeating their achievement, winning the double of League and FA Cup. It also proved to be her last contribution to the Gunners cause.

'I was still an England international and I had won a number of honours as a player,' she said. 'I was looking for a new challenge when I was approached by Croydon.'

The following season, as player-manager,

Bampton made another breakthrough. 'I became the first woman to manage a team to the League and Cup double,' she said. 'It meant a lot to me to prove a point in this way.' The League title was won on goal difference from Doncaster Belles after Croydon completed the fixture list unbeaten.

'I spent six seasons at the club as player-manager, and we won the League title three times. I kept on playing throughout my time at Croydon. By the time I finished I had achieved everything I wanted in the game.'

Back in 1988 Bampton had joined a small exodus of British players to Italy, where she trained full-time with Trani, who finished runners-up in both the League and the Cup at the end of her only season at the club, playing in front of home crowds of up to 3,000 against the likes of Milan, Napoli and Roma.

Overall, though, it proved to be a bitter-sweet experience. 'I was definitely a better player for my time overseas, but I also found myself frustrated by the culture surrounding Italian football,' she said.

Several other Italian clubs offered her a contract to stay on but it made no difference. 'I enjoyed the football itself, but I was homesick,' she said. 'It was time to come home.'

'The English game suited me. I considered myself a box-to-box player,' Bampton said. 'I worked hard to win the ball, and I was always looking to make forward runs. I was not a natural goalscorer, but I did look to set up chances for others.'

Debbie Bampton prepares to shoot, 1983.

IAN RUSH

▶▶▶▶▶▶▶▶▶▶▶▶▶▶▶▶

1961–

Wiry thin and whippet-quick, Ian Rush was the most prolific goalscorer to wear the red shirt of Liverpool and an instrumental figure in their relentless pursuit of honours over a period of 15 years.

In 658 appearances for the club, the Welshman scored 346 goals. 'A phenomenal record,' said Kenny Dalglish, his one-time strike partner and later manager.

'They used to say it was my vision that opened up the chances for Ian to put away. But really, it was his vision, his knowing when to run and where to run,' Dalglish said. 'That was the vital ingredient. I would just hit the ball into space, knowing that he would have the pace and the instinct to be moving there.'

Roger Hunt, the Liverpool goalscoring hero of the 1960s, said: 'The game is so much more defensive these days. If Ian had been playing in my time he might have scored a hundred more goals than he has already.'

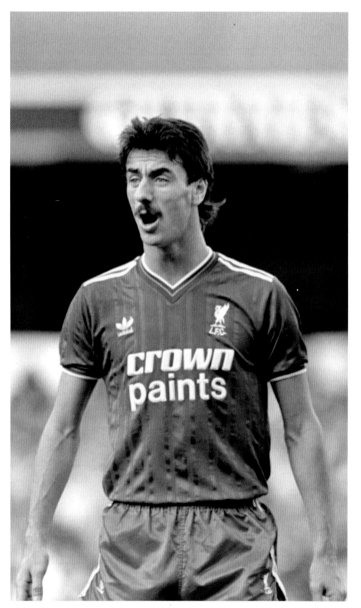

Ian Rush, 1985

PLAYER • INDUCTED 2006 • 73 CAPS • 1 EUROPEAN CUP • 5 DIVISION ONE CHAMPIONSHIPS

3 FA CUPS • 5 LEAGUE CUPS

'A player with his qualities could turn a hopeful pass into a great one.' – Kenny Dalglish

One season above all stands out: in 1983–84 Rush rewrote the Anfield record books when he scored 47 goals in all competitions, three of which – the European Cup, the League championship and League Cup – were claimed by Liverpool.

On a personal level, Rush was awarded the Golden Boot as Europe's leading goalscorer; at home, his fellow professionals and the football writers voted him Footballer of the Year.

It was the start of an incredible run. Over the next six seasons Rush scored nearly 200 goals, at an average strike-rate of two goals every three games. Nothing like this had been seen at the highest level since the heyday of Jimmy Greaves two decades earlier.

'Overseas, players and fans give him the same kind of adulation we give the likes of Maradona, Cruyff, Pele and Van Basten,' Mark Hughes, a Wales team-mate said. Ron Atkin-

↗
Ian Rush celebrates scoring in the FA Cup final, 1989.

son, the Manchester United manager, described Rush somewhat graphically as 'a killing machine in front of goal'.

In the FA Cup Rush eclipsed Denis Law's record of 41 goals. Five of them were registered in Wembley finals, another record. As everyone knew, whenever Rush scored, Liverpool did not lose, a remarkable run that lasted until 1987.

After one season with Juventus, Rush returned to Anfield a better player, according to Dalglish. Rush had always worked hard on behalf of the team, winning possession and harassing defenders. Now he was making goals with his clever passing and selfless running, as well as scoring them, prompting Dalglish to state: 'Ian is the best striker I've ever seen'. Howard Kendall the Everton manager said: 'The number of times Ian forces defenders into mistakes is remarkable.'

↖
Ian Rush scores against West Ham United, 1983.

In May 1996, Rush, now no longer an automatic choice at Anfield, accepted a free transfer to Leeds. As he took the field before his last home game, Liverpool's opponents formed a guard of honour. 'It was no more than he deserves,' said Middlesbrough manager Bryan Robson. After a stint with Newcastle United, Rush played out his career with Wrexham, before joining Chester as manager.

Summing up his Liverpool career, and his partnership with Dalglish, a typically modest Rush said: 'I just made the runs knowing the ball would come to me. Once we were on the same wavelength, it all clicked.'

▶ key match

Everton 1 Liverpool 3, FA Cup final, Wembley Stadium, 10 May 1986

When Ian Rush scored Liverpool's equaliser, he delivered a stunning psychological blow. As if the painful memory of his four goals at Goodison Park in 1982 wasn't bad enough, there was the inescapable thought: when Rush scores, Liverpool never lose.

'Once that happened, we knew, deep down, there was nothing going for us,' Gary Lineker said later.

At 2–1, Rush struck again. 'I hit that shot so hard it took the goal netting with it and smashed a photographer's camera,' he recalled.

In 1989, Rush, though not fully fit, was named substitute for another Cup final against Everton. 'They fear you,' said Kenny Dalglish. Rush got on, and scored twice again in a 3–2 win.

HOWARD KENDALL

▶▶▶▶▶▶▶▶▶▶▶▶▶▶▶▶

1946–

Howard Kendall enjoys the distinction of winning a championship title as both player and manager with the same club, ensuring his status as an idol in the eyes of successive generations of Everton supporters.

The feeling of appreciation is mutual. 'You can have love affairs with other football clubs,' Kendall once said, 'but for me, with Everton, it's a marriage.'

Under his leadership, Everton were European Team of the Year in 1984–85, after clinching a double of First Division championship and European Cup-Winners' Cup. At Wembley, the Blues lost in the FA Cup final, ruining their dream of a treble.

'Howard created a fantastic, fluent side,' said Andy Gray, the Everton forward and future television pundit. Unbeaten for five months, Everton won the title by a margin of 13 points despite several defeats once the title had been secured.

↖
Howard Kendall celebrates championship success, 1987.

MANAGER • INDUCTED 2005 • 2 DIVISION ONE CHAMPIONSHIPS • 1 FA CUP

1 EUROPEAN CUP-WINNERS' CUP

'An unshakeable bond had formed during my playing days. Everton was in my blood. The fascination for the club never wavered.' – Howard Kendall

Two years later, Everton finished top again, earning Kendall a second Manager of the Year award. Furthermore, in the mid 1980s, the team reached three successive FA Cup finals, winning once: a 2–0 victory over Watford in 1984.

As a player, Kendall was signed from Preston North End in 1967 for a fee of £85,000, a record for a wing-half. Three years later he won a championship medal, playing alongside Alan Ball and Colin Harvey in midfield.

After learning his trade as a manager at Blackburn Rovers, Kendall arrived at Goodison Park in 1981, a time of crisis for the club. In rebuilding the side, he proved himself to be an outstanding judge of talent: nine of the players he introduced went on to become full internationals.

Howard Kendall gives a thumbs up, 1990.

In 1981 Kendall paid Bury £150,000 for Neville Southall. 'It was my first signing, and my best,' Kendall said. 'In his prime, Neville was the best keeper in the world.' Other inspirational signings followed – at equally bargain prices.

Peter Reid was burdened by a reputation for being injury-prone, but Kendall ignored the midfielder's past medical record in signing him for a knockdown fee of £60,000 from Bolton Wanderers.

Similarly, Andy Gray, once the most expensive footballer in Britain, saw his value in the transfer market plummet following a succession of injuries. His transfer from Wolverhampton Wanderers, for a fee of £250,000, lifted the mood at Goodison Park.

Other players were plucked from near-

Howard Kendall celebrates with Kevin Ratcliffe, 1985.

> **▶ key match**
>
> **Everton 3 Bayern Munich 1 (agg. 3–1), European Cup-Winners' Cup semi-final, second leg, Goodison Park, 24 April 1985**
>
> Howard Kendall sat up all night watching a video tape of this pulsating victory over the best team in Germany that season.
>
> The previous evening, Everton had gone in a goal down at half-time. They now had to score twice to go through. 'We were totally shell-shocked,' Andy Gray recalled.
>
> 'Keep playing at a pace Bayern don't like,' Kendall told his players. 'I guarantee you that the Gwladys Street will suck one in.'
>
> Goals from Gray, Graeme Sharp and Trevor Steven sealed victory on a tumultuous night. Kendall did a jig of delight on the touchline. 'What a magnificent night,' he said. 'It is my most precious memory in football.'

obscurity, including Liverpool reserves Kevin Sheedy and Alan Harper, and Derek Mountfield from Tranmere Rovers; meanwhile, Trevor Steven was switched to a wide midfield role following his transfer from Burnley.

At the back, Gary Stevens and Kevin Ratcliffe came up through the ranks at Goodison Park.

For a sum of money not much greater than the record transfer fee at the time – £1.7 million – Kendall built an entire championship-winning side.

After a stint in Spain and at Manchester City, Kendall returned to Everton for the second of three spells in charge at Goodison Park. There were also brief stays at Sheffield United and Notts County. Kendall has since been officially named Everton's greatest manager.

BRYAN ROBSON ▶▶▶▶▶▶▶▶▶▶

1957–

Bryan Robson was a talismanic midfield player for both club and country; but his courage and commitment took a heavy toll in terms of injury, denying him the possibility of winning a record number of international caps for England.

Robson played 90 times for his country between 1980 and 1991, finishing his international career as the fifth most-capped player in history, despite suffering more than 20 fractures or dislocations during his career.

Notably, for a ball-winning, aggressive midfield player, Robson added another dimension to his game going forward: impeccable timing and anticipation when making late runs into the opposition penalty area – attributes that lifted him to ninth position on the all-time list of goalscorers for England, with 26 goals.

An automatic choice when fit during the eight years that Bobby Robson was in charge, he was never named as a substitute for England. On 65 occasions he captained the side. 'Lesser players have won more, but none have given as much,' Bobby Robson wrote. 'England were a taller, prouder team when he played. I could see no failing in him as a player. Bryan missed out on 35 caps under me alone and had he had a normal, relatively trouble-free career he would have broken the all-time British record.'

Ron Atkinson, the Manchester United manager, made Robson the most expensive footballer in Britain when he paid West Bromwich Albion £1.5 million to bring him to Old Trafford in 1981. 'The best half-backs ever were Duncan Edwards and Dave Mackay, and Robbo is right up there with them,' Atkinson said.

'There was an aura about Bryan,' Alex Ferguson, the successor to Atkinson as manager said. 'When I arrived here in 1986 there was a feeling around the club that winning or losing largely depended on whether or not he was playing.'

Bryan Robson captains Manchester United in the FA Cup final, 1990.

PLAYER • INDUCTED 2002 • 90 CAPS • 2 PREMIER LEAGUE TITLES • 3 FA CUPS

1 EUROPEAN CUP-WINNERS' CUP

'Bryan is a miracle of commitment, a human marvel who pushed himself through every imaginable limit on the field.' – Alex Ferguson

Bobby Robson regarded his namesake as being indispensable to England's cause at the 1986 World Cup in Mexico, even at the risk of his own future as national team manager. Robson took a massive gamble on the Manchester United midfield player when he named him for the opening fixture of the tournament against Portugal in Monterrey on 3 June.

Bryan Robson had dislocated his shoulder for the third time in a warm-up game in Los Angeles, but his manager decided his inclusion was a risk worth taking. The manager acknowledged that his captain's all-action, versatile style might be hampered by the dislocation, but he played down his own doubts, concealing the extent of the player's injury, and the risks involved in playing him, from the media.

Two years work and planning appeared to have been destroyed when, late in the first half, Robson fell awkwardly and his shoulder popped out for a fourth time, ruling him out of the tournament. The media was biting in its criticism of Bobby Robson.

It made no difference to the England manager. 'My heart bled for Bryan when he suffered the injury,' Robson said. 'I knew the risks involved in playing him, but I believed it was worthwhile given his importance to, and influ-

↗

Bryan Robson celebrates victory over Yugoslavia with Bobby Robson, 1987.

ence on, the team. Bryan was as important to England as he was to Manchester United.'

Bryan Robson commanded a remarkable degree of respect inside the dressing room of England and Manchester United, on the strength of his leadership quality as captain and competitive nature as a player.

Alex Ferguson described him as a hero, and a competitor without equal. 'Bryan is a miracle of commitment, a human marvel who pushed himself beyond every imaginable limit on the field. The combination of his stamina and perceptive reading of movement enabled him, in his prime, to make sudden and deadly infiltrations from midfield and score vital goals.'

Robson did more than any other player to keep Manchester United competitive in the early Ferguson years. 'He was known as "Captain Marvel" for a good reason,' Ferguson said.

↖

The shirt worn by Manchester United for the FA Cup final against Crystal Palace, 1990.

Bobby Robson praised his unrelenting competitiveness and refusal to give up. 'He would hunt a rival down and get in the tackle, face to face. He challenged fairly, powerfully, correctly.'

Paul Gascoigne described Robson as the greatest midfield player in the world. 'When he was captain of England, it always felt so good knowing he was there.'

A cult figure himself at Old Trafford, Eric Cantona adopted Robson as his new idol on arrival at Old Trafford. 'An awesome player,' Cantona said. 'The fans love him. They cheer him even when he is warming up. The people don't forget those who have made them dream.'

↖

Bryan Robson, (Trevillion).

And Roy Keane, one of Robson's successors as Manchester United captain, described him as 'the main man in the dressing room'.

'Bryan was respected to the point of awe by every other player,' Keane said. 'His courage in the face of injury or any other adversity was bottomless. When Alex Ferguson struggled in his early years at Old Trafford, Robson fought like a lion to drive the team forward. He was a great player for the club.'

↖

Bryan Robson at the 1986 World Cup finals.

GARY LINEKER

▶▶▶▶▶▶▶▶▶▶▶▶▶▶▶

1960–

Gary Lineker enjoys the distinction of being the only Englishman to lift the Golden Boot – the coveted FIFA award for the leading goalscorer in a World Cup finals tournament. He earned the accolade – and worldwide media attention – for his tally of six goals in Mexico in 1986, when England reached the last eight. At Italia '90, he added four more goals, including a famous equaliser against West Germany in the semi-final.

In all, Lineker scored 48 times for his country, a total that fell one shy of Bobby Charlton's record. 'Gary was simply the best finisher I've ever seen,' said Bobby Robson, the England manager in 1986 and 1990.

All six goals in Mexico illustrated his greatest asset as a striker: a poacher's instinct to be in the right place when it mattered. Each one of them involved a one-touch finish from close range. As he said himself: 'I was what we call in the trade a box-player.'

Gary Lineker on the ball, 1991.

PLAYER • INDUCTED 2003 • 80 CAPS • 1 FA CUP

'I looked to pounce on defenders' mistakes, and made repeated runs into space in the hope that the ball would come to me.'
– Gary Lineker

Three times Lineker finished leading goalscorer in the top flight – with, in turn, Leicester City, his hometown club, Everton and Tottenham Hotspur. In 1986, at the end of his brief stay at Goodison Park, he was voted Footballer of the Year by both the press and his fellow players.

In realising his technical limitations, Lineker was able to concentrate on making the most of his natural gifts: lightning pace, keen anticipation and outstanding positional sense. 'I developed my own style,' he explained.

It was all about getting that vital half-yard on his marker, most often at the near-post. Alternatively, if released with an early pass from midfield, he rarely came off second best in the chase for a through-ball. 'No one could match Gary's pace over 40 yards,' said Howard Kendall, the Everton manager who paid £800,000 to bring him to Merseyside.

As a consequence of his success in 1986, Lineker came to the attention of Barcelona, who invested a record £2.2 million fee for his transfer. On leaving Spain, Lineker rejected a more lucrative move to Monaco in favour of a return home with Spurs. In 1991 he collected an FA Cup winners' medal, reversing his experience of defeat with Everton at Wembley five years earlier.

At both Spurs and Barcelona he played under the managership of Terry Venables, who noted the striker's habit of 'always keeping the

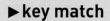

ball low and always hitting the target'.

In 1991–92, his farewell season in English football, the former England captain was voted Footballer of the Year for the second time.

When the end came, Lineker had a spotless disciplinary record, without a booking, let alone a sending-off to his name. In recognition, FIFA presented him with a Fair Play Award in 1991.

Such sportsmanship on the field, and polite demeanour off it, cemented an enduring popularity for the future *Match of the Day* presenter. Hard-bitten football reporters weren't immune to his appeal either; at the conclusion of his last appearance for England they gave him a standing ovation in the press room.

Gary Lineker shows off his 'lucky' boots, 1986.

BOBBY ROBSON

▶▶▶▶▶▶▶▶▶▶▶▶▶▶▶

1933–2009

By guiding England to their best performance in a World Cup finals on foreign soil, Bobby Robson lifted the reputation of English football in troubled times.

When England came within two penalty kicks of reaching the final of Italia '90, it was the closest the national side had come to winning the trophy since the days of Alf Ramsey.

Knighted for his services to the game in 2002, Robson had an instinct for adventure. For him football was a vibrant, attacking game. His teams at their best were direct, energetic and stylish. He inspired loyalty because his players signed up to his ideals.

An honest patriot, Robson respected and promoted the best traditions of English football. He believed the game was all about speed, technical ability and stamina. Sportsmanship mattered; there was no place for cynicism, nor malice in his approach, which is why England's exemplary behaviour in winning the FIFA Fair Play Award in 1990 meant so much to him.

↖
Bobby Robson watches from the dug-out in Copenhagen, 1982

MANAGER • INDUCTED 2003 • 1 FA CUP • 1 UEFA CUP

'It was a joy working with England at the World Cup in Italy ... It was an experience I would never swap.' – Bobby Robson

The former England international began his career in management at Fulham, before moving on to Ipswich Town where he won the FA Cup in 1978 and the UEFA Cup in 1981, the same season in which a challenge for the championship fell agonisingly short.

On their way to that UEFA Cup success, Ipswich gave what was arguably their finest performance for Robson in overwhelming a St Etienne side that included Michel Platini and Johnny Rep 4–1 in the away leg of their quarter-final, prompting a standing ovation by French fans.

Bobby Robson signs an autograph, 1980.

Under Robson, the modest Suffolk club achieved a level of consistency between 1969 and 1982 that was bettered only by Liverpool. Ipswich were bright, inventive and forward thinking, a boldness best illustrated by the pioneering move to sign Dutchmen Arnold Muhren and Frans Thijssen following the lifting of an import ban in 1978. Robson's reward: a 10-year contract at Portman Road.

His subsequent eight, turbulent years in charge of the national team coincided with a succession of crises in English football: the disasters at Hillsborough and Bradford, and the fatal outbreak of hooliganism at Heysel that led to a ban on English clubs in Europe.

Throughout it all, Robson led England with a calm authority, despite being subject to bouts of media and public vilification unprecedented in their intensity, most notably during successive disappointments in European Championship campaigns. He would eventually leave the job 'with dignity, and grey hair,' according to the Football Association.

The rehabilitation of English football began in earnest in 1986 when England reached the quarter-final of the World Cup in Mexico, only to be denied by Argentina and Diego Maradona, whose infamous 'Hand of God' goal prompted Robson to reflect later: 'It wasn't the Hand of God, it was the hand of a rascal. God had nothing to do with it.'

When the Football Association allowed his contract to run out in 1990, Robson enhanced his standing on the Continent by winning

major honours for PSV Eindhoven in Holland, Porto in Portugal and Barcelona in Spain.

In 1999 Robson made a sentimental return to his native north-east, whereupon he lifted his beloved Newcastle United out of the doldrums, securing three consecutive top-five finishes. When he became an honorary freeman of the city of Newcastle in 2005, he described the award as 'the proudest moment of my life'.

Following his death in 2009 at the age of 76, Sir Alex Ferguson led the tributes, saying: 'It has been one of the privileges of my life to have met Bobby and to have been so enthused by him.'

In 1968 Arthur Hopcraft wrote the seminal book *The Football Man*. The moniker sums up Bobby Robson.

MARK HUGHES

▶▶▶▶▶▶▶▶▶▶▶▶▶▶▶

1963–

Sir Alex Ferguson once described Mark Hughes as 'the most courageous striker in the game and the greatest big-game player I have ever seen'.

The Wales striker's combination of power, verve and relish for battle made Hughes a terrace hero at Manchester United and Chelsea – the two English clubs he served with such distinction during his peak years as a player.

At Old Trafford Hughes was likened to Denis Law, the great hero of the Stretford End masses during the 1960s. 'They like Mark's commitment and see in him a present-day Law, especially as a scorer of spectacular, often vitally important goals,' Ferguson said.

Physically, Hughes could look after himself – always giving as good as he got. 'The bottom line is that I don't like great, hulking defenders who think that they can get away with anything,' he once wrote.

Mark Hughes celebrates his goal in the FA Cup final, 1990.

PLAYER • INDUCTED 2007 • 72 CAPS • 2 PREMIER LEAGUE TITLES • 4 FA CUPS

3 LEAGUE CUPS • 2 EUROPEAN CUP-WINNERS' CUPS

> **'Mark has always scored marvellous goals, so you can understand why he is such a hero in the eyes of so many fans.'**
> **– Alex Ferguson**

Voted Footballer of the Year by his fellow professionals in 1989 and 1991, Hughes climbed the steps to the Royal Box as an FA Cup winner a record four times: as a United player in 1985, 1990 and 1994, and then in a last Wembley hurrah with Chelsea in 1997. The following season he collected a second European Cup-Winners' Cup medal.

Mark Hughes holds aloft the European Cup-Winners' Cup, 1991.

Remarkably, the now veteran Hughes wasn't finished yet. In a final flourish, the striker helped Blackburn Rovers, the club he would later manage, to lift the League Cup – the last of his 11 honours in the game.

Sandwiched in the middle of all this came stints at Barcelona and Bayern Munich, the German club where he enjoyed a renaissance after a frustrating experience in Spanish football.

On one celebrated occasion, Bayern organised a private jet to whisk him back to Munich for an evening kick-off – only hours after he played in an international fixture for Wales. 'The more important the occasion,' Hughes once said, 'the more I relished the challenge. The big games seemed to bring the best out of me.'

In his second stint at Old Trafford, following his loan spell in Germany, Hughes was a vital figure in United's resurgence under Ferguson, culminating in 1992–93, the club's break-through, title-winning season.

The following season Hughes kept United on track for the club's first ever double with a last-gasp equaliser against Oldham Athletic in an FA Cup semi-final. His spectacular volley into the top corner remains an indelible memory for United fans.

Outside the penalty area Hughes excelled as a 'link-man' on account of his outstanding technique, strength and skill in retaining possession as United built their attacks.

When a niggling knee injury began to restrict his appearances, Hughes, now in his early thirties, moved on to Stamford Bridge in order to secure more first-team football. 'If I leave him out he is like a bear with a sore head for about three weeks,' Ferguson said. 'He doesn't want explanations, just the shirt.'

Soon after his departure in 1995, Hughes was described by Ferguson as 'a sort of British warrior, whose willingness to compete up the middle on his own, and his refusal to shrink from the most punishing markers is like waving a flag of courage for the rest of the team.'

Assessing his former player's contribution to the United cause, Sir Alex added: 'Anybody who sees himself as a centre-forward of the old type should come and watch Mark.'

▶ key match

Manchester United 2 Barcelona 1, European Cup-Winners' Cup final, Rotterdam, 15 May 1991

Mark Hughes proved a point when he scored both goals against his former employer.

Having nudged a Steve Bruce header over the line for the opener, Hughes added a stunning second goal: an unerring, arrow-straight shot on the turn from a narrow angle.

After Barcelona reduced the deficit, Hughes finally broke their resolve when his direct running on the break drew a professional foul that led to the sending-off of his marker.

Hughes was the talk of Europe, but he dismissed the possibility of a return overseas and committed his future to Manchester United. 'All I wanted to do was show Barcelona that I'd matured into a good player,' he said.

KENNY DALGLISH

▶▶▶▶▶▶▶▶▶▶▶▶▶▶▶▶▶

1951–

Kenny Dalglish won the League title and FA Cup double in his first season as player-manager – and he built on this early success in later years by becoming only the fourth person in history to lead two different clubs to championship success.

Indeed, over a period spanning four decades, few individuals in history can claim to have made such a significant impact on English football – as player and then manager.

During his six years in charge at Anfield – starting in 1985 – Dalglish won three titles and two FA Cups; a decade later, having moved on to Blackburn Rovers, he brought the Premier League trophy to Ewood Park. Four times along the way, his peers in the dug-out voted him Manager of the Year.

In January 2011, Dalglish returned to Anfield as manager. 'We could not have made a better choice,' said principal-owner John Henry.

Kenny Dalglish watches the action, 1991.

MANAGER • INDUCTED 2010 • 3 DIVISION ONE CHAMPIONSHIPS • 2 FA CUPS

1 PREMIER LEAGUE TITLE

In winning the title with two different clubs, Dalglish followed in the footsteps of three towering figures in football management: Tom Watson (Sunderland and Liverpool) more than a century ago; Herbert Chapman (Huddersfield Town and Arsenal) during the inter-war years; and Brian Clough (Derby County and Nottingham Forest) in the 1970s.

Promoted to the top job from within, in line with established club policy, the Scot proved himself a respectful custodian of Anfield tradition. As player-manager, Dalglish maintained the 'Boot Room' ethos shaped by Bill Shankly and Bob Paisley – a trusted early adviser.

At Blackburn, in contrast, Dalglish was effectively starting from scratch, having been handed the responsibility of investing the tens of millions of pounds being pumped into the club by Rovers benefactor and lifelong supporter, Jack Walker.

Once promotion had been achieved, Dalglish raised the stakes dramatically in 1992 by signing Alan Shearer from Southampton for a British record fee of £3.5 million. In their second season back in the top flight, Rovers finished runners-up, by which time England internationals David Batty and Tim Flowers had been added to the playing staff.

Emboldened by this success, Dalglish backed his own judgement again by signing striker Chris Sutton from Norwich City for £5 million, once again breaking the transfer record.

When Rovers finally secured their first title in 81 years, a tearful Jack Walker said: 'We won because we have the best manager in the game.' As it happened, the title was secured at Anfield, and after captain Tim Sherwood lifted the trophy, the entire ground echoed to the chant: 'Dalglish! Dalglish!'

Dalglish began his managerial career as successor to Joe Fagan in the most demanding circumstances: the immediate aftermath of the Heysel disaster in 1985.

Within two years, Dalglish had built his own team, following the signing of midfielder Ray Houghton, and forwards Peter Beardsley, John Aldridge and John Barnes. On their way to the title, Liverpool went unbeaten for 29 League matches at the start of the season – equalling the Football League record.

Having nursed the club through the grief and trauma of the Hillsborough disaster in 1989, an exhausted Dalglish resigned two years later.

After leaving Rovers, Dalglish guided Newcastle United to a qualifying position for the Champions League and a losing FA Cup final appearance.

▶talking point

Kenny Dalglish shouts his orders, 1989.

GILLIAN COULTARD

▶▶▶▶▶▶▶▶▶▶▶▶▶▶▶▶▶

1963–

Gillian Coultard, the diminutive dynamo whose energy and ambition propelled Doncaster Belles to the pinnacle of the domestic game, played more games for England than any other woman in history.

On the way to amassing 119 caps, Coultard secured a place in the record books when she scored the first goal ever netted at Wembley Stadium in a women's international.

Prodigiously talented as a child, Coultard was training with the senior national team at the age of 13; two decades later, she was a member of the first England team to reach a FIFA World Cup finals tournament.

Once into her thirties, Coultard switched roles from central midfield to sweeper, in order to prolong her career. When she retired in 2000, she was captain of England. She had played the game at the highest level for 16 years.

Gillian Coultard evades a defender, 1983.

PLAYER • INDUCTED 2006 • 119 CAPS • 2 PREMIER LEAGUE CHAMPIONSHIPS • 4 FA CUPS

**'To reach the landmark of a century of caps was a fantastic feeling, and an honour that no one can take away from me.'
– Gillian Coultard**

Her competitiveness, relentless will to win and discipline were vital factors in keeping the Belles at the top of the domestic game during the 1980s and 1990s.

↖
Gillian Coulthard in action, 1997.

A loyal servant to the club, she turned down various offers to play professional football in Sweden, Italy and Belgium. And to play for England on tour, she used up annual leave from her factory job.

The prominent woman footballer of her generation, Coultard was a mainstay of the Doncaster Belles side that secured the double of national League and FA Cup in 1994 – a decade after taking the captain's armband.

The youngest of eight children, Coultard was identified as a potential future international whilst still studying at school. Training alongside established England players at such a tender age proved to be a 'frightening' experience, however invaluable in football terms.

Five years later, in May 1981, Coultard made her debut for England in a 3–1 win over the Republic of Ireland.

She had, meanwhile, switched from right-winger to a ball-winning role in central midfield – the position she would make her own with both club and country.

Five foot nothing tall, Coultard combined a low centre of gravity with strength in her upper body – attributes that gave her an advantage going into the tackle.

A combative 'box-to-box' runner, she was often described in the papers as 'the Bryan Robson of women's football'. And like Robson, she captained her country, leading by example in terms of work-rate. 'The amount of ground she covered was astonishing,' Mark Bright,

the Sheffield Wednesday striker and future media pundit said, after watching one Belles performance. 'Gill was outstanding. Scoring one goal and running the game.'

All in all, Coultard played in four European Championship tournaments between 1984 and 1995. Runners-up in 1984, England reached the semi-finals twice and the quarter-finals once.

When England qualified for the 1995 World Cup in Sweden, Gillian Coultard fulfilled her greatest ambition in the game. This would be her first – and last – World Cup – and it ended at the quarter-final stage with defeat against Germany.

PETER BEARDSLEY

▶▶▶▶▶▶▶▶▶▶▶▶▶▶▶▶▶▶

1961–

A pioneer in the role of withdrawn striker – operating in the so-called 'hole' behind a recognised goalscorer – in the modern era, Peter Beardsley followed an unusual path on his way to establishing himself as the most valuable footballer in the country.

His shoulders habitually hunched, the quick-witted, incisive Beardsley created a sequence of scoring opportunities for a succession of strike partners, including Kevin Keegan, Alan Shearer and, most notably, Gary Lineker.

A proud Geordie and product of the famous Wallsend Boys' Club, Beardsley attained hero status in Newcastle, where he enjoyed a glorious renaissance late in his career. On Merseyside, meanwhile, he holds the distinction of scoring the winning goal for both Liverpool and Everton in derby matches. 'I will probably be best remembered for my enthusiasm,' the ever-modest Beardsley said.

Peter Beardsley in possession for Newcastle, 1985.

PLAYER • INDUCTED 2007 • 59 CAPS • 2 DIVISION ONE CHAMPIONSHIPS • 1 FA CUP

Following a record £1.9 million transfer from Newcastle United in 1987, Beardsley spent his peak years at Anfield, where he won all his major honours – two championship medals and an FA Cup winners' medal. For many fans on the Kop, this was Liverpool's most vibrant attack since the war – and such a far cry from Beardsley's early days in the game.

After a halting start to his professional career, with spells at Carlisle United and Vancouver Whitecaps, and rejection by Manchester United, Beardsley made his breakthrough at Newcastle, alongside Kevin Keegan in attack. Promotion to the top flight duly followed.

His emergence in international football was also belated; Beardsley was already 25 when Bobby Robson awarded him his first cap during the build-up to the 1986 World Cup. Once in Mexico, he quickly established himself as a regular, in partnership with Lineker up front. A goal against Paraguay helped England reach the last eight, and subsequent defeat against Argentina.

Four years later, Beardsley and Lineker were automatic choices as England progressed to the semi-final of Italia '90. 'The two of them complemented each other perfectly,' Bobby Robson said.

After a lengthy absence from international football in the early 1990s, Beardsley experienced a resurgence during the build-up to Euro '96 when Terry Venables identified him as a key tactical figure. 'With that one selection, our football became more fluid and attractive,' Venables wrote.

By now he was back for a second spell at St James' Park, following a £1.5 million move from Everton. In two productive years at Goodison Park, his valuation in the transfer market had risen 50 per cent – a rare achievement for

a player on the so-called 'wrong' side of 30.

Back in the black and white of Newcastle United, Beardsley provided a creative spark as Kevin Keegan's side thrillingly challenged Manchester United for supremacy in the mid 1990s. But for a decision by Ron Atkinson, a former manager at Old Trafford, it might have been a different story.

In the early 1980s, an emerging Beardsley was released by Manchester United after making only one appearance. It proved a costly mistake which Alex Ferguson twice made efforts to put right, to no avail. 'It wasn't to be,' Ferguson said. 'I would have loved to see Peter play in our team.'

Peter Beardsley scores against Paraguay, 1986.

THROUGH THE AGES
FOOTBALL IN THE 1980s

▶▶▶▶▶▶▶▶▶▶▶▶▶▶▶▶▶▶▶▶▶▶▶▶▶▶▶▶▶

THIS PAGE: **Above** England players don Basque-style berets for photographers, 1982. **Right** Vinnie Jones gets to grips with Paul Gascoigne, 1988.

OPPOSITE: **Above left** Terry Venables answers questions from reporters, 1987. **Above right** Andy Gray, of Everton, escapes a pitch invasion at Highbury, 1984. **Below left** Glenn Hoddle, on bass, and Ray Clemence, on piano, accompany singers Chas and Dave, 1982. **Below right** Brian Talbot, of Arsenal, poses for photographers, 1980.

PAUL GASCOIGNE ▶▶▶▶▶▶▶▶

1967–

Paul Gascoigne was identified as the most famous man in Britain in the aftermath of his performances for England at the World Cup in 1990. Football fans were enthralled by his ability on the ball, and his tears of disappointment in defeat had a million mums reaching for the tissues.

His popularity and commercial value soared to such an extent that, upon his return home from Italia '90, he licensed his own nickname as a commercial brand. 'Gazza' had graduated from footballer to business trademark. 'Paul was a sensation – the finest player in the tournament,' England manager Bobby Robson said.

Gascoigne cried in frustration after being booked by the referee during the semi-final against West Germany. In that moment he realised that he would miss the final – should England get through – because of suspension. 'I was devastated,' he recalled, 'and the tears just came. I resolved to give my all for England in whatever time there was left. So I played my heart out.'

Those performances in Italy catapulted Gascoigne onto the world stage. Two years later, Lazio paid Tottenham Hotspur £5.5 million for his transfer – a move that had been delayed for more than a year after Gascoigne suffered a serious cruciate knee ligament injury playing for Spurs in the FA Cup final. Carried from the field on a stretcher, he watched his colleagues defeat Nottingham Forest from a hospital bed.

A free-spirited practical joker, Gascoigne was famously described by Bobby Robson as being 'daft as a brush'. Celebrated, most of the time, by team-mates for this playful nature, he also gained their respect for his work ethic in training and during matches.

'He succeeds in keeping the company happy, but he is also a man who works on the field with great dedication and seriousness,' Dino Zoff, the Lazio coach, said.

Paul Gascoigne shields the ball from a Czechoslovakia defender, 1990.

PLAYER • INDUCTED 2002 • 57 CAPS • 1 FA CUP

'Paul was a great trainer and a great player. But off the pitch he was a riot. He kept everyone laughing.' – Terry Venables

Paul Gascoigne always had a strong belief in his own ability. As a schoolboy he would practise his signature during lessons. 'I'm going to be a professional footballer,' he told his teachers. That confidence as a player never left him.

Before the semi-final of the 1990 World Cup, Bobby Robson had a quiet word in private; he wanted to stress the scale of the challenge facing him. 'You do realise you'll be playing against the best midfield player in the world,' Robson said, referring to Lothar Matthäus of West Germany. Gazza replied: 'No, Bobby, you've got it wrong. He is.' Gascoigne was 23 at the time.

↗
The trophy for the BBC Sports Personality of the Year. Paul Gascoigne won the award in 1990.

Several weeks earlier, during the build-up to the tournament, his England team-mates presented Gascoigne with a birthday cake. He finished his speech in gratitude by saying, 'So, here I am, a legend at my age.'

Gascoigne had been marked out for greatness since his early days as an apprentice at St James' Park by Jackie Milburn, the great

Newcastle United forward of the 1950s. 'We've got one here you should look out for,' wrote Milburn in a message to Bobby Robson, the then England manager.

Alerted, Robson went to watch Gascoigne in action. Ninety minutes later he realised that Milburn had been right in his assessment. 'This lad is a little gem,' Robson told his fellow Geordie. More proof of Gascoigne's outstanding potential was gathered in 1984–85 when he captained Newcastle's FA Youth Cup-winning side.

At the age of 21 Gascoigne ignored the overtures of Manchester United in favour of Tottenham Hotspur in a deal worth £2.3 million. At White Hart Lane he thrived under the coaching regime of Terry Venables. 'I loved every minute of my time at Spurs,' he wrote later, 'and I improved leaps and bounds as a player.'

By 1991, when Gascoigne injured his knee so badly at Wembley, he had established himself as an indispensable member of the England set-up. Sadly, the injury ruled him out of international football for two years. These were dark days for both player and country.

'All that time we've been trying to eke out results without Paul,' Graham Taylor, the then England manager, said on his return. 'You find yourself saying, "Don't let anything else go wrong with him". He's that important to us.' Without him, England failed to qualify for the 1994 World Cup.

In what proved to be his last significant

↖
Paul Gascoigne evades the challenges of Switzerland players, 1996.

A puppet featured on the satirical television programme *Spitting Image* in the 1990s.

contribution for England, Gascoigne played a crucial role as playmaker when England reached the semi-final of the European Championships on home soil in 1996.

One highlight, above all, remains vivid in the popular imagination: the spectacular turn and volley for the goal that sealed victory against Scotland in a group game at Wembley. 'That was not only the best goal of Euro '96,' Terry Venables, the then England coach said, 'but the best goal of the last two or three major tournaments.'

Running onto a pass from Darren Anderton, Gascoigne had feinted in order to commit the defender, flicked the ball over his opponent's head, skipped round him, and then volleyed the ball into the bottom corner.

'I just knew where Colin Hendry would be and when he would commit himself,' Gascoigne recalled. 'So I knew what to do. It felt brilliant when it all worked. I went to look like I would knock the ball past him and try to go round the outside, but I changed direction and lobbed it, and he ended up on the deck.'

Venables said the display of skill was comparable to those normally associated with the best Brazilians. 'Gazza always gives you that touch of the unexpected that the opposition don't like,' he said.

England won the game 2–0. 'After this goal, our opponents were making plans about how to play against him, right up to the semi-final against Germany,' Venables said.

Although there would be more highlights – most notably during his time in Scotland with Rangers – Gascoigne endured a gradual decline in his fortunes, first with Middlesbrough, then Everton. Psychologically, his omission from the England squad for the World Cup in 1998 was a particularly heavy blow.

Above all, perhaps, injury took its toll. 'During my career, I had 31 operations,' he said. Through all the setbacks, however, and despite his increasing dependence on alcohol

▶talking point

Paul Gascoigne was invited to Buckingham Palace and 10 Downing Street in celebration of England's performance during the 1990 World Cup.

His profile soared. Franco Zeffirelli, the Italian film director, announced that he loved Gascoigne's sense of humour; Osvaldo Ardiles, the Argentina international, named his dog after him; Madame Tussaud's made a waxwork figure; and his puppet caricature appeared on the television satire programme *Spitting Image*.

'Everyone was competing for a bit of me, wanting my presence at events,' Gascoigne recalled. 'It was overwhelming.'

Gascoigne put his name to lunchboxes, calendars, t-shirts, key rings, books, videos, bedroom rugs and newspaper columns. His cover of 'Fog on the Tyne' sold 100,000 copies. 'We registered the name "Gazza" so that people couldn't instantly rip us off,' he recalled.

The celebrity status brought its rewards: a gold disc for his pop song, and the award as BBC Sports Personality of the Year. Bobby Charlton presented the trophy. 'I had a hard job keeping back the tears,' Gascoigne said.

But there was also the downside. Gascoigne often found himself besieged. 'I hid in the car boot when I was driven away from my home or White Hart Lane,' he recalled. 'The only time I feel safe now is in the middle of a football pitch. At least there I know I can escape for a couple of hours.'

and other drugs, his love of the game never wavered. 'I accomplished my dreams, but not my potential,' he once said.

Paul Gascoigne, (Trevillion).

JOHN BARNES

▶▶▶▶▶▶▶▶▶▶▶▶▶▶▶▶

1963–

John Barnes joined a select group of past greats when he was voted Footballer of the Year for the second time. Only four other players – Stanley Matthews, Tom Finney, Danny Blanchflower and Kenny Dalglish – had previously been two-time winners.

Bobby Robson, who awarded him the bulk of his 79 England caps, described Barnes as 'a match-winner' and a vital member of both his 1986 and 1990 World Cup squads.

A remarkable run and dribble through the Brazil defence during a friendly in Rio de Janeiro in 1984 launched Barnes' profile on the international stage. 'I loved that goal,' he said later. One Brazilian newspaper described his individual effort as 'the greatest goal ever scored at the Maracana'. Meanwhile, Zico, the great Brazil number 10 declared that 'Barnes is the future of English football'.

Summing up his approach, Barnes said: 'My first instinct is always to pass. Only if there's nothing on do I keep running with the ball.'

John Barnes runs with the ball, 1993.

PLAYER • INDUCTED 2005 • 79 CAPS • 2 DIVISION ONE CHAMPIONSHIPS • 2 FA CUPS • 1 LEAGUE CUP

'The future of English football.' – Zico, 1984

Signed by Graham Taylor from obscure non-League side Sudbury Court in return for a new set of kit, Barnes became a prominent figure in the rise of Watford.

After winning promotion in 1981–82, Watford finished runners-up in the top flight the following season. By now Barnes was an England player; and another year on, he was an FA Cup finalist. 'Graham Taylor always drummed into me, as a winger: "Take them on, John, take them on." '

Bertie Mee, the double-winning manager at Arsenal in 1970–71 and then senior figure at Vicarage Road, looked to the past in his praise of Barnes, likening his dribbling ability to that of Tom Finney, the Preston and England winger. 'John has the same way of gliding past his marker,' Mee said.

↖
John Barnes in the stand at Vicarage Road, 1985.

↗
John Barnes beats two defenders, 1988.

Following his transfer to Anfield for £900,000 in 1987, Barnes was voted Footballer of the Year, as Liverpool won another title – an individual and collective double repeated by player and club in 1989–90. The shameful racial abuse that greeted his arrival in the city had been drowned out, with neutrals joining the Kop in praising his ability, and the dignified manner in which he triumphed over bigotry.

The Liverpool passing game suited him perfectly. So much so that Barnes always thought of himself as a better, more effective player for his club than his country. 'I often felt inhibited with England,' he wrote later.

However, there were many memorable moments: notably his performance as a late substitute in 1986 when he almost single-

handedly rescued the quarter-final against Argentina. But in other England games, in his own words, he found himself 'marooned on the wing a lot, feeling frustrated'.

'I never saw myself as just that for Liverpool,' Barnes said. 'I was a more all-round player. In one season I scored 22 goals in 34 League games.' Tactically, Barnes formed the vital link between defence and attack.

Alan Hansen had previously looked for Kenny Dalglish when distributing the ball from the back. Now he had a new outlet. 'John's first touch was so good, it didn't really matter if he was closely marked. I gave him the ball anyway.'

After operating in a deeper, anchor role in the latter years of his decade at Anfield, Barnes moved on to Newcastle United and then Charlton Athletic.

HOPE POWELL

▶▶▶▶▶▶▶▶▶▶▶▶▶▶▶▶▶▶▶

1966–

Hope Powell, a former England international and double-winning captain with Croydon, broke new ground by becoming the first woman in the world to gain the UEFA Pro Licence, the highest qualification in the game.

On her retirement as a player in 1998, Powell was appointed England women's national team coach, with responsibility for the senior, Under-19s, Under-17s and Under-15s sides. At the age of 31 she was the youngest ever person to be given the job.

A football prodigy, Powell made her debut for England at the age of 16. 'As soon as Hope joined the squad she stood out as an exceptional talent,' said Gillian Coultard, the former England captain. 'As a creative player she had this outstanding technical ability, and it was obvious to everyone that she would make the step up into the England team.'

Hope Powell controls the ball, 1998.

PLAYER • INDUCTED 2003 • 66 CAPS • 1 NATIONAL LEAGUE TITLE • 2 FA CUPS • 1 LEAGUE CUP

'She had this rare quality of being able to know where the other players were without even looking.' – Gillian Coultard

In a career disrupted badly by injury, Powell played 66 times for her country as an attacking midfield player or occasional striker between 1983 and 1998, scoring 35 goals at a ratio of more than one goal every two games.

Powell made her debut for England in a 6–0 thrashing of the Republic of Ireland at Reading in a European Championships qualifier on 11 September 1983. England went on to the reach the final of the competition, losing against Sweden the following year.

It was the closest Powell came as a player to winning a major honour with England. The squad reached the semi-finals in the tournament in 1987 and 1995, and the quarter-finals in 1991 and 1993.

At club level, Powell enjoyed her greatest success in 1996 when, in addition to being appointed England vice-captain, she lifted both the League and FA Cup with Croydon.

She spent nine years of her career with Millwall Lionesses, winning the FA Cup in 1991. Previously, during a two-year stint with Friends of Fulham, she ended up on the losing side in the 1989 final despite scoring twice.

For most of her time in international football Powell formed a central midfield partnership with Coultard, the most capped female England player in history.

The team tactics were formulated in order to take best advantage of Powell's attacking ability and finishing talent. 'Her skill set her apart,' said Coultard. 'She was a creative

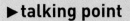
player in the mould of Paul Gascoigne. Hope was two-footed and a good dribbler. She could see a pass and she could also score goals, and I rated her very highly, both for her ability and her contribution to the team on and off the field.'

In 2002, Powell was awarded an OBE in the Queen's birthday honours list in recognition of her services to women's sport. 'This is a great honour for women's football,' Powell said.

The following year she gained the UEFA Pro Licence at the end of a 12-month programme. 'I consider it a tremendous privilege to have this role as England head coach and I feel very fortunate to do this work for a living,' she said.

Hope Powell with England players, 2002.

TEDDY SHERINGHAM

▶▶▶▶▶▶▶▶▶▶▶▶▶▶▶▶▶▶▶▶▶▶▶▶▶▶▶▶▶▶▶▶

1966–

Teddy Sheringham was one of the great servants of English football: a player whose skilful scheming and remarkable longevity revived memories of a previous age, the age of Stanley Matthews and Tom Finney; and along the way, he won a bagful of medals and played a hero's role in the most important match in European club football.

Playing across the divisions – first with Millwall, then Nottingham Forest, Tottenham Hotspur, Manchester United, Spurs again, Portsmouth, West Ham United and Colchester United – Sheringham was 42 by the time he finally hung up his boots in 2008. At the time he joked: 'My dad wanted me to carry on and beat Sir Stanley Matthews' record of playing at 50 years of age, but I feel this is the right time to bow out.'

Reflecting upon all his experiences in football, one memory stood out: victory in the 1999 Champions League final. 'We celebrated for so long I forgot how many laps of honour we'd done,' he wrote later.

Teddy Sheringham is mobbed by England team-mates, 1996.

PLAYER • INDUCTED 2009 • 51 CAPS • 3 PREMIER LEAGUE TITLES • 1 FA CUP • 1 CHAMPIONS LEAGUE

**'Sheringham is the most intelligent strike partner I have played alongside.'
– Jürgen Klinsmann**

In a tribute, *The Times* praised Sheringham's 'rare combination of intense hunger and calm authority'. At a time when pace assumed ever greater importance, Sheringham, though never one of the quickest forwards, flourished as a result of his vision, technique and eye for

Teddy Sheringham celebrates winning the Champions League with David Beckham, 1999.

goal. Jürgen Klinsmann, the Germany striker, was once quoted as describing his one-time Spurs team-mate as the 'most intelligent strike partner I have played alongside'.

Notable highlights of his career included telling and timely contributions – first at Wembley and then the Nou Camp – for treble-winners Manchester United in 1999, and a match-turning appearance as a substitute for England that ensured participation in the 2002 World Cup in Japan and South Korea.

At the age of 35, Sheringham scored a crucial equaliser in the vital qualifier against Greece at Old Trafford – one of 51 appearances he made for his country between 1993 and 2002. Meanwhile, at club level his goals helped Manchester United win another title. In tribute, both the football writers and his fellow professionals voted him their Footballer of the Year in 2001 – making him the oldest player to win this notable double.

Five years earlier, Terry Venables selected Sheringham to play in the vital, and much-vaunted 'hole' behind Alan Shearer as England reached the last four of the European Championships.

His lengthy career began at Millwall, where Sheringham finished top-scorer four times, including 1987–88 when the Lions reached the top flight for the first time. In the 1990–91 season he scored 37 times, making him the highest scorer in the League. Those goals were not enough to win promotion, but they

impressed Brian Clough who invested £2 million to bring Sheringham to Nottingham Forest that summer.

In August 2006, during a three-year stint with West Ham United, Sheringham became the oldest outfield player in the history of the Premier League, at the age of 40 years 139 days. On either side of his stay at Upton Park, the former Spurs idol played for Portsmouth and Colchester United, where he ended his career.

Reflecting on this career, former Millwall striker partner and Republic of Ireland forward, Tony Cascarino wrote of Sheringham's 'sharp football brain', then added: 'He had the ability to pass the ball where and when team-mates wanted it, a talent for finding space and time amid the mayhem of a match.'

ALEX FERGUSON ▶▶▶▶▶▶▶▶▶

1941–

Alex Ferguson, the first manager in history to win the championship title three seasons in a row, bore the heavy burden of expectation at Old Trafford and then resurrected Manchester United as a dominant force in domestic and European football.

Three times within a decade Ferguson led his side to the double of League title and FA Cup, a unique feat for a manager in England. In the triumphant 1998–99 season, the European Cup (Champions League) was added to complete an unprecedented treble.

'There have been some wonderful times at Old Trafford under Alex,' Bobby Charlton said. 'He has been successful, while maintaining a great tradition for attacking football at the club.'

In December 2010 – 24 years, one month and 14 days after his appointment – Ferguson became the longest-serving manager in the club's history, eclipsing the record of Matt Busby. Asked about the similarities between the two Scots, Ferguson joked: 'Sir Matt was a bit calmer than me.'

However, for almost seven years following his appointment in 1986, Ferguson was weighed down by history. More than 25 years, dating back to the days of Busby, had elapsed since the last title success. In 1992–93, the club finally broke through. 'The barrier that had defied so many talented people, world-renowned players as well as managers, had been breached,' Ferguson said. Twenty-six years of 'collective cursing and frustration', were at an end.

Over the following decade Manchester United won the title seven more times. In 2000–01, they completed a hat-trick of championship wins, a feat no other manager had achieved.

A one-time Glasgow Rangers centre-forward, Ferguson learned his trade in Scottish football. At Aberdeen, he first smashed the seemingly entrenched Rangers-Celtic duopoly, and then guided the Pittodrie club to European success.

↖ Alex Ferguson smiles in victory, 1999.

▶ key match

Bayern Munich 1 Manchester United 2, Champions League final, Barcelona, 26 May 1999

As his players prepared to leave the dressing room at half-time, Alex Ferguson knew he had one last opportunity to influence their thinking.

'Lads, when you go out there, just have a look at that cup,' he said. 'It will be about five yards away, but you won't be able to touch it. Think about the fact that if you lose this game, you'll have been so close. So, just make sure you don't lose!'

With 24 minutes left, Bayern still led 1–0. Time for a change. First, substitute Teddy Sheringham was told to give the opposition problems down the left flank. Next came Ole Gunnar Solskjaer. 'Ole has got lightning quick reactions, and their defenders were exhausted,' Ferguson wrote later.

Two goals in injury time – scored by Sheringham and Solskjaer – changed everything. His reaction has since entered football folklore. 'I can't believe it,' he said. 'Football – bloody hell.'

MANAGER • INDUCTED 2002 • 2 CHAMPIONS LEAGUES • 1 EUROPEAN CUP-WINNERS' CUP

11 PREMIER LEAGUE TITLES • 5 FA CUPS • 4 LEAGUE CUPS

'Alex has this personality. He makes things happen. Every part of the club is buzzing.' – Bobby Charlton

Manchester United were stuck just above the relegation zone when Alex Ferguson left Aberdeen to take over as manager on 6 November 1986. The team 'lacked fitness, ambition and morale was poor,' Ferguson quickly concluded. 'Too many physical lightweights,' he said.

Ferguson began by strengthening the defence. Viv Anderson, the first signing, added experience and resilience at full-back, and Steve Bruce came in as a reliable and robust centre-half from Norwich City.

Other problems were less easily remedied. By the third anniversary of his appointment, and with no trophy to show for his time in charge, the pressure was mounting. Frustrated supporters unfurled a banner at one home game. 'Three years of excuses; Ta-ra, Fergie,' it read.

Results did not improve. 'Black December', as Ferguson came to refer to the last four weeks of 1989, was the 'lowest, most desperate point in my career'.

One of the earliest lessons he had learned in management was: 'Never seek confrontation; confrontation will come to you.' And so it was at Old Trafford.

A drinking culture had enveloped the club and Ferguson eventually sold two established first-team players, Paul McGrath and Norman

The Manager of the Month award, 1994.

Whiteside, as a signal of intent to others.

Ferguson was unrelenting in his demands. Several former players have spoken of the 'hairdryer treatment', a torrent of 'in-your-face' criticism delivered at close quarter. Cups, bottles and boots have been hurled in the dressing room. Ferguson himself has expressed concern 'at the quickness of my temper and depth of my anger'.

Several players, though, have noted a mellowing in Ferguson over the years. Bryan Robson, captain of the 1992–93 side said: 'he is much calmer these days.'

Bobby Charlton has likened Alex Ferguson to Matt Busby in terms of their philosophy to football. 'Matt would never think about playing defensively,' Charlton said. 'He always used to say that the game must never be boring for the public, and that legacy has continued with Alex.'

The parallels in the careers of the two men, the only managers to be knighted solely for their work at club level, are striking.

Sir Alex Ferguson, 2010.

Manchester United had not won the championship title for 34 years when Matt Busby took over in 1945; when Ferguson arrived at the club the supporters had already been waiting 19 years since the success of 1966–67.

Both managers won the FA Cup as their first major honour at the club: Busby in 1948; Ferguson in 1990. Both had previously finished runners-up in the League. Both men also broke up a championship-winning side to introduce a generation of young players. It was a particularly bold decision on Busby's part back in the 1950s. 'You'll never win anything with a bunch of kids,' to use Alan Hansen's famous phrase, was even more entrenched as a managerial philosophy.

Manchester United reached the FA Youth Cup final two seasons in succession in the early 1990s, a throwback to the run of success in the competition enjoyed by the 'Busby Babes' in the 1950s.

Both European Cup-winning sides had a solid core of local lads and players brought up through the ranks. Ryan Giggs, Paul Scholes,

↗
Sir Alex Ferguson makes a point, 2008.

Gary Neville, David Beckham and Nicky Butt were following an example set by Nobby Stiles, Brian Kidd, Bill Foulkes, David Sadler, Bobby Charlton and George Best in 1968.

'Our victory against Bayern Munich, the miracle of the Nou Camp, came on what would have been Sir Matt's 90th birthday,' Ferguson said. 'That was very important to everyone at Manchester United.'

In 2008, Ferguson and his players celebrated in the Moscow rain as Manchester United won Europe's most coveted prize for a

↖
A Manchester United shirt, 1999.

third time – a victory made all the more poignant as it occurred 50 years on from the Munich disaster. Ferguson had fulfilled his ambition: to bring the trophy back to Manchester in honour of the victims and survivors of the tragedy.

TONY ADAMS

▶▶▶▶▶▶▶▶▶▶▶▶▶▶▶▶▶

1966–

Tony Adams, the great servant of Arsenal Football Club and a celebrated one-club man, is the only player to captain a championship-winning side in three different decades.

Twice, in 1997–98 and 2001–02, Adams led his team to the League and Cup double. 'An exceptional player who is highly respected at the club because of his commitment,' Arsène Wenger said.

Adams lifted the championship trophy for the first time in 1988–89, after being appointed the club's youngest ever captain at the age of 21. 'He is my sergeant-major on the pitch,' said George Graham, the Arsenal manager at the time. 'A colossus.'

Inevitably there would be a price to pay physically for all those years of committed service. Announcing his retirement, Adams said: 'The body has packed up on me, really. I want to be able to walk in a few years' time, so best I get out now.'

↖
Tony Adams salutes fans at Highbury, 1998.

PLAYER • INDUCTED 2004 • 66 CAPS • 2 DIVISION ONE CHAMPIONSHIPS • 2 PREMIER LEAGUE TITLES

3 FA CUPS • 1 EUROPEAN CUP-WINNERS' CUP • 2 LEAGUE CUPS

'The greatest of all Arsenal men, as simple as that.' – Bob Wilson

Over a period of 19 years Adams played 421 League games at the heart of the Arsenal defence. A cult hero at Highbury, tickets for his testimonial sold out within two days.

Adams played 66 times for England, including 15 appearances as captain. David Seaman, the Arsenal and England goalkeeper said: 'He's a born leader and there's not many of those around.'

Off the field, however, an increasing dependence on alcohol blighted his private life, leading to a prison sentence for drink-driving in 1991. He publicly admitted his health problems five years later. Once sober, he established a charity in aid of players suffering addiction.

Adams made his debut in 1983 at the age of 17 years and 26 days, making him the second youngest player to appear in an Arsenal shirt. 'I was so nervous I put my shorts on the wrong way round,' Adams recalled.

In 1987, Adams was voted Young Player of the Year. 'If we had that boy,' one First Division manager said privately, 'we'd conquer the world.'

After taking over as manager at Highbury in 1986 George Graham founded his challenge for the championship on a sound defence, with Adams at its core. Rigorously applying 'flat back four' tactics, the Arsenal defenders compressed play as high up the pitch as possible in a bid to restrict space to opponents in midfield. Pushing up in a line, they relied heavily on the offside trap.

Hence the abiding memory of Adams, standing, arm raised, appealing to the officials. 'I thought their goal was offside,' he said after one match in 1991. 'But then I always do.'

In the second double season, 1997–98, injuries restricted Adams to 26 League appearances. But he did play in the final home game, and he even scored the fourth, celebratory, goal against Everton.

Tony Adams holds aloft the League trophy, with John Lukic and Lee Dixon, 1989.

▶ key match

Liverpool 0 Arsenal 2, First Division, Anfield, 25 May 1989

Tony Adams made the last rallying call to his team-mates before they left the dressing room for the most dramatic game in the club's history.

'We've come this far, lads,' Adams said, smacking the palm of his hand, 'and we're not letting the title slip now.'

After earlier heading the table, Arsenal needed to win 2–0 at Anfield to secure their first title since 1971. 'They have all written us off,' Adams said. 'Now let's prove them all wrong. Let's go.'

George Graham said: 'Everything Liverpool tried foundered on the rock of our defence. Tony was typically determined and committed.'

Adams duly lifted the famous trophy. 'It was a proud moment,' he said.

In 2001–2002 Adams played only 10 games, but again he was there to lift the Premier League trophy at Highbury, just as he had been when the FA Cup was won the week before.

The physical toll of playing for almost two decades finally caught up with Adams in 2002 when he announced his retirement. 'He does everything 100 per cent,' Ian Wright said. 'He's not one to shirk a challenge.'

Alex Ferguson, manager of Arsenal's fierce rivals, Manchester United, said in 1999: 'He's the defining spirit of their team, a classic English defender – brave, reliable and capable not only of fulfilling his own responsibilities superbly but of organising and inspiring others.' Adding: 'I can't wait for him to retire.'

TERRY VENABLES

▶▶▶▶▶▶▶▶▶▶▶▶▶▶▶▶

1943–

The only footballer to play for his country at every level, Terry Venables was the overwhelming choice within the professional game for the top job in English football – and he then guided England to the brink of European Championship glory.

'He is not only the outstanding coach in the country, he is also a clever, shrewd and motivated tactician,' Sir Alf Ramsey wrote, prior to Venables' appointment in 1994.

At club level he achieved success at home and abroad, notably with Tottenham Hotspur and Barcelona, where he set a club-record for longevity in the manager's chair, after guiding the Catalan giants to the 1986 European Cup final.

Football has always fascinated Venables. As a player he once travelled to Yorkshire to watch Pelé play for Santos against Sheffield and then drove back through the night to be ready for training the next day.

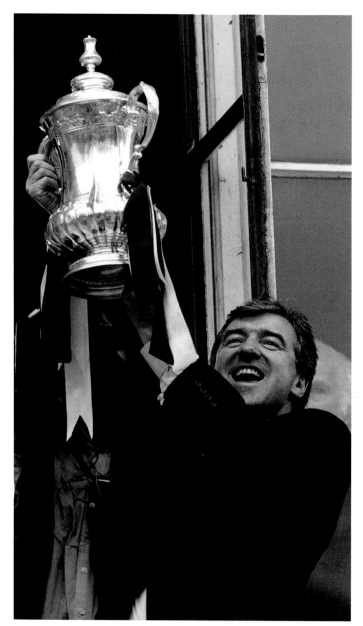

Terry Venables holds aloft the FA Cup, 1991.

MANAGER • INDUCTED 2007 • 1 FA CUP

**'I loved my time working with Terry at Tottenham Hotspur and with England. In my opinion, he is a truly world-class manager.'
– Paul Gascoigne**

Following his return to England, Venables guided Spurs to success in the FA Cup in 1991, nine years after they had defeated his Queens Park Rangers side at Wembley in the same competition. But a subsequent internal dispute within the club would cut short his time at White Hart Lane. Then came the call from the Football Association.

After England fell agonisingly short of reaching the final of Euro '96, losing on penalties against Germany, the players pleaded

Terry Venables takes training, 1992.

with Venables to reverse his decision to stand down. 'There is not one footballer, from the humblest journeyman to Premiership star, who wanted him to go,' Teddy Sheringham wrote soon after.

In an earlier group game, Venables masterminded England's 4–1 demolition of Holland. Those 90 minutes provided 'the greatest, most satisfying experience of my career', Venables said. Guus Hiddink, the Dutch coach said later: 'Terry made a fool of me. England taught us a lesson.'

Given his first chance of management at Crystal Palace, Venables guided a young and talented side to the top flight as Division Two champions in 1978–79. Great times lay ahead, the papers predicted: this Palace side, they said, would be the 'Team of the Eighties'. By now, Venables was coaching the England Under-21s on a part-time basis, in partnership with Dave Sexton.

Moving on, Venables repeated the trick at QPR, winning promotion in 1982–83 – the year after Rangers lost against Spurs in the FA Cup final. During his time at Loftus Road, Venables helped pioneer artificial pitches, but ultimately that experiment failed: the high bounce frustrated fans and the rock-hard surface put enormous strain on joints and muscles.

But the surface did at least encourage the type of football Venables – a gifted midfield player himself, notably with Chelsea and Spurs – always favoured: vibrant, flexible,

attacking. A fierce and tireless critic of the 'long-ball game' that swept English football during the 1980s, Venables wanted the ball 'on the deck'. His innovative methods and consistent success soon attracted the interest of senior figures at the Nou Camp.

As a coach and manager, his involvement with the England set-up spanned four decades, culminating in a stint as assistant to Steve McClaren for the Euro 2008 qualification campaign.

Assessing his career, Venables unhesitatingly singled out his experience in 1996 as the highlight. 'England were the best team in that tournament, and I would contend that we, derided not so long ago as technical and tactical dinosaurs, showed the rest of Europe how the game should be played in the future.'

MARIEANNE SPACEY

▶▶▶▶▶▶▶▶▶▶▶▶▶▶▶▶▶

1966–

The great star of her generation, Marieanne Spacey devoted the bulk of her career to making Arsenal the most successful women's team in the country, and her goals lifted the Gunners to four titles, five FA Cups and seven League Cups during her nine years at the club.

The highlight of an outstanding career at club level came in 1991 when Spacey was voted Player of the Season and topped the goalscoring charts. Meanwhile, at international level, after making her debut for England at the age of 18 in 1984, she amassed 91 caps and scored 28 goals in two spells.

Then, nearing the end of her career, she joined Fulham as a figurehead for the first fully professional side in the women's game, before taking over as manager for three seasons. Under her leadership, Fulham also enjoyed success.

↖
Marieanne Spacey holds aloft the FA Cup, 1998.

PLAYER • INDUCTED 2009 • 91 CAPS • 4 PREMIER LEAGUE TITLES • 5 FA CUPS • 7 LEAGUE CUPS

**'Marieanne was one of the most feared forwards in the game.'
– Vic Akers, Arsenal manager**

Her involvement with the game began at the age of 11 when she got in trouble at the local youth club for using a netball for a kick-about with her friends. The youth leader suggested that the girls form a five-a-side team, and it was only then that she began to take the game seriously. Before long, the teenage Spacey came to the attention of Friends of Fulham.

With the launch of the Women's Premier League in 1993, Friends of Fulham and Doncaster Belles emerged as the top two sides in the country. During more than a dozen years with Friends of Fulham, Spacey also played for Lazio in Italy and enjoyed a stint in Finnish football. Then came the move to Arsenal in the summer of 1994, following a conversation with Vic Akers, the Gunners manager.

'Vic had a very good understanding with the players,' Spacey recalled, before explaining her position with Arsenal. 'He gave me a free role, behind the two main strikers. It meant that I was facing the goal when I received the ball, which I loved. I would go into the box, and then drop back out again and pick up the loose pieces.'

Spacey made her debut for England in 1984, and she went on to win 76 caps during her first stint with the national side. Then came an unexpected swansong: in the build-up to the 1999 European Championship campaign, when England coach Hope Powell identified Spacey as the experienced leader the team needed in midfield. 'She did an outstanding job for the team,' Powell said.

Two years later, at the age of 36, Spacey retired from international football. 'I may well be the oldest player to represent England in the modern era,' she said.

Vic Akers has praised her contribution to the English game: 'She had good technique, ability on the ball, pace and power, and she was capable of scoring goals from all over the pitch – many of them from distance. If I had to sum her up, I would say this: Marieanne was a match-winner.'

▶ talking point

Vic Akers watched from the sidelines as Marieanne Spacey struggled for form in the FA Cup final against Liverpool in 1985. The Arsenal manager was worried. Then, with only a few minutes remaining, she popped up to score the winner.

'Marieanne had a marvellous attitude, and here was a great example,' Akers said. 'She never hid and always wanted the ball, even if she was off her game. The younger players saw that and learned a valuable lesson.

'Then came that one bit of magic we needed: a terrific shot from the edge of the penalty area. Like all great players, she found a way to win the game.'

Marieanne Spacey focuses on the ball, 1998.

PETER SCHMEICHEL

▶▶▶▶▶▶▶▶▶▶▶▶▶▶▶▶▶▶▶▶▶▶▶▶▶▶▶▶▶▶▶▶▶▶▶▶▶

1963–

Sir Alex Ferguson has described the £505,000 transfer fee Manchester United paid the Danish club Brondby for a goalkeeper – whom he nicknamed 'The Viking' – as the 'buy of the century'.

'At his best, I don't believe a better goalkeeper than Peter Schmeichel has played the game,' Ferguson said. 'He is a giant figure in the history of Manchester United and our debt to him will never be forgotten.'

When Schmeichel arrived at Old Trafford in 1991, United were still chasing their first championship title since 1967. When he departed seven years later, they were crowned the best team in Europe in the last game he played in their colours.

Over the years one character trait proved useful. 'My temper keeps me alert and focused,' he explained. 'Without it, I'd be quite ordinary. Trust me, I've tried to restrain myself and it just didn't work.'

↗ Peter Schmeichel celebrates saving a penalty, 1997.

PLAYER • INDUCTED 2003 • 129 CAPS • 1 CHAMPIONS LEAGUE • 5 PREMIER LEAGUE TITLES

3 FA CUPS • 1 LEAGUE CUP

**'I want my opponents to feel
intimidated simply by my
presence between the posts.'
– Peter Schmeichel**

Roy Keane spoke approvingly of Schmeichel's 'act' as a goalkeeper who was handed the nickname 'Mr Clean Sheet'. In order to gee himself up, the Dane behaved like 'a poser who fancied himself in a big way and played to the crowd', his Irish team-mate said.

Peter Schmeichel dives for the ball, 1999.

All the mannerisms, including the finger-pointing and gestures of frustration directed at team-mates, were deployed as weapons in a psychological battle. 'Everything I do in goal is aimed at undermining the self-confidence of my opponents. Even a fraction of a second delay in shooting can make all the difference.'

A member of the Denmark side that unexpectedly won the European Championships in Sweden in 1992, Schmeichel drew upon his sporting roots as an outstanding junior handball player to introduce a novel technique to English football: the 'star-jump'.

This involved the spread-eagling of his arms and legs when facing a shot from close range. It was a method that proved to be highly effective in one-against-one situations in football. 'He blocks so much of the goal,' Alan Hansen said. 'His ability in these situations must be worth 12 points a season. He is in a class of his own in this respect.'

Schmeichel played a vital role in helping Manchester United secure their historic treble – at both ends of the pitch.

Before the quarter-final second leg in the Champions League, Inter players tried to intimidate their opponents before the game in Milan. In response Schmeichel rallied his team-mates in the tunnel: 'When the great Peter raises his voice, the walls shake,' Ferguson said. 'The Inter players certainly got the message.'

Then, in the dying seconds of the final, with United facing defeat against Bayern Munich in Barcelona, Schmeichel famously raced upfield

▶key match

Manchester United 2 Arsenal 1, FA Cup semi-final, Villa Park, 14 April 1999

In the last minute of normal time, with the scores level at 1–1, Peter Schmeichel readied himself for what he would later describe as 'one of the most important moments in my career'.

Dennis Bergkamp strode up and hit a firm shot, about waist-high, to Schmeichel's left. 'I gambled correctly and hit the jackpot.'

Instead of there being seven minutes left, as Schmeichel believed, only seconds remained in normal time. Had Bergkamp scored, it would have dashed Manchester United's dream of an unprecedented treble – and handed Arsenal the initiative in the title race. In extra-time, a wonderful individual goal by Ryan Giggs settled an engrossing tie that had lasted four hours.

for a corner. Sitting on the bench at Nou Camp, Ferguson turned to Steve McClaren, the assistant manager, and said: 'What the hell is he doing?'

Schmeichel was acting on his own initiative. 'I knew that my green goalkeeper's jersey would cause considerable confusion,' he recalled. 'It was the kind of chaos defenders dread, and the ball eventually fell to Teddy Sheringham to score. We were never going to lose after that.'

In eight seasons at Old Trafford he played 292 League games, in more than 40 per cent of which he kept a clean sheet. After a spell in Portugal, Schmeichel had stints with Aston Villa and Manchester City.

DARIO GRADI

▶▶▶▶▶▶▶▶▶▶▶▶▶▶▶▶

1941–

Dario Gradi earned the fulsome praise of a host of high-profile figures for his outstanding record in working at the difficult end of professional football – and his longevity.

For almost three decades Gradi has worked for Crewe Alexandra, including two spells as manager, during which time he lifted the modest Cheshire club from the bottom of the old Fourth Division to a place in the second tier of English football.

'Dario is honest, diligent and remarkable,' Sir Bobby Robson said in a tribute to the longest serving manager in English football. 'He has done a great job at Crewe and proved himself to be one of our best managers.' Arsene Wenger, the Arsenal manager, describes Gradi's working relationship with Crewe as 'a great marriage'. Asked to define his role, Gradi said: 'I am a teacher. I try to help players get better.'

↖
Dario Gradi prepares for training, 2001.

MANAGER • INDUCTED 2004

'Dario is honest, diligent and remarkable. He has done a great job at Crewe and proved himself to be one of our best managers.' – Sir Bobby Robson

He arrived in 1983 to find a club lacking a coaching system and youth team, so he set them up himself. Since then Gradi has coached more than 20 youngsters who have gone on to play for their country at full, Under-21 or Under-18 level.

Those foundations enabled Gradi to establish an outstanding reputation as a coach, or 'teacher', as he described his role in the development of young players. Danny Murphy, Robbie Savage, Neil Lennon, Seth Johnson and Geoff Thomas and, most notably, David Platt, all came through the system at Crewe.

Before Gradi took over, Crewe had spent the entire twentieth century languishing in the bottom two divisions of the Football League. In contrast, in seven of the eight seasons up to

Dario Gradi, Crystal Palace manager, 1981.

the end of 2004–05 the club was one promotion away from the Premier League.

In doing so, Crewe were competing against clubs whose support base dwarfed the then average 7,000 home attendance at Gresty Road.

When Gradi started his project in the summer of 1983, he had no contract; the board could sack him with two weeks' notice. Crewe finished the previous season in 91st place in the Football League. 'The team was struggling and the ground was a dump,' Gradi recalled. 'But the only way was up.'

In 2007 Gradi stood down as manager in order to take up a role as technical director. When the team's fortunes slumped, he returned to the dug-out in 2009 and results soon improved.

Gradi is a chairman's dream manager:

Dario Gradi, left, playing for Sutton United in the Amateur Cup final, 1969.

During his time in charge he has brought in more than £20 million in transfer fees, 10 times the outlay on new players; the team has won promotion four times, and average crowds at Gresty Road more than tripled.

Almost half of the transfer funds injected into the club have been spent on facilities at the ground. A new main stand cost £5 million, with £500,000 spent on the rest of the stadium. The training ground took up another £2 million.

'I think about what we've achieved every time I walk into the place,' Gradi said. 'It means an awful lot to me. The ground is a lasting legacy to my work here, and perhaps they might name some part of the ground after me when I'm dead and gone.'

ERIC CANTONA ▶▶▶▶▶▶▶▶▶▶▶▶

1966–

Eric Cantona, the charismatic Frenchman nicknamed 'Le King' by the Stretford End, added the final, vital ingredient to the mix of talent that lifted Manchester United back to the top of English football – ending 26 years of frustration.

When Cantona arrived at Old Trafford in November 1992, for a modest fee of £1 million, Manchester United were lying in sixth place in the Premier League. The following May they were crowned champions for the first time since 1966–67. 'We were an inspired and transformed team,' wrote Sir Alex Ferguson, reflecting the scale of the forward's contribution. 'Eric had a priceless presence.'

Remarkably, Cantona had managed a repeat of his earlier, equally dramatic experience at Leeds United the previous season. Here, too, the outspoken rebel of French football acted as a catalyst. Arriving mid-season, he added the spark that lifted Leeds to the title. 'I was a hit with everyone,' Cantona said, referring to his brief spell in Yorkshire, an outcome that followed his decision to end a brief, self-imposed retirement. 'Eight goals for Leeds that season – I had become the leader.'

After crossing the Pennines, heading west, Cantona immediately impressed Roy Keane by his presence as a footballer – the aura of supreme self-confidence. 'Collar turned up, back straight, chest stuck out, Eric glided into the arena as if he owned the place.'

'Straightaway, he illuminated Old Trafford,' Ferguson recalled. 'The place was a frenzy every time he touched the ball.' Cantona often cut an imperious figure, deliberately posing in order to milk the applause of his audience; English football had its greatest showman since Len Shackleton, the skilful, crowd-pleasing entertainer of the 1950s.

Eric Cantona, 1997.

▶ key match

Liverpool 0 Manchester United 1, FA Cup final, Wembley Stadium, 11 May 1996

Roy Keane was thankful that the ball fell to Eric Cantona. If it hadn't, Manchester United might not have completed their second double in three seasons – and he might not have become the first foreign player to lift the trophy as captain.

'That winning goal,' Keane recalled, 'no one else would have been capable of scoring that goal. His knack of scoring important goals always stood out. As an individual, Eric was a legend.'

'Looking back, it seems inevitable that the ball would somehow come to him,' Alex Ferguson recalled. 'But when it did, the ball bounced up at quite an awkward height. Eric needed good foot movement and perfect body position to execute a scoring shot.'

PLAYER • INDUCTED 2002 • 43 CAPS • 1 DIVISION ONE CHAMPIONSHIP • 2 FA CUPS

4 PREMIER LEAGUE TITLES

'I sometimes have the impression that if Eric can't score a beautiful goal he would rather not score at all.' – Michel Platini

Eric Cantona packed an extraordinary amount of experience into the nine years he spent playing football in his native France. On the plus side, he played 43 times for France, scoring 19 goals, including one on his debut.

In June 1988, Cantona joined Marseille, the club he supported as a boy, from Auxerre, for a French record fee of £2.3 million. In 1989–90 he won a French Cup-winners' medal with Montpellier.

Off the field, however, his reputation was tarnished by a number of confrontations with authority. His outbursts were directed at a number of targets: Henri Michel, the national team coach, referees, the ruling body of French football. Fines and suspensions usually followed.

Cantona spoke his mind. As in the time he reacted to the announcement of a four-week ban for throwing a football at a referee by calling each member of the disciplinary panel an idiot to their face. They promptly doubled the length of the suspension.

Throwing his shirt to the ground in protest after being substituted led to disciplinary action at Marseille; at Montpellier, Cantona fought with a team-mate in the dressing room. By now his career was in crisis. Cancelling his own contract in a mix of frustration and despair, he announced his retirement at the age of 25 in 1991.

Michel Platini, who once said he had 'the impression that if Eric can't score a beautiful

Le Rouge Devil, a sculpture by David Hughes, 2000.

goal he would rather not score', eventually persuaded Cantona to return, then suggested a new start. 'What about a move to England?' Platini asked.

After a brief trial at Sheffield Wednesday, he signed for Leeds United. By the age of 25, Eric Cantona had been employed by six clubs in France and one club in England.

Then came the transfer to Old Trafford. For the remaining five years of his career he put an end to his nomadic ways. 'I value truth, honesty, respect for one another, sincerity, compassion and understanding,' he said. 'These qualities are found at Manchester United.'

Cantona formed a menacing partnership with Mark Hughes. In the 20 games they started together in 1992–93, United scored 39 goals. The team had managed barely a goal a game before his arrival. 'It had the best defence, but not the best attack,' Cantona said.

Eric Cantona holds aloft the FA Cup, 1996.

Roy Keane, the United captain, attributes the success of Cantona at Old Trafford to the man-management of Alex Ferguson. 'The manager gave Eric the freedom to be himself without undermining his own authority,' Keane said.

Cantona felt valued and wanted in Manchester. 'The other players accepted this special treatment because he could justify it with his brilliance on the field,' Keane said.

Only once did Cantona threaten to walk out. In 1995 he was suspended for eight months for an infamous 'kung-fu' attack on a supporter of Crystal Palace. Convicted of common assault, the Frenchman was eventually sentenced to 120 hours' community service.

When he subsequently fled the country, threatening to quit the game, Ferguson made a special trip to Paris in a bid to dissuade him. The manager kept faith with Cantona, offering him a new three-year contract and later, in 1996, the captaincy. Cantona responded by leading the club to a second double in three seasons.

For all his showmanship on the field, Cantona worked tirelessly and conscientiously in training. After watching the Frenchman score the winning goal in the 1996 FA Cup final with an outstanding piece of technique, Alex Ferguson said: 'That vital volley was a dramatic demonstration of the value of all Eric's devotion to practice.'

Recalling the sight of Cantona working alone on the training ground after hours, David Beckham stressed the importance of his status as an example and role model for young players at the club. 'Eric had a huge influence on my attitude to the game – and the same was true for the likes of Ryan Giggs and Paul Scholes.'

As a senior professional, Cantona became a trusted voice in the dressing room when it came to tactics. Before the 1996 FA Cup final, for instance, he suggested that Roy Keane play a more defensive role in front of the back four, to counter the attacking threat posed by Liverpool. His manager agreed. 'It was a good idea,' Ferguson said later.

There have been two 'Kings' of the Stretford End – Denis Law and Eric Cantona. The

Eric Cantona shields the ball, 1996.

▶ **talking point**

Eric Cantona spoke of a deep and abiding respect for the history and rituals of English football.

The experience of playing at Wembley for the first time in 1992, fulfilled all the expectations the Frenchman had harboured since childhood.

On 8 August, Cantona lined up for Division One champions Leeds United against Liverpool, the FA Cup winners, in the Charity Shield. As a boy growing up in France, Cantona had been entranced by the traditions surrounding the old stadium.

'To play at Wembley, for a footballer, in terms of the prestige and the honour that emanate from playing there, is a little like Wimbledon for a tennis player,' Cantona said, describing the pitch as 'the most wonderful playing surface in the world'.

'I will never forget that day in what I call the temple of football. I scored three goals, and Leeds won. All in all, it was one of the best days in my career.'

'The national anthem, the chants and shouts of the supporters, the stadium full of the colours of both teams playing against each other, the presentation of the trophy – I remember everything,' he wrote later.

contribution made by the latter to the Manchester United cause in recent history is best summed up by Roy Keane when he said: 'Eric did more than any other player to deliver success for the manager of this football club.'

In the mid 1990s, Nike ran a poster campaign featuring Cantona's image. Referring to the World Cup win of 30 years earlier, the caption read: '1966 was a great year for English football. Eric was born.'

BRENDA SEMPARE

▶▶▶▶▶▶▶▶▶▶▶▶▶▶▶▶

1961–

As a coach and manager at club and international level Alan May gained a deep respect for the qualities of Brenda Sempare as a footballer – and he likened her ability to dominate proceedings on a football field to that of a 'star' performer on stage.

'If Brenda Sempare was a ballet dancer,' May said, expounding his point, 'she would always be in the role of prima ballerina. She had a balance and grace in her movements on the ball that made her a pleasure to watch. There was something else: when you watched a game in which Brenda was taking part, your eye was continually drawn to her. She had a presence on the field.'

May, the former Croydon Ladies manager and now head scout with the England women's division at the Football Association, noted other attributes. 'Brenda combined pace with frightening power. There was skill mixed with steel. She was not physically big as a player, but she certainly packed a punch – both verbally and when she was competing for the ball.'

Brenda Sempare shields the ball.

PLAYER • INDUCTED 2010 • 53 CAPS • 1 LEAGUE CHAMPIONSHIP • 1 FA CUP

'One of a kind of her generation in the game, in terms of ability and presence. A football architect.' – Alan May

Capped 53 times, Sempare began her career as an attacking midfield player with Friends of Fulham. Successful stints followed at Wimbledon Ladies, and finally and most notably, Croydon. Once she had passed the age of 30, when her legs began 'to go', Sempare played out her career in a defensive role.

Sempare left arguably her greatest moment until last. It was the last day of the 1995–96 season. Her team, Croydon Ladies, needed to win to pip Doncaster Belles for the title on goal difference. It was also to be her last game before retirement.

With 10 minutes to go, up she popped in the Arsenal Ladies penalty area to score the goal that secured not only the title – unbeaten, to boot – but a notable League and Cup double.

Success in the FA Cup was secured with a 2–0 victory in the final against Doncaster Belles. In November 2001, Hope Powell, a Croydon team-mate, recalled the game. 'Brenda's performance in that final was the best all-round display I have ever seen,' the England coach wrote in *The Times*.

At international level Sempare played in all four of England's matches at the 1995 Women's World Cup in Sweden. Having emerged from a group that included Canada, Norway and Nigeria, England were defeated 3–0 by Germany in the quarter-finals.

In its match report, *The Independent* praised the 'heroic' goalkeeping of Pauline

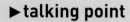
▶talking point

Brenda Sempare played a crucial role in the development of Hope Powell as an international footballer – actions that highlighted her leadership qualities according to Alan May.

'Although she was only in her early twenties herself, Brenda was established with the England team when Hope emerged as a player of great potential,' May recalled.

'In terms of caps, if not age, Brenda was a senior player, and she made a point of befriending Hope and showed her what it meant to be an England player and how to conduct oneself on international duty. That helped Hope enormously.'

Cope and the tireless efforts of Sempare in midfield 'as she worked valiantly to stem the tide of German attacks'.

Asked to sum up Sempare's career in women's football with a single recollection, Alan May unhesitatingly cites a moment from the victorious FA Cup final. 'We were under a lot of pressure late in the game, and the ball was played into our penalty area. There was Brenda. She pulled the ball down, brought it under control, looked up, and then calmly passed the ball to a colleague.

'There were a lot of players around her, but she had so much confidence in her own decision-making. She trusted her own ability. And that gave everyone else in the side such confidence.'

↖
Brenda Sempare prepares to shoot, 1983.

STUART PEARCE

▶▶▶▶▶▶▶▶▶▶▶▶▶▶▶▶▶▶

1962–

Stuart Pearce exemplified the positive attributes so often associated with English football: loyalty, fearlessness, ferocious determination to win and an indefatigable spirit – character traits that earned him recognition by five England managers.

The combative left-back was renowned for his shuddering tackles, surging runs and thumping free-kicks during a career spent largely at Nottingham Forest under the tutelage of Brian Clough, who said: 'At his peak, Stuart was awesome. There is no other word for it.'

A fierce patriot, Pearce gained great satisfaction from his longevity at international level. 'Someone told me that I am the fifth oldest player to represent England,' he said. 'I treasure the memory of every single appearance I made for my country. Far too many players pay lip service to playing for England. It meant everything to me.'

Stuart Pearce celebrates his successful penalty, 1996.

PLAYER • INDUCTED 2010 • 78 CAPS • 2 LEAGUE CUP'S

'At his peak, Stuart was awesome. There is no other word for it.' – Brian Clough

After making his international debut in 1987, at the relatively late age of 25, Pearce collected 78 caps – putting him just outside the top 10 on the all-time England appearance list at the time.

During the latter stages of an England career spanning a dozen years, his consistency twice earned the veteran defender a recall from international retirement at the request of Glenn Hoddle, then Kevin Keegan.

In 1996 Pearce created one of the most memorable images in the history of English football. Six years after being reduced to tears over his failure to convert his spot-kick in a losing penalty shoot-out in a World Cup semi-final, Pearce faced another test of nerve.

This time a place in the semi-final of the European Championships was at stake. After unerringly finding the net with his penalty, Pearce, his face distorted by emotion, let out a

Stuart Pearce clenches his fist on a Wembley lap of honour, 1989.

scream from the gut – part exorcism, it seemed, part rallying cry to the nation.

A working-class lad born in Hammersmith, London, Pearce was a late starter in football, having trained as an electrician – hence his first nickname 'Sparky'. Those origins as a tradesman helped explain his popularity. 'I believe the fans see a little bit of themselves in me,' he wrote.

After starting his career on a part-time basis with non-League Wealdstone in 1983, Pearce was signed by Coventry City for a fee of £30,000. However, not even a subsequent move to the City Ground dispelled all the doubts he harboured about his ability to make the grade. Famously, he took out an advert as an electrician in the Forest programme.

Few shared his uncertainty. In all, Pearce spent 12 years at Forest, most of them as

Stuart Pearce crosses the ball past Ruel Fox of Tottenham Hotspur, 1996.

captain. Twice Pearce collected a League Cup winners' medal, and he gave his side the lead with a trademark free-kick in a losing FA Cup final appearance in 1991.

Despite their relegation from the top flight in 1993, Pearce decided to stay at the City Ground, helping Forest to gain promotion the following season. By now, he was far and away the club's most popular player.

In later years, as his career wound down, Pearce helped Newcastle United qualify for the Champions League and reach another FA Cup final. Spells at West Ham United and Manchester City followed.

Rivals understood only too well the value of Pearce to England. 'We respect Pearce as the heartbeat of their team,' Germany and Bayern Munich defender Christian Ziege said in 1996. 'He competes to the limit. He is a fearsome sight.'

IAN WRIGHT

▶▶▶▶▶▶▶▶▶▶▶▶▶▶▶

1963–

Ian Wright installed himself as an instant idol at Highbury on the strength of his showmanship, competitive spark and exceptional finishing ability.

'Ian has all the qualities you want from a striker: lightning pace, sharp reflexes, courage and an eye for goal,' said George Graham, the then Arsenal manager.

Graham considered the effervescent Wright an indispensable cog in a team that reached four major Cup finals over a period of three seasons. 'No successful Arsenal side had ever been so dependent on one man,' he wrote. In 1997–98, as a last hurrah at Highbury, under the leadership of Arsène Wenger, Wright helped the club win the Premier League title.

It was Steve Coppell who gave Wright his big break in the game. 'When I offered him his first professional contract I have never seen anybody so happy in all my life.'

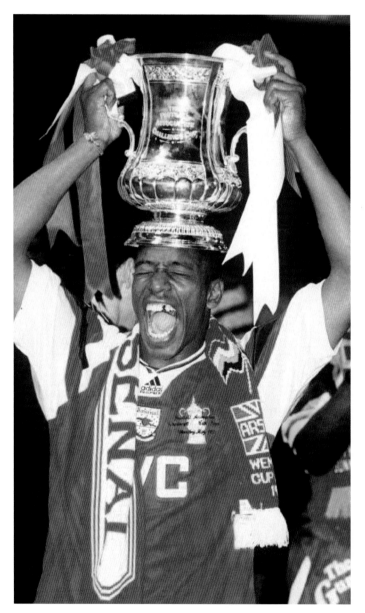

A jubilant Ian Wright rests the FA Cup on his head, 1993.

PLAYER • INDUCTED 2005 • 33 CAPS • 1 PREMIER LEAGUE TITLE • 2 FA CUPS • 1 LEAGUE CUP

1 EUROPEAN CUP-WINNERS' CUP

A hat-trick on his League debut for the Gunners was a portentous start: six years later Arsenal had a new record goalscorer in their ranks.

Graham described Wright as an instinctive finisher in the mould of Jimmy Greaves and Denis Law. 'Just like them, Ian is a natural,' he said.

Wright had something else in common with Law: a fiery temperament that fuelled his competitive zeal – and occasionally boiled over. This combative, effervescent spirit made Wright, like Law before him, a huge favourite with fans. 'There is not a thimbleful of cowardice in him,' Graham said. 'He goes in where it hurts.'

Following his £2.5 million transfer from Crystal Palace in 1991, Wright finished the season as the leading goalscorer in Division One, with 29 goals. In the autumn of 1994, he scored in 12 consecutive games, an Arsenal record.

Wright played in two FA Cup finals, both of which went to a replay, scoring four times in all. In 1993, the latter of those Wembley occa-

↗
Ian Wright celebrates a goal at Wembley, 1993.

sions, he netted in both games as Arsenal defeated Sheffield Wednesday.

In European competition, Wright experienced mixed fortunes. In 1993–94, he missed the victory over Parma in the final of the European Cup-Winners' Cup because of suspension. The following season he scored in every round up to the final, only for Arsenal to fall dramatically at the last hurdle against Real Zaragoza in Paris.

Wright was already 21 years of age before he made his breakthrough into full-time professional football. He then made up for lost time in spectacular fashion. Wright had been working as a plasterer when Crystal Palace invited him for a two-week trial in 1985. Three days in, Steve Coppell, the Palace manager, offered him a contract.

'On his first day at Selhurst Park, Ian told me that he wanted to play for England, which was quite a bold statement for someone who

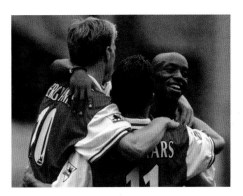

↙
Ian Wright celebrates with his team-mates, 1997.

had just walked in off a building site,' Coppell recalled.

Less than five years later Wright fulfilled his ambition when he won the first of his 27 caps, scoring seven goals. In his six seasons at Palace, Wright scored 90 League goals in 225 appearances, helping the club to promotion from the Second Division in 1988–89.

In his first 79 games for Arsenal, Wright scored a remarkable 56 goals. Within two years of his arrival, he became the quickest player to register 100 goals for the Gunners, beating the record set by Ted Drake six decades earlier. In total, he scored a then club-record 185 goals for Arsenal, before moving on to West Ham United.

▶ key match

Crystal Palace 3 Manchester United 3 (aet), FA Cup final, Wembley Stadium, 12 May 1990

As a boy Ian Wright loved everything about the FA Cup final. 'It was always something I wanted to experience,' he wrote later.

Wright fulfilled that ambition as a late substitute. Palace were losing. 'Do anything you like to spark something,' manager Steve Coppell told him. 'Try and make a difference.'

With virtually his first touch he created a shooting chance. 'I knew it was going in as soon as I hit it,' he said. Wright was so overjoyed that tears streamed down his face in celebration.

During extra-time, Wright gave Palace the lead with a far-post volley. 'It was such an amazing moment that I didn't know how to celebrate,' he said.

THROUGH THE AGES
FOOTBALL IN THE 1990s

▶▶▶▶▶▶▶▶▶▶▶▶▶▶▶▶▶▶▶▶▶▶▶▶▶▶▶▶▶▶▶▶▶▶

THIS PAGE: Above Ryan Giggs, David Beckham and Paul Scholes line up with other first-team graduates and youth team coach Eric Harrison, 1995. **Right** Eric Cantona models on the catwalk in Paris, 1993.

OPPOSITE: Above left England celebrate a goal by Paul Gascoigne against Scotland, 1996. **Above right** Kevin Keegan watches Labour leader Tony Blair head the ball, 1995. **Below left** Peter Beardsley, John Barnes and Des Walker record the official England World Cup song, 1990. **Below right** Gary Lineker and Michael Owen appear in a television advert for a snack food product, 1998.

KAREN WALKER

▶▶▶▶▶▶▶▶▶▶▶▶▶▶▶▶

1969–

Often hailed as the best header of a ball in the game, Karen Walker ended her career as the leading goalscorer in the history of the England women's team.

'A big, strong, old-fashioned centre-forward who knew where the goal was' – to quote her own words – Walker found the net 40 times in 83 appearances for her country between 1987 and 2003.

Walker bowed out at the top: voted Player of the Year in a poll of her team-mates and backroom staff, she was captain of England when she retired from international football.

At club level, she also ended on a high note. In her last game before hanging up her boots she played for Leeds United in the Cup final – her 12th appearance in the showpiece fixture, a record in the women's game.

↖
Karen Walker, 2002.

PLAYER • INDUCTED 2007 • 83 CAPS • 2 PREMIER LEAGUE CHAMPIONSHIPS • 5 FA CUPS

**'I was asked to go along for a trial. I was 15 years of age, and I stayed for 20 years.'
– Karen Walker on her time at Doncaster Belles**

Walker made all but the last of those appearances in the colours of Doncaster Belles, the club she joined at the age of 15. Within a year or so she had established herself in the first team, playing against women twice her age.

↖
Karen Walker in action for England, 1998.

For much of the ensuing two decades, the Belles were the outstanding team in the country. 'I played 11 FA Cup finals with them, winning five and losing six,' she recalled. 'We won the national title twice and one double.'

During one remarkable Cup run with the Belles, Walker scored a hat-trick in every round, including the final against Southampton. 'Hopefully,' she said, 'no one will ever match that particular record.' Her third goal in the final was a trademark header, delivered from a position near the penalty spot.

A county-standard basketball player in her teens, Walker had a prodigious leap. As many as two-thirds of her goals were headers, especially in the early years at the top level. 'I nearly always went to the back post, then attacked the ball,' she said. 'I jumped well, and I was very brave', as the cuts, bruises and occasional concussions she sustained testified.

'Karen terrified defenders with her ability in the air,' Hope Powell, the England coach said. 'She had a great team spirit and passion for the game.'

In 2004, nearing the end of her career, Walker left the Belles in order to join local rivals Leeds United. 'It was a big step to leave, but I needed a new challenge,' she said. In her first seven games with Leeds, she scored 12 goals.

Following her retirement as a player, Walker was a guest pundit for the BBC during the Women's World Cup in China in 2007.

Writing in the *Daily Telegraph*, several years earlier, the sports columnist Julie Welch commented: 'If Karen Walker talks as she scores goals, it would be good to hear her views about the game.'

Of her experience in front of the cameras, Walker commented: 'When it came to my turn, I simply said what I thought. Overall, it was a wonderful opportunity. Something that I can always say that I've done.'

Summing up her career, Walker said, modestly: 'I was never the fastest or the most skilful player but I knew where the goal was, and I was never scared to miss.'

ALAN SHEARER

▶▶▶▶▶▶▶▶▶▶▶▶▶▶▶

1970–

Alan Shearer justified his status as the most expensive footballer in the world when he established a record for goalscoring during the Premier League era.

In his prime, Shearer became the first player since the 1930s – the heyday of the bustling, robust English centre-forward – to score more than 30 goals in the top division in three successive seasons.

His tally of 34 goals in the 1994–95 season, the middle campaign in this exceptional run of form, helped Blackburn Rovers win the championship title for the first time in 81 years. On a personal note, he was voted Player of the Year by his fellow professionals, an award he lifted again two years later.

'Alan is in a class of his own,' Kenny Dalglish, the then Blackburn manager said. 'He lifts the whole team and turns draws into victories. In a word: priceless.' Another football Hall of Famer, John Barnes once described Shearer's value as 'incalculable'.

Alan Shearer runs with the ball, 1994.

PLAYER • INDUCTED 2004 • 63 CAPS • 1 PREMIER LEAGUE TITLE

'Alan had everything in his armoury. At his very best he could do everything you could ever want in a striker.'
- Andy Gray

After starting his career with Southampton, Shearer scored 260 goals in the Premier League for Blackburn Rovers and Newcastle United, the club he supported as a boy.

In the space of five years Shearer's value in the transfer market increased almost five-fold – from the £3.3 million Dalglish paid the Saints in 1992, to £15.6 million, the sum Newcastle United invested in 1996. Two transfers, two records: one British; the other

marking a new high for world football.

'Alan is a superstar, but without a superstar's temperament,' said Kevin Keegan, who managed Shearer at both club and international level. 'He is such a great asset in the dressing room.'

John Barnes listed Shearer's qualities as a forward. 'Alan is a nightmare to defend against because if a cross comes in he will always be there. He is very clinical at hitting the target, and he can also drop his shoulder and score from 30 yards.'

On 9 April 1988, a raw Shearer made a stunning impact on top-flight football. His three goals on his debut for Southampton made him the youngest player – at 17 years and 240 days – in the modern era to score a hat-trick in the top division.

A key turning point came in 1992, the year he signed for Blackburn Rovers and made his England debut. Meanwhile, his scoring rate rose dramatically; over a four-year period at Ewood Park, Shearer found the net 112 times in 138 appearances. With England, he averaged a fraction under a goal every two internationals.

As a boy, Shearer, the son of a sheet metal-worker and celebrated product of the Wallsend Boys Club, queued for four hours to witness Kevin Keegan's debut as a Newcastle player in 1982. Fourteen years later, when Shearer signed for the club, an estimated 15,000 fellow Geordies gathered at the ground on a non-match day to celebrate his homecoming.

Alan Shearer celebrates a goal, 2002.

Fully aware of the club's proud traditions, Shearer made one demand before signing: to wear the number nine shirt, just as Hughie Gallacher, Jackie Milburn, Wyn Davies and Malcolm Macdonald had done before him. 'As a Newcastle fan, I knew what it meant,' he said later.

In the end, Shearer eclipsed them all, scoring 206 goals in all competitions, a club record. Those goals helped Newcastle United reach the Champions League and two FA Cup finals.

On announcing his retirement after a decade at the club, Shearer said: 'When I was a boy I wanted to wear the number nine shirt and score goals at St James' Park – I've lived my dream.'

ARSÈNE WENGER

▶▶▶▶▶▶▶▶▶▶▶▶▶▶▶▶▶▶▶

1949–

A decade after arriving at Highbury with little fanfare, Arsène Wenger was talked about in the same reverential tones as Herbert Chapman, in terms of his importance as a manager in the history of Arsenal Football Club.

By guiding the Gunners to two League and FA Cup doubles, the urbane French manager revived memories of the 1930s, when Chapman established Arsenal as the dominant force in English football for the first time.

In the process, Wenger – a studious, innovative thinker in the same mould as Chapman – revolutionised English football in terms of diet, preparation, training and scouting.

After Arsenal's double success in 1997–98 – Wenger's first full season in charge at Highbury – the club offered him a new contract. 'Arsène can stay here for as long as he wants,' Peter Hill-Wood, the chairman, declared.

↖
Arsène Wenger gives instructions from the sidelines, 2010.

MANAGER • INDUCTED 2006 • 3 PREMIER LEAGUE TITLES • 4 FA CUPS

'For me, football is first and foremost a game. It has a framework, yet it should leave a part for freedom of expression.' - Arsène Wenger

On his arrival in North London, Wenger set out to fuse, as he put it, 'continental sophistication with the indefatigable spirit' of English football. That way, he said, Arsenal would have 'the best of both worlds': a battle-hardened, home-grown defence led by Tony Adams; the French pairing of Patrick Vieira and Emmanuel Petit in midfield, with the two Dutchmen Dennis Bergkamp and Marc Overmars providing the flair up front.

Over time, Wenger introduced a more continental style of play. Gone was the direct, long-ball game that defined the Gunners previously, in favour of intricate passing movements. Fans at Highbury began referring to their side's fluent, effervescent brand of play as 'Wengerball'. For him, football is never simply about winning. 'The imprint you make in the spirit of people is more important than the result,' Wenger once said.

In 2003–04, Arsenal went unbeaten throughout the season in winning another Premier League title. Not since Preston North End, more than a century earlier, had football witnessed such authority and consistency. In tribute the newspapers dubbed Arsenal 'The New Invincibles'.

In 2006 Arsenal reached the final of the Champions League for the first time, and came agonisingly close to victory against Barcelona, despite being reduced to ten men.

By now, the scouting net had been spread even wider, particularly in Africa. 'We represent a football club which is about values, not passports,' Wenger said.

Thierry Henry had been converted from a winger into a goalscoring striker. Later, Spaniard Cesc Fabregas and Dutchman Robin Van Persie made their names. In recent years, more home-grown talent has been unearthed and nurtured, with the emergence of Theo Walcott, Aaron Ramsey, and Jack Wilshere.

Arsène Wenger holds aloft the FA Cup, 2005.

▶ **talking point**

From day one of his tenure as Arsenal manager, Arsène Wenger challenged the conventions of English football – everything from training methods, to diet and pre-match preparations.

A stickler for detail, Wenger replaced gruelling, sweat-inducing tests of stamina, with training sessions shorter in duration, less competitive, and timed to the second. Stretching was paramount. 'Training is not about winning five-a-sides,' he told the players. 'It is about a prepared, organised and structured sequence of actions, to make you better able to play a game.'

Off the field, the menu in the training ground restaurant was re-written. Fatty foods were out; in came vegetables, pasta and vitamin supplements.

Under his stewardship, Arsenal have been successful – and profitable, year on year. And those riches were invested in youth development and infrastructure: a new 60,000-seat stadium and a £12 million training complex, the building of which Wenger planned and oversaw in minute detail.

Once described by club vice-chairman David Dein as a 'miracle worker', Wenger outlined his philosophy: 'For me, football is first and foremost a game. It has a framework, yet it should leave a part for freedom of expression.'

Famously, a bust of Herbert Chapman was displayed in the marble halls of Highbury. In 2007, a similar tribute to Wenger – the longest serving manager in the club's history – was unveiled at the Emirates Stadium.

ROY KEANE

▶▶▶▶▶▶▶▶▶▶▶▶▶▶▶

1971–

Roy Keane can properly be described as the 'heart and soul' of the Manchester United side that enjoyed unprecedented success in English League and Cup football during the 1990s, according to Sir Alex Ferguson.

'Roy is a legend who will always be revered by fans at Old Trafford for what he did for this club,' Ferguson once said. With Keane driving them on from his position in central midfield, United claimed three doubles in the space of five years.

'If I could have any individual player in the world in my team, money no object, it would be Roy,' said Brian Clough, the manager who signed Keane as a teenager for Nottingham Forest in 1990.

Three years later, when Keane became available for transfer, Ferguson acted swiftly, telling the player: 'Roy, with you at our club, we can win the biggest prize in Europe.' Keane accepted the challenge, and in 1999 he proved his manager correct.

Roy Keane lifted on the shoulders of his team-mates, 1999.

PLAYER • INDUCTED 2004 • 60 CAPS • 7 PREMIER LEAGUE TITLES • 4 FA CUPS

1 CHAMPIONS LEAGUE

'I worked for every second with complete determination and absolute concentration. Determination was my trademark.' – Roy Keane

'I didn't think I could have a higher opinion of any footballer than I did of Roy, but he rose even further in my estimation with this performance,' Sir Alex said, recalling the Irishman's display at Juventus in the Champions League semi-final, second leg in 1999.

When Keane was cautioned in Turin it meant an automatic suspension for the final. He would miss out on the biggest game of his career. His reaction to this disappointment 'defined him as a player', Ferguson said.

Roy Keane celebrates his goal, 2002.

'Roy seemed to redouble his efforts against Juventus. It was the most emphatic display of selflessness I've seen on a football field, inspiring all around him,' Ferguson said. Two goals adrift at one stage, United eventually went through 3–2 on aggregate.

The childhood boxer always relished a challenge. 'During my time in the ring as a lad I developed a certain confidence when confronted by physical aggression,' he said.

Keane loathes complacency, in himself and in others. Relentlessly over the years he drove his team forward. His fierce will to win has since been identified by Ferguson as perhaps the biggest factor behind the rise of the club.

'I worked for every second with complete determination and absolute concentration,' Keane said of himself as a youngster. 'Determination was my trademark.'

The constant striving for improvement did

Roy Keane escapes his marker, 1997.

lead, at times, to controversy. Keane had a history of red cards and confrontations with referees. By his own admission, he sometimes went too far. 'The psycho with veins bulging in his head is me,' he said disapprovingly, referring to a photograph of one infamous incident.

A native of Cork, Keane was playing for semi-professional Cobh Ramblers when a Forest scout first spotted him. Less than a year later Keane was playing international football. Jack Charlton, the Republic of Ireland manager, was soon describing him as 'the best midfielder in Britain'. Graham Taylor said: 'I just wish he was English.'

Bryan Robson, a predecessor in the leadership role at Old Trafford said: 'I haven't seen him have an average game yet. He's outstanding, a legend. If I had to pick a World XI, Roy would be in it.'

PAULINE COPE

▶▶▶▶▶▶▶▶▶▶▶▶▶▶▶▶

1969-

From the moment Pauline Cope put on a pair of goalkeeper's gloves for the first time as an emergency replacement in her late teens, she displayed the natural ability that made her an automatic choice for England for a decade, during which time she amassed 60 caps, establishing a record tally for a custodian in the women's game.

A World Cup veteran, Cope won domestic Cup honours during a career that encompassed stints at four of the major clubs in the country – Millwall Lionesses, Arsenal, Croydon and Charlton Athletic.

And yet her outstanding career as a keeper came about pretty much by chance. In her early days as a junior at Millwall, Pauline turned up for a game expecting to play centre-half as usual, only to be given the number one shirt when the regular keeper failed to turn up. Before that day, she'd never spent a moment between the sticks. However, it turned out that she was a natural.

Pauline Cope playing for England, 2000.

PLAYER • INDUCTED 2008 • 60 CAPS • 2 PREMIER LEAGUE CUPS • 4 FA CUPS • 3 LEAGUE CUPS

Fearless and aggressive, Pauline soon gained a reputation for bravery, especially when the boots started flying in the penalty area. 'I'm a bit of a nutter, really,' she once joked.

Born in 1969, she made her debut for England in the 2–1 defeat against Germany. 'I was in my mid twenties when I won my first cap. Pretty much from then on if I was fit I played. For friendlies, they might give someone else the chance to get some experience. In the big games, though, I played.'

During her two stints as an Arsenal player, under the management of Vic Akers, Cope was able to train occasionally alongside club-mate David Seaman, the then England number one.

She also benefited from the specialist coaching of Bob Wilson, the last line of defence in the Gunners' double winners of 1970–71. 'Both Bob and David were extremely generous and helpful to me, and they passed on a few tips which I found very useful during games,' Cope said.

It was during her time at Arsenal that Cope enjoyed her greatest achievement in domestic football: the League Cup and FA Cup double in 1994–95. And at the end of that memorable season she was selected in England's squad for the World Cup finals tournament in Sweden.

'Pauline had a tremendous presence in goal for England,' Hope Powell, the national team coach and former England team-mate, told the audience when Cope was officially inducted into the Football Hall of Fame at a ceremony in London in September 2008.

'She had no fear, which is a great attribute,' Powell added. 'But there was more to her goalkeeping than courage – she also had great ability in terms of positioning and shot-stopping.'

Pauline Cope, right, holds aloft her FA Cup winners' medal, 1995.

'As a character in the dressing room, she was very competitive, and she had a huge influence on the side in this respect. In some ways we still miss her in the England set-up. And it is not possible for me to pay Pauline a bigger compliment than that.'

'Pauline had a tremendous presence in goal for England. She had no fear. But there was more to her goalkeeping keeping than courage – she also had great ability in terms of positioning and shot-stopping.' – Hope Powell

DENNIS BERGKAMP

▶▶▶▶▶▶▶▶▶▶▶▶▶▶▶▶▶

1969–

After Arsenal completed the double in the 1997–98 season, Arsène Wenger was asked by a journalist to comment on Dennis Bergkamp, the Arsenal forward and playmaker. 'Can you not say he is the best player in the world right now?' the Gunners manager asked, rhetorically. 'If there is a better one, then I have not seen him.'

The football writers and Bergkamp's fellow professionals obviously concurred with Wenger; they voted the Dutchman Player of the Year in their respective polls that season. The evidence in support of his claim for such lofty recognition was compelling: 19 goals in 39 games; at least as many 'assists'; and innumerable flashes of brilliance.

Sir Bobby Robson saw something of Jimmy Greaves and Denis Law in him. 'As a player I marked Jimmy and Denis,' the then Newcastle United manager said. 'You think you have them in control, but then they destroy you in the space of five minutes. Bergkamp is the same.'

Dennis Bergkamp lifts the FA Cup, 2005.

PLAYER • INDUCTED 2007 • 79 CAPS • 3 PREMIER LEAGUE TITLES • 4 FA CUPS

His exploits in one extraordinary match against Leicester City at Filbert Street created television history: an unprecedented first, second and third finish in one Goal of the Month competition on *Match of the Day*; one of those strikes – a stunning juggle and volley – duly won the programme's annual award. 'Dennis only scores best-sellers,' Wenger said.

'There is a fluidity about his game that is unique,' said Patrick Vieira, the Arsenal midfielder. 'He allows the team to live and breathe.'

When Bergkamp joined Arsenal in 1995, it marked a turning point for English football. Never before had an established international star, with the best years of his career still ahead of him, committed his future to the top flight of English football.

A graduate of the Ajax academy, Bergkamp endured an unhappy spell with Internazionale in Italy, where his career stagnated.

It was a different story in North London, following his £7.5 million transfer. Having seen him demonstrate his ability at close hand for the first time in training, a few of his teammates bowed before him, arms outstretched,

↗
Dennis Bergkamp celebrates a goal, 2004.

quoting a line from the cult movie *Wayne's World*. 'We're not worthy! We're not worthy!'

Describing his number 10 as 'super-talented', Wenger considered Bergkamp indispensable on account of 'his ability to deliver the final ball'. By the time he retired 11 years later, the wiry Dutchman enjoyed iconic status at Highbury.

Gradually, as his career began to wind down, Bergkamp increasingly took on the role of 'impact player', coming off the bench, invariably entering the fray to a standing ovation from the Highbury crowd.

There was to be one more tribute: a testimonial against Ajax that doubled as an official opening for the club's new Emirates Stadium.

Several weeks earlier, Bergkamp made his last appearance on the team-sheet in a competitive match, at the age of 37: the

↖
Dennis Bergkamp chips the ball, 2005.

Champions League final against Barcelona in Paris. 'It could not be a better script,' Wenger said beforehand, but sadly for Bergkamp, Arsenal lost the match.

Gary Lineker was an admirer of Bergkamp's 'Great vision, awareness, touch, finish, not to mention selflessness, which for a striker is almost a contradiction in terms.'

Another famous goal involving an almost inconceivable turn and calm finish against Newcastle United in 2002 left the *Match of the Day* presenter in awe. 'This wasn't just a great goal, it was genius,' Lineker said.

'A great player is one who makes his team win,' Wenger once stated. 'Anything else is just talk. Dennis is a great player.'

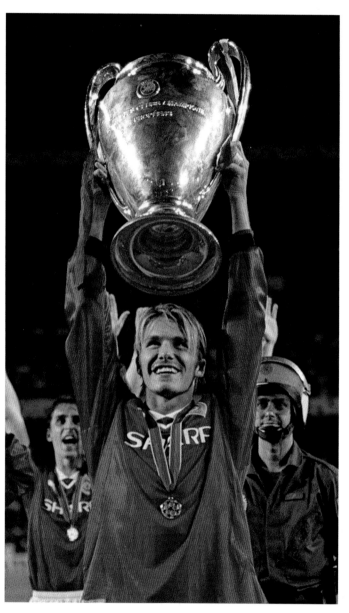

DAVID BECKHAM

▶▶▶▶▶▶▶▶▶▶▶▶▶▶▶▶▶▶

1975–

David Beckham lifted himself above Bobby Moore, Bobby Charlton and Billy Wright when he became the most-capped England outfield player in history, an achievement that enhanced yet further his status as the most famous sportsman in the world.

A set-piece specialist, expert, diligent technician and exemplary crosser of a ball, the former Manchester United player enjoys the additional distinction of being the first England player to score a goal at three different World Cup tournaments.

When injury ended his hopes of playing in the 2010 World Cup in South Africa, Beckham had 115 caps to his name – second only to goalkeeper Peter Shilton on the all-time list. In 1997 Beckham gave an interview to the *Sunday Times*. 'To me, Glenn Hoddle, Bryan Robson and Bobby Charlton are legends,' he said. 'If I can reach their level, I will be very happy.'

↖
David Beckham holds aloft the European Cup, 1999.

PLAYER • INDUCTED 2008 • 115 CAPS • 6 PREMIER LEAGUE TITLES • 2 FA CUPS

1 CHAMPIONS LEAGUE

Of all his goals for both club and country, the most memorable and celebrated remains the strike against Greece that took England to the 2002 World Cup – a stunning, trademark free-kick that flew unerringly into the top corner of the net at Old Trafford.

Four years after being publicly vilified in the wake of his sending off in the defeat against Argentina at France '98, Beckham was soon to be voted BBC Sports Personality of the Year, sealing his rehabilitation as a national sporting hero.

A second remarkable comeback was to follow. Having already relinquished the captaincy, Beckham was dropped by Steve McClaren in the wake of England's exit from the 2006 World Cup in Germany. A year later, he had fought his way back into the side.

David Beckham, 2002.

Then, in 2008, Fabio Capello handed back the captain's armband on his recall to the national side – the 59th time Beckham enjoyed the 'honour and privilege' of leading his country. Capello thus became the sixth manager to select Beckham since his international debut in 1996 – another record for an England player.

Born in Walthamstow, north-east London, Beckham trained with Tottenham Hotspur before joining Manchester United, the club he supported as a boy. At Old Trafford he joined the 'golden generation' of Youth Cup winners, alongside Paul Scholes and Gary Neville.

In 1996, having already won Premier League and FA Cup honours, the floppy-haired Beckham established himself as a household name with one audacious piece of skill against Wimbledon. Spotting the Dons' goalkeeper off his line, he scored with a shot from just inside his own half – a feat that famously, in 1970, had proved beyond even the great Pele. In the dressing room afterwards Eric Cantona shook Beckham's hand. 'What a goal,' the Frenchman said.

Three years later, Beckham delivered the corners from which United scored both of their goals in the famous comeback against Bayern Munich in the Champions League final. 'David was the most effective midfield player on the pitch,' Alex Ferguson told reporters.

After his sending-off for an innocuous kick against the calf of Argentina midfielder Diego Simeone in 1998, Beckham faced Argentina

▶key match

England 2 Greece 2, World Cup qualifier, Old Trafford, 6 October 2001

With only a few seconds remaining, and with England facing the prospect of a play-off, David Beckham stood over a free-kick some 30 yards from goal.

The instant he made contact with the ball he knew that it was going in. 'I lost it completely after scoring,' he recalled. 'It was the best feeling ever.'

Beckham, a tireless and inspirational presence on the right side of midfield, had shown an indefatigable spirit; five times previously he'd tried and failed with free-kicks from distance. 'You saw how much he wanted to see us through,' said England coach Sven Goran Eriksson. 'He is a really great captain.'

again in a World Cup group match four years later. This time a single goal settled matters – and it was Beckham who scored it from the penalty spot under intense pressure.

Following his transfer to Real Madrid in 2003, Beckham spent four successful years in Spain, before moving on to LA Galaxy. When Fabio Capello recalled him to the England side, Beckham made history again – as the first England international to be playing outside Europe.

'David Beckham deserves all the respect you can give him. He is a really great England captain.' – Sven Goran Eriksson

GIANFRANCO ZOLA

▶▶▶▶▶▶▶▶▶▶▶▶▶▶▶▶▶▶▶▶▶▶▶▶▶▶▶▶▶▶▶▶▶▶▶▶

1966–

A diminutive Italian with an ever-ready, impish smile, Gianfranco Zola provided the creative spark that transformed Chelsea into a side capable of winning honours on a regular basis.

During his seven seasons at Stamford Bridge, Zola earned cult status; and in 2003, Blues fans voted him the club's best-ever player. 'Amazing,' said Zola, on hearing the news. Perhaps even more revealing, Zola was immensely popular with rival fans. At away grounds, spontaneous applause greeted his emergence from the Chelsea team bus.

His impact was both dramatic and immediate: at the end of his first season in England, 1996–97, Zola was voted Player of the Year by the football writers – the first Chelsea player to be so honoured.

Off the field, Zola was a model professional: modest, enthusiastic, respectful, loyal and uncomplaining. He often made a decisive impact from the substitute's bench. John Terry, the future Chelsea captain, described him as 'just perfection'. 'Chelsea are in my heart,' Zola said simply.

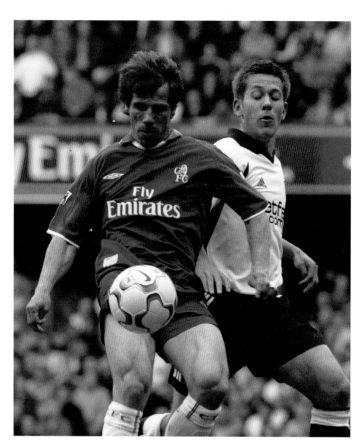

Gianfranco Zola controls the ball, 2003.

PLAYER • INDUCTED 2006 • 35 CAPS • 2 FA CUPS • 1 EUROPEAN CUP-WINNERS' CUP • 1 LEAGUE CUP

**'Gianfranco was a player of pure quality. His vision and range of passing were second to none.'
– Ryan Giggs**

Standing five-foot-six-inches tall and wearing the playmaker's number 10 shirt – a habit initiated during his days as understudy to Diego Maradona at Napoli – Zola regularly conjured up moments of sublime improvisation.

Perhaps one example, above all, lingers in the collective memory at Stamford Bridge: the audacious back-heel from a near-post corner against Norwich City. In his post-match interview, the Blues manager, Claudio Ranieri, described the goal by the man nicknamed 'The Wizard' as 'a fantasy, magic'. Forced to improvise by the path of the ball as it came to him, Zola later described his inspired finish as 'a thing of the moment'.

'I think my way around the pitch, always changing my pattern of movement, to make it

↗
Gianfranco Zola celebrates a goal, 2000.

difficult for opponents,' the Italian once said, explaining his methodology.

Over the years, Zola developed an abiding passion for the traditions of English football, particularly the FA Cup, and he later described the victory over Middlesbrough at Wembley Stadium in 1998 as 'the greatest experience of my career'.

The following season, Zola created another indelible memory for Chelsea fans when he scored the winning goal in the European Cup-Winners' Cup final against Stuttgart, barely 20 seconds after coming off the bench. Afterwards, he created a lasting image by donning an over-sized blue-and-white hat for the press photographers.

But for injury, he would undoubtedly have started the final in Stockholm. But it all ended well. Voted man-of-the-match, Zola told reporters afterwards: 'When the ball came to

↖
Gianfranco Zola prepares to shoot, 2002.

me, I remember thinking: "This is it, Gianfranco. Hit the target." It was a fantastic moment when the ball went into the net.'

Awarded an OBE in recognition of his football prowess and charity work, Zola – now aged 37 – agreed to join Cagliari in 2003. Belatedly, Chelsea offered him almost four times as much money to stay. For all his deep-felt affection for the club, however, the honourable Sardinian refused to go back on his word.

According to Ryan Giggs, Zola was the only player in English football whom Manchester United routinely man-marked, on the orders of their manager. 'Gianfranco was an exceptional player,' Sir Alex Ferguson wrote later. 'All in all, a clever little so-and-so.'

PAUL SCHOLES

▶▶▶▶▶▶▶▶▶▶▶▶▶▶▶▶▶▶

1974–

Paul Scholes has quietly and unobtrusively gone about the business of establishing himself as one of the most highly rated – and honoured – players of the Premier League era, garnering fulsome plaudits from all quarters for his all-round ability in midfield.

A graduate of the Manchester United youth system and a loyal one-club man, the Salford-born midfielder made a vital contribution in bringing the Champions League trophy back to Old Trafford in 1999, after an absence of 31 years.

Nine years later, in the same competition, Scholes was reportedly the first name on the United team-sheet for the final against Chelsea in Moscow. In-between times, he was once described by Sir Alex Ferguson as 'the best player on our books'. In 2010 Ferguson added: 'Paul has retained his appetite for the game over the years. He's never lost his enthusiasm. He is blessed with something special.'

Paul Scholes runs with the ball, 2004.

PLAYER • INDUCTED 2008 • 66 CAPS • 9 PREMIER LEAGUE TITLES • 2 LEAGUE CUPS

3 FA CUPS • 2 CHAMPIONS LEAGUES

↗
Paul Scholes scores against Barcelona, 2008.

With England, Scholes amassed 66 caps between 1997 and 2004, when he announced his retirement at international level. Glenn Hoddle, who handed him his England debut, said: 'Paul thinks quickly – he's mobile, versatile and always looking for space. The guy oozes confidence.'

It is a measure of Scholes' value that successive England managers tried, unsuccessfully, to persuade him to change his mind about standing down, most recently in 2010, when he was in his mid thirties.

France midfielder Patrick Vieira, a combative opponent in many heated tussles with rivals Arsenal, nominated Scholes as 'the best passer in English football'. This theme was echoed by Sir Bobby Charlton, who once said: 'Paul is always in control, and he is pinpoint accurate with his passing – a beautiful player to watch.'

His ability to read and then break up the opposition's pattern of play once prompted Sir Alex to describe Scholes as 'a right nuisance'. He was courageous, too. When he had to put his foot in, he was 'tough and resilient', a player who 'never shirks a tackle', said Roy Keane, his long-time midfield partner.

Going forward, Scholes was once described by his manager as 'the best finisher in the club'. In recent seasons, the outstanding range of his contribution was highlighted when he adapted with aplomb – and without fuss – to a deeper, more defensive role in midfield.

A member of the youth side that included David Beckham and the Neville brothers, Phil and Gary, Scholes was compared to Kenny Dalglish by Eric Harrison, the youth coach. 'It's just like watching Dalglish in his prime,' Harrison once said. 'Paul can score any sort

of goal with his craft, intelligence, vision and the vital acceleration over five yards.'

Though listed by UEFA as a Champions League winner, Scholes suffered the disappointment of missing the final against Bayern Munich in 1999 because of suspension. When, nine years later, the chance came to put the record straight, he took full advantage.

In the second leg of the semi-final against Barcelona, it was Scholes who scored the decisive goal at Old Trafford with a trademark strike from distance. Sir Bobby Charlton was watching from his seat in the stand. 'Only Paul can score that kind of goal from that distance, smashing a shot from long-range into the top corner like that. It was really wonderful,' Sir Bobby said.

↖
Paul Scholes celebrates his goal, 1998.

THIERRY HENRY

▶▶▶▶▶▶▶▶▶▶▶▶▶▶▶▶

1977–

Thierry Henry sustained a level of excellence over a longer period of time than any other player in the post-war era, in the view of both his fellow professionals and the journalists who cover the game.

In 2003 and 2004, the Arsenal and France striker became the first individual to be voted Footballer of the Year in successive seasons by the football writers.

'I always said that I wanted to make history,' Henry said. 'Winning it twice in a row is unique. It is very special.' A third, record-breaking award followed in 2006. No one had done that before. In one of those polls, he received an astonishing 90 per cent of the votes. At the time, Arsène Wenger said: 'I would not swap Thierry for anyone in the world.'

So what makes him so exceptional? 'Thierry can be in his own half with the ball and he still terrifies the opposition,' Wenger explained. 'He can hurt them from that far out. Only the greatest players pose that kind of threat.'

Thierry Henry celebrates a goal, 2003.

PLAYER • INDUCTED 2008 • 123 CAPS • 1 WORLD CUP • 1 EUROPEAN CHAMPIONSHIPS

2 PREMIER LEAGUE TITLES • 3 FA CUPS

**'Thierry is the best striker in the world because he can score the goals that make a difference.'
– Patrick Vieira**

His peers were equally impressed by his performances over those two campaigns, voting him PFA Player of the Year by huge margins.

Alan Shearer led the praise. 'Thierry's technique is fantastic: he can score goals with either foot, he can run in behind you, he can come short, too. He takes people on, he can dribble and is simply superb. His record

↗
Thierry Henry leaps over a defender, 2007.

proves that he is so consistent. Some of his play has been simply breathtaking.'

A century of goals in the Premier League was achieved in his 160th game, the second-fastest strike-rate since the competition began, behind only Shearer. It wasn't just a question of quantity. Many of Henry's goals linger in the memory: the swivel and volley on the turn against Manchester United at Highbury; a mesmerising run and finish against Tottenham Hotspur; an audacious back-heel against Charlton Athletic.

All this marked a remarkable turnaround from his uncertain early days in North London. Signed by Wenger – the man who nurtured his talent as a youngster during their time together at Monaco – from Juventus in August 1999, for a fee of £10.5 million, Henry struggled to adapt when Wenger switched him from a wide role to

↖
Thierry Henry applauds Arsenal fans, 2006.

central striker. 'You're a natural goalscorer,' Wenger told him. The manager did not waver in that belief. Henry also struggled to come to terms with the physical side of English football. 'A real battleground,' he called it. Gradually, he adapted to the unfamiliar conditions.

By the time the Frenchman left for Barcelona in 2007 for a fee of £16 million, Henry was the club's record goalscorer, with a tally of 226 goals.

Over the years, his performances earned the respect and admiration of opposition fans. Towards the end of his time with Arsenal, Henry was playing in an away game against Portsmouth when the Pompey supporters began chanting his name in praise.

After the game, Wenger said: 'Thierry is the best in the world. We are running out of words to describe him.'

▶talking point

Thierry Henry had not played as a central striker for 10 years when Arsène Wenger told him: 'You're wasting your time out wide on the wing.'

After a disappointing stint in Italy, Henry had his doubts about the switch. Indeed, the transition proved difficult. 'After one match, the manager told me that I had been rubbish and he was right,' Henry recalled.

On the training ground, defender Martin Keown made sure that Henry came to understand the physical nature of English football. Keown also advised Henry to watch the play of Ian Wright. It was a piece of advice that helped enormously. 'I studied his runs and positioning,' Henry said. 'Solid, very solid.'

RYAN GIGGS

▶▶▶▶▶▶▶▶▶▶▶▶▶▶▶▶▶▶

1973–

Ryan Giggs holds two remarkable records: no one has played more times in a Manchester United shirt; and no footballer in history has won as many honours in the English game.

Since making his debut at Old Trafford on the left wing as a 17-year-old, Giggs has won a record 11 championship medals, to add to his four FA Cup, four League Cup, and two Champions League gongs.

Fittingly, the veteran Welshman marked his achievement in overhauling Sir Bobby Charlton's total of 758 first-team appearances by converting the decisive strike in the penalty shoot-out against Chelsea in the 2008 Champions League final.

Ten days earlier, on the final day of the Premier League season, Sir Bobby was present at Wigan Athletic when Giggs came off the bench to score the goal that secured the title, again at the expense of Chelsea.

Ryan Giggs shields the ball, 2008.

PLAYER • INDUCTED 2005 • 64 CAPS • 2 CHAMPIONS LEAGUES • 11 PREMIER LEAGUE TITLES

4 FA CUPS • 4 LEAGUE CUPS

'Ryan is an incredible human being.' – Sir Alex Ferguson

'Ryan's record with United is unbelievable,' Sir Bobby told reporters. 'I'm really proud of him. He is a great athlete and a great person. The day he came here, I knew he was special.' Sir Bobby wasn't alone in coming to that conclusion.

'Whatever the club has paid me in my time as manager was justified at a stroke by securing Ryan as a player for the club,' Sir Alex Ferguson once wrote. 'When he runs at people, he can leave the best defenders in the world with twisted blood.'

In 1999, Giggs was the first player to embrace Ferguson in the wake of Manchester United's 2–1 victory over Bayern Munich in the Champions League final in Barcelona. 'The strain Ryan put on the opposition was one of the factors that steadily drained them in the second half,' Ferguson said later, referring to the part Giggs played in United's remarkable comeback.

Little had changed in fact since Ferguson first saw Giggs in action. Standing on the touchline at the Manchester United training ground, the Scot watched with increasing excitement as a young, wiry teenager tore the opposition to shreds in a trial match.

'That day Ryan gave one of those rare and priceless moments that make all the sweat and frustration and misery of management worthwhile,' Ferguson wrote. 'I shall always remember my first sight of him, floating over the pitch at the Cliff so effortlessly that you would have sworn his feet weren't touching the ground.'

A United fan as a boy, Giggs had been training at the Manchester City school of

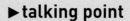

▶ talking point

There were several Arsenal players and more than half the length of the pitch in front of Ryan Giggs when he took possession during extra-time in the semi-final of the FA Cup at Villa Park in 1999.

With no support from team-mates available, Giggs decided to go with instinct. So he began running at people, as David Seaman, the Arsenal keeper later recalled, in his description of the winning goal.

'I expected him to lay it off, but he just kept on coming, and it was a real shock when he beat the lot and was right in on goal. His finish was exceptional, too. Ryan just smashed his shot past me from a narrow angle.'

excellence, more often than not donning a red shirt for the purpose. On his 14th birthday the Giggs family received a visitor: Ferguson had made a special journey in order to persuade the teenager to sign schoolboy forms. Within four months of turning professional in November 1990, he made his first-team debut.

Before long, United fans were singing 'Giggs will tear you apart again,' re-working the lyrics of the cult Joy Division song.

George Best, the great United idol of the 1960s and the player against whom Giggs has been compared throughout his career, watched the Welshman's progress with interest. 'One day they might even say that I was another Ryan Giggs,' Best said in 1992.

Ryan Giggs runs with the ball, 1994.

THROUGH THE AGES
FOOTBALL
IN THE 2000s

▶▶▶▶▶▶▶▶▶▶▶▶▶▶▶▶▶▶▶▶▶▶▶▶▶▶▶▶▶

THIS PAGE: **Above** England players launch the new England kit, 2007. **Right** Bobby Robson signs copies of his autobiography, 2000.

OPPOSITE: **Above left** Local children put on a show for the England squad at their World Cup training base, 2010. **Above right** David Beckham launches a line of children's clothing – DB07 – for a high street retailer, 2002. **Below left** Sir Alex Ferguson shares a joke with fellow manager Sam Allardyce at Aintree, 2010. **Below right** A statue of Bobby Moore stands outside Wembley Stadium, 2010.